The First Lady of Mulberry Walk

The First Lady of Mulberry Walk

The Life and Times of Irish Sculptress Anne Acheson

David Llewellyn

Matador
5 Weir Road
Kibworth Beauchamp
Leicester LE8 0LQ, UK
Tel: 0116 279 2299
Email: books@troubador.co.uk
Web: www.troubador.co.uk/matador

ISBN 978 184876 405 7

British Library Cataloguing in Publication Data.
A catalogue record for this book is available from the British Library.

Typeset in 11pt Garamond by Troubador Publishing Ltd, Leicester, UK

Matador is an imprint of Troubador Publishing Ltd

Printed in Great Britain by the MPG Books Group, Bodmin and King's Lynn

Dedicated to Harriet Emily Rhys-Davies MBE
whose inspiration and enthusiasm made this a reality

Contents

Introduction   ix
Acknowledgements   xiii

1   A Model Pupil...   1
2   ...and a Model Teacher   17
3   The Bronze Age   28
4   A Small Corner of England   38
5   Superintendent of the Baths   46
6   The Presiding Genius   60
7   The Roaring Twenties   71
8   Leading Light   80
9   The 'Queen' of Iraq   89
10 Indian Summers   99
11 She's a Jolly Good Fellow   112
12 The Balloon Goes Up   124
13 Plus ça Change   133
14 Blitz and Pieces   142
15 A Wish is Granted   153

16 Home and Away   163
17 The Monkey Club   171
18 In Memoriam   178
19 The Mould is Broken   190
20 Innocence and Health   202
21 Post Mortem   211

Appendix   219
Index   221

Introduction

~~~))) ~~~

It would be intriguing to know how the 21st Century would have dealt with someone such as Anne Acheson. The all-intrusive media would almost certainly have labelled her a celebrity, possibly even a heroine, and her praises would have been sung – but for how long?

So it is probably just as well that Anne Acheson lived when she did, even if she was not a 'celebrity' by present day criteria. However, she was undeniably a woman of her times, and she did attain a certain amount of fame, although what celebrity that did cloak her did not exactly thrust her into the public spotlight, indeed her renown was confined chiefly to just a couple of specialised spheres – orthopaedics and art.

It is right and proper that Anne Acheson's achievements should be set down in print. She deserves her modest place in history. She also merits a certain amount of focus on her life, even posthumously, because hers was a full life, one of achievement and success. There was an element of the pioneer to Anne as well. Having supported the Feminist Movement, albeit as a more moderate Suffragist, rather than as an extreme Suffragette, it must have been particularly satisfying for her to become the first female Fellow of the Royal British Society of Sculptors. She was also among the earliest women to have been admitted as an associate to the same professional body in the first place.

Her work in the First World War, apart from showing that she had a broad streak of humanity and selflessness running through her, also revealed a logical, pragmatic approach to problems; while the way she applied her sculpting skills to the challenges that were daily presented to the Surgical Requisites Association demonstrates a great deal of imagination and intelligence.

This book began as a private project, a family affair, because apart from her relatively unknown status almost fifty years after her death and a perceived lack of glamour in her life, there just did not seem to be the material to allow anything more than a thumbnail sketch of an extremely high achiever. Too many letters and papers had long since been discarded, mislaid or destroyed, many by Anne Acheson herself when making her various moves of residence and studio. All her peers, familial, social and professional, had long since shuffled off their mortal coils, so contemporaneous memories were also lost to the researcher, while the next and subsequent generations remembered less and less. And memory is far from perfect. In this case the earliest memories would be based on childish perceptions, the later ones distorted by the passage of time.

As things turned out though, there was more than enough documentary evidence of her life that had survived, in some cases for more than a century, and, as ever and as per Parkinson's Law, 'Work expands to fill the time', so this modest project grew into something quite different, and rather more sizeable than had at first been anticipated. Firstly this was because the surviving members of oldest generation of the family had their memories poked and prodded by myself and by Harriet Rhys-Davies, my chief researcher, and also because documents and little gems to corroborate or even reveal, various actions or facts about Anne were unearthed in the unlikeliest of places.

But throughout, the purpose of the book was to try to get some idea of Anne Acheson's life, both professional and voluntary, and the times in which she lived; it was also hoped to shed a little light on her personal life, however, given that the most obvious omission in this work is any mention of a romantic liaison, it was never intended for this biography to become prurient, to try to uncover, or worse, imply, anything salacious. That is because there is simply nothing, well almost nothing, to indicate that she did or didn't have a relationship with anyone, and as a consequence no attempt has been made to speculate, conjecture or otherwise assume something where there is no evidence to say or confirm either way. Not until her death did anything emerge which suggested at least a closer friendship with one man, but even then any correspondence between Anne and the gentleman in question has not survived. Furthermore, while he states that they did many innocent, sociable things together, not once is there even a hint from Anne in any of her letters to her friends or family, which backs this up. The man is never mentioned by her.

Ultimately anyway, in the context of this book, Anne Acheson's romantic episodes, if there were any, would have been an irrelevance, since they would hardly have set her apart from the rest of the human race. The focus of this book has been on the things that did make her stand out from the crowd, namely her war work and her art, coupled with her intense, and innate, sense of duty each time a world war broke out.

This book does not pretend to analyse anything about Anne Acheson's thought processes. It is not an attempt to 'get in the mind of' the woman. A biography, any biography, cannot truly make such a claim, even more so when the subject of it is no longer alive to give the odd helpful pointer. A biography merely has the available material, and in some fortunate cases, witnesses, albeit a generation, or even two, below the subject.

In this instance all that has been attempted is to chart the deeds, the acts, state the facts and place them in the context of the world at that particular time, using, wherever possible, Anne Acheson's own words from those letters that did survive. The task then has been to present them in an interesting and entertaining way, and this is what I hope I have achieved.

If I have not even partially succeeded in that then the failure is mine, not Anne Acheson's. If I have succeeded then the credit is Anne Acheson's, not mine.

David Llewellyn
Kent
February 2010

Acknowledgments

So many patient people have helped in the production of this book. In no particular order I should like to thank, Celia Pilkington, Archivist at The Honourable Society of the Inner Temple Treasury Office in London; Martyn Anglesea BA, M Litt, Curator at the Ulster Museum; Tess Watts of the Mary Evans Picture Library; Victoria Rea, archivist at the Royal Free Hospital Archive Centre in London; Stephen White, Assistant Curator, Fine Art, National Museums Liverpool and his successor Charlotte Keenan. There was also some invaluable help from Mark Pomeroy, Archivist for the Royal Academy of Arts in London, who supplied complete lists of exhibits for both Anne Acheson and Amy K Browning, and was in general extremely tolerant of my numerous requests for this and that.

Dr Emmanuel Minne, Archivist and Historian of the Royal British Society of Sculptors (formerly the Royal Society of British Sculptors), was particularly assiduous in providing detailed information regarding Anne Acheson's Associateship and ultimate Fellowship of the RBS.

Without the input of Jane Rosen, librarian at The Imperial War Museum in London, and her staff, it would not have been possible to uncover so many treasures pertaining to the Surgical Requisites Association, including the confirmation of the name and rank of Major, later Colonel, Edward Randolph Armstrong of the Indian Medical service, the generous benefactor of No 17 Mulberry Walk. Ms Rosen also had the added problem of my late mother-in-law Harriet Rhys-Davies suffering a fracture-dislocation of her left hip, during our time spent in Lambeth on this vital research, but she and the staff remained calm and helpful throughout the ordeal.

A special mention must go to Christopher and Arianwen Neve, for their hospitality and help as I retraced Anne Acheson's journey to their wonderful home Coggers in Benenden, formerly owned by Mrs Marion Cran; it was at Coggers that I was able to see the pond beside which '*Sally*' had been placed by Anne. My gratitude also goes to the team at Matador for their patience and professionalism.

Members of the family also deserve praise and thanks for their indulgence. George Faris, the Rev. John Faris and Paul Faris all supplied me with useful anecdotes. The Rev. Malcolm Acheson provided some superb research material, most notably his grandfather Sir James Acheson's memoir; Professor John and Mrs Mary Faris a veritable sackload of letters and documents, as well as memories and their own family researches. Professor Faris went even further, being a glutton for punishment, he read the manuscript closely in its very raw stages and suggested some wise changes as well as picking up on some glaring errors. Sandy Faris also braved a reading of the manuscript, again making some sensible suggestions; Virginia Ironside is responsible for making me realise that my idea of a structure for the book did not work. Virginia's own vast experience of authorship also helped me with sorting out numerous other snags and pitfalls. Her suggestions were all well-received, and, in general, acted upon.

Neil Faris provided luxurious accommodation and hospitality in Belfast, as well as risking chest infections by rooting through various family attics for ever more vital documents and correspondence; he lurked in and frequented the Northern Ireland records office and obtained birth and death certificates almost to order; he also gave me an immense amount of support, enthusiasm and encouragement throughout the whole project. My wife Hilary Llewellyn was the first to suggest that the original structure was wrong. She also gave priceless support throughout, tolerating long absences and lonely evenings and weekends while I worked on the biography. I am indebted to her for her tolerance, her support and her input.

The last word though has to go to my late mother-in-law. This book was the idea of Dr Harriet Rhys-Davies MBE, and it was her cajoling, coaxing and indeed confidence in my ability to produce something worthwhile, which underpinned this whole project.

She had initially persuaded a raft of relatives to send her any papers, letters and memories of Anne Acheson that they may have stored about their house or their person. The pity of it is she did not live to see it reach fruition. The fact that she had such faith and belief in me was remarkable, but that was nothing to her resilience at reading, re-reading, then reading again and again, each early attempt to get the biography on to the page. She it was who attempted to get me to try to put it all together in as interesting a way as possible. I hope she has succeeded.

Copyright acknowledgements

Extracts from Janey By Janey Ironside (Michael Joseph, 1973) © published by kind permission of Virginia Ironside.

Extracts from The Times (July 15th 1929 and March 3rd 1962) © published by kind permission of News International.

Extracts from The British Journal of Nursing (February 24th 1917 and December 24th 1917) © published by kind permission of The Royal College of Nursing Archives.

Extracts from Essex at War, edited by Hervey Benham, published by Benham and Co., Essex County Standard, © published by kind permission of the Essex County Standard.

Extract from the Illustrated London News (December 3rd 1927) © published by kind permission of Mary Evans Picture Library.

Extract from The Glasgow Herald (February 8th 1932) © published by kind permission of the Herald & Times Group.

Extracts from The Queen (August 9th 1923, September 23rd 1925 and July 31st 1929) © published by kind permission of The National Magazine Company).

Extracts from The Lady (August 11th 1927) © published by kind permission of the Lady Magazine.

Extract from The Daily Mail (February 16th 1928) © published by kind permission of Associated Newspapers Ltd

Extract from The Daily Sketch (January 24th 1917 © published by kind permission of Associated Newspapers Ltd

Extracts from Amy K Browning, An Impressionist in the Women's Movement, by Joanna Dunham (Boudicca Books, 1995) © published by kind permission of the author.

Photograph of Anne Acheson at work in later life reproduced by kind permission of The Belfast Telegraph

1

A Model Pupil...

T here is a grainy black and white photograph, in an early Twentieth Century newspaper, of some largely indistinct figures. It was taken just after the end of the First World War, outside Buckingham Palace. To most people it was just another smoggy day in London town. But for one of the fuzzy figures captured by the photographer on that chilly February morning in 1919, the day held special significance. It was the day the Irish sculptress Anne Acheson was presented with the insignia of the CBE by His Majesty King George V. A well wrapped-up and behatted Anne is captured by the photographer outside the gates of the Palace with a couple of friends, helpfully holding out the insignia in the direction of the camera lens.

However, the award, Commander of the British Empire, was not in recognition of Anne Acheson's artistic prowess, but rather it was to mark her considerable contribution to the war effort, her sculptor's inspiration, which was to lead – before the end of the war – to the replacement of the crude war-time splint, first by a papier maché version, then finally by the plaster cast, which is still used today.

While it was a notable achievement for this young Ulsterwoman, there was also a seeming inevitability to it, given her background and her upbringing.

Anne's parents had instilled into her and her siblings much of the deep-seated work ethic which was to drive her professionally and voluntarily throughout her life. Her patience and her tolerance were born of an innate understanding of people. She was a sensitive person and was sensible of others' feelings and wishes. However she and her brothers and sisters were always encouraged to express themselves, not just in discussion or by writing, but in art as well. They were brought up to believe in liberal principles and not to fear holding a view on something, provided that opinion was based on an ethical or spiritual foundation.

Anne Acheson was born into her loving and supportive family in Portadown, County Armagh in Ireland, on August 5th 1882 – the Census of 1911 gives her year of birth as 1884, but that must surely have been a mistake on the clerk's part, a mis-reading of her handwriting perhaps, since her birth certificate reveals the former date, and from what can be deduced from her writings she was anything but vain, so she would hardly have lied about her age, particularly not in something as important as the National Census. Her parents, John and Harriet, christened her Anne Crawford, although for most of her life she was known variously as Annie or Nan to the family, and as Acheson or Ach by her fellow artists.

Harriet was the daughter of the Reverend Professor James Glasgow, who was the first missionary of the Presbyterian Church in Ireland to be sent to India. He set sail with a colleague, the Reverend Alexander Kerr, who had, briefly, been the Minister of First Portadown Presbyterian Church from June 1838 to July 1840. The pair left Liverpool in August 1840, arriving in Bombay, now Mumbai, on February 26th 1841. Later that same year the Rev Kerr sadly died, but the Rev James Glasgow, who was eventually joined by his brother Adam, stayed in India until 1864, returning home that year. He died in 1890. James Glasgow was an extremely distinguished scholar: learned in many languages, he translated the Bible into Gujarati, and he is still revered in the Presbyterian Church in South India (now amalgamated with the Anglican Church there).

Harriet Acheson was a talented, literate woman. She was born in Belfast in 1851 and, once old enough, attended a boarding school that had been established by the directors of the London Missionary Society for the education of the daughters of missionaries of all societies. The school was based to the east of London in Walthamstow. According to family records one of the requirements of Walthamstow Hall was for each pupil to choose a chapter of the Bible and repeat from memory one verse every day. During her time at the school Harriet, or Harrie as she was affectionately known, displayed an aptitude for verse. This was to blossom in adulthood, but she still had poetry published while a teenager, her first effort having appeared in McComb's Almanack in 1867, when she was still only 15 (she worked as an assistant to William McComb, a well known Belfast bookseller, who every year published an Almanack containing his own, and other people's, poetry). Harriet repaid McComb's encouragement by helping him to produce his Almanack in his declining years.

Several of Harriet's poems appear in a contemporary anthology entitled Modern Irish Poets and in the introduction to the selected verses published the editor describes her work: "Mrs. Acheson is a fluent, vigorous, and graceful writer, both in prose and poetry. She is a warm advocate of Temperance, and makes herself acquainted with the current public questions of the day, including land reform, on which she has written a series of ballads that have enjoyed much popularity."

On leaving Walthamstow Hall Harriet Glasgow returned to Belfast where she attended the Ladies Collegiate School (the name was changed in 1887, the year of Queen Victoria's Golden Jubilee, to Victoria College and School by Royal command), which had been founded in 1859.

Diligent research by Professor John Faris, a nephew of Anne Acheson, and his wife Mary has uncovered correspondence which reveals that, although, in those unenlightened Victorian times, a woman's place was anywhere but at university, Harriet Glasgow was still able to sit certain examinations set by Irish university colleges. This was due in part to the fact that Margaret Morrow Byers, the founder of Victoria College, had ensured that there would be an advanced, or university department at the school, which provided honours and pass classes for matriculation in the various universities for the first and second arts examinations, as well as for BA and MA degrees of the Royal University of Ireland, formerly the original Queen's University, which had been founded in 1850, before being closed in 1888 to be replaced by the Royal University of Ireland.

The Faris research unearthed a letter from the secretary of the Queen's University dated Dublin Castle July 14th 1871 in which Harriet was informed that following a recent examination held by the university she had been awarded first class in history, language, and literature, Latin, French, German and geometry, and second class in algebra. According to an entry in her father's diary at the time Harriet was top among the women entrants in the exam.

On completion of her exams Harriet took up a teaching post at Victoria College, thus beginning a long family connection to one of the most prestigious educational establishments in Ulster, which was to end with her daughter Grace becoming the headmistress and her granddaughter Katharine Faris teaching modern languages and becoming the careers mistress there in the mid- to later-twentieth Century.

Then, at the age of 26, Harriet Glasgow married John Acheson.

Anne's father John was the fourth of eight children by the Rev Joseph Acheson, the minister of Castlecaulfield Presbyterian Church, and his wife Amelia Brown, who came from Donaghmore. John was born in 1845 and was educated at another prestigious Belfast school, 'Inst' (the Royal Belfast Academical Institution). When he became engaged to Harriet he was in partnership with his brother Joseph and their brother-in-law Joseph Beatty (husband of their sister Bella) in a druggist's business in Portadown, which employed at the time some nine apprentices. John successfully sat an examination in Latin and botany at the Royal College of Surgeons in Kildare Street, Dublin, an important step on the way to becoming a fully fledged pharmacist.

The trio was also involved in the grain trade and in general provisions in the town. In addition to his business interests, John Acheson was also a volunteer fireman, and by the time John and Harriet were married on December 26th 1877, he had expanded his business interests by entering the linen industry with his brother Joseph, the pair of them setting up J&J Acheson in the Bann View works on the Garvaghy Road in Portadown. After the death of Joseph, John's cousin Robert Brown was made a partner in the business. Sadly only the factory chimney has survived into the 21st Century.

John Acheson was a liberal, eventually becoming a member of the executive council of the Ulster Liberal Association, and his young wife was equally fervent in her espousing of the liberal movement; she was also an enthusiastic supporter of the Temperance Movement and edited 'Echoes of Erin', the magazine of the Irish Women's Temperance Union. Harriet also wrote a series of ballads in support of the Reform of Irish Land Acts; these were eventually incorporated in a collection of her verse which bore the title 'Ulster Ballads of Today', by Harriet Acheson. As a supporter of home rule John, who was in favour of a parliament in Dublin, which would rule all Ireland, was labelled as a Gladstone liberal, but in principle the concept of 'Home Rule' for Ireland caused consternation among the Protestant population in the north of the country, despite the fact that many of them were Ulster liberals.

However, according to Neil Faris, his great-grandfather John Acheson, who was also a Justice of the Peace, was not a hard-line adherent of Home Rule. "He simply supported home rule for rational reasons," explains Neil. "He felt that much of the government of Ireland could be dealt with locally and did not need to go to London for resolution. But this did not entail any diminution of the link between Ireland and the rest of the United Kingdom." Neil recalls his grandmother Grace Faris saying that her father had thought it ludicrous that Parliament at Westminster should debate the position of a pillar box on the Carrickblacker Road in Portadown (the address of Dunavon, the eventual Acheson family home).

John Acheson did not join the rush of many Ulster Liberals into 'liberal unionism' and ultimately into the Conservative and Unionist Party – the 'Unionists' sought to preserve the link between Ireland and the rest of the United Kingdom, and they wanted to maintain it without any kind of devolution. John, however, did remain a member of the Ulster Liberal Party, although the division among the liberals caused by the question of Home Rule did prompt him to resign as a member of the Ulster Reform Club, which had just been established in Royal Avenue, Belfast. He had been a foundation supporter and major donor to the Club, but, when a majority of the Club voted to support the unionist position of opposition to any form of home rule, he and some other remaining supporters of the Ulster Liberal Party left the club.

John Acheson's radical streak also showed itself in his opposition to the Boer War. Neil Faris adds: "I can recall Granny telling me about this, and that his stance made him unpopular with his business colleagues in Portadown who were fervent supporters of the British Empire."

He was certainly an enlightened man and did not appear to harbour petty prejudices. For example it is family lore, according to Neil, that John Acheson was the largest employer in Portadown and somewhere there exists a newspaper report of Unionist criticism that he was "overly fond of employing from the Roman Catholic community of the Garvaghy Road area".

The couple had a fruitful relationship raising seven children in all, five girls and two boys; Emily was the eldest, born in 1878, just a year after John and Harriet were married; Mary (known familiarly as Molly) followed two years later; then came Anne after another two-year interval; the arrival of Grace, in 1885, broke the sequence, and there was an even longer gap before James (Jimmy) appeared in 1889. He was followed more swiftly by John Edgar (known as Edgar) in 1891, then finally came the baby of the brood, Harriet Elizabeth (known initially as Harrie, then later, in adulthood, as Hazel). Five of the children went on to get married: Emily, Molly, Grace, Jimmy and Edgar, leaving Anne and Hazel to embrace spinsterhood.

It was also in 1885, some eight years after their marriage, that John Acheson had a house built, at an initial cost (excluding architects' fees) of £1,070 – an enormous sum in those days. This was the much-loved family home 'Dunavon', which commanded a panoramic view of the River Bann, on which John had a fleet of half a dozen barges. As the years went by John and Harriet would be seen habitually, after dinner, walking arm-in-arm around the garden, of which John was particularly proud, supervising the work of a team of gardeners. The youngsters and their cousins used the river as their playground more often than not in Jimmy's home-made canvas canoe, constructed according to instruction in the Boy's Own Paper.

They had a happy childhood according to James, who went on to enjoy great success in the Indian Civil Service, eventually gaining a knighthood.

In his memoirs, which he entitled 'An Indian Chequerboard', he recorded: "We were a very closely-knit family, wisely and gently ruled by mother, but not interfered with too much by her or my father." John Acheson, linen mill owner and JP, was, according to James "a kindly and generous father." His mother Harriet, he claims "was a talented writer and poetess." She was also someone who was "greatly beloved by the poor people of the whole mid-Armagh countryside."

The most significant factor of the radicalism of the Achesons of 'Dunavon' Portadown, and something which underpinned Anne's whole life thereafter, lay in their attitude to education. John and Harriet ensured that all their daughters, with the exception of Emily, their eldest child, received a university education. This was extremely unusual for middle class people in late Victorian and Edwardian Britain. Tertiary education was primarily a male preserve. Janey Ironside, James' daughter, states in her autobiography 'Janey': "Fortunately the tradition in my father's family was of equal opportunity for women." There is no doubt at all that down the generations that tradition has been maintained.

Initially the children all attended Alexandra School in Portadown, which was run by two sisters, the Misses Kinkead. The school was based in a converted hay loft, at the top of a building housing the Bank of Ireland. A photograph taken perhaps around 1894 or 1895, with a view of a seated Grace Acheson's back, shows a wood panelled room with boys and girls, around 16 or 17 in all, of various ages. All of them are busily pursuing their studies, overseen by two youngish and vaguely stern-looking, female teachers. There is a blackboard in one corner, a map of the world, or more likely of the British Empire, on one wall and other maps of what appears to be Europe on another wall.

The focal point of the photograph however is the stove, which appears to be lighted, the sole source of heat for the classroom. A couple of years earlier the photograph might well have featured Anne as well, since she would have been in the same classroom along with her younger sister. By the time of this photograph, however, Anne was already a pupil at Victoria College in Belfast.

No actual school reports have survived; however, there is no doubting Anne's academic abilities. A report in a local newspaper of the time reveals that she earned the second highest mark in Ulster and the third highest in the whole of Ireland in the preparatory grade of the Education Board of Ireland's Intermediate Examinations, that era's equivalent of the Eleven-Plus. Her overall mark of 2,693 in all subjects won Anne an exhibition. The newspaper article reports: "The Alexandra School, Portadown, appears to have done extremely well. In the preparatory grade no fewer than three of the pupils gain the much coveted exhibitions, one of them, Miss A C Acheson, daughter of Mr John Acheson JP, of Dunavon, taking third place in Ireland."

There exists a surprising amount of early evidence of Anne's artistic aptitude, in addition to various childish, but still impressive, drawings, including a study in pencil of her sister Grace in 1892, another rather good study, possibly of Grace or Hazel, shows a young girl, ribbon in her long hair, lying on her stomach, right fist supporting her head under her cheek, while she reads a book, and Anne has given the sketch the title 'It's awfully interesting.'

There are other more mature sketches, including a couple in pencil of a bearded man in profile; one is of his left profile, the other of the right side, and this latter, in which he is sitting back in a chair, also shows him wearing spectacles. The first of these sketches has been made on the family's embossed notepaper, which gives the address simply as 'Dunavon, Portadown'. There are also two delightful watercolours, one of a girl most probably under eight, who is sitting, with her back to the artist, totally engrossed in doing something with her hands. The only visible leg is her left one, but it is straight out in front of her, in typical child-like fashion, and already it would seem that Anne's ultimate interest in children as subjects is manifesting itself. There is another watercolour depicting a thatched cottage and a further pencil sketch of a striking looking young woman, with serious eyes and a wavy fringe covering part of her deep forehead.

Her skills were not confined to art, Anne obviously enjoyed creative writing as well. There is a short story, written when she was 10½ according to her sign-off at the end. It is entitled 'Willie's Dream', and has been painstakingly written in her impressive, copperplate cursive handwriting. Another short story, 'The Wonder-Working Bell', which carries illustrations, showed off her literary and her artistic gifts.

There are also a couple of charming poems. She clearly possesses her mother's bardic genes. They are written in a slightly more mature hand. One has been written by a twelve year old Anne. The poem, untitled, is dated October 24th 1894, and is addressed to her parents.

"Dear Mammy I was last night at the lecture/About those fine webs of such delicate structure/That are made by an animal cunning and wise/ All for the purpose of catching some flies/Mary was there and Pappy was too/And a great many people I very well knew./Mary said that while writing to you I could tell/That the black and red blouses are made very well./It's hard to write poetry, as everyone knows/So I think I will write my next letter in prose." It reveals a delicious sense of humour even in the schoolgirl.

The other one is a rather more fanciful, five stanza effort about a small stream. The first four verses are written in ink, the fifth in pencil and it looks as if Anne had started making corrections to the scansion and the words in pencil, before, presumably giving up on it

There exists far weightier evidence of her academic prowess during her secondary education. According to Miss Anna Matier, the legendary and formidable headmistress of Victoria College, Anne Acheson covered herself with academic distinction while at the school. "She was most successful," wrote Miss Matier, in a testimonial for Anne when she was applying for a teaching post in Putney, "in the various examinations of the Irish Intermediate Board, gaining many distinctions, some of them of the highest order."

But Victoria College also educated undergraduates of the Royal University of Ireland and according to Miss Matier: "In the severely testing examinations of the R.U.I. Miss Acheson secured further honours, finally graduating ... in 1904."

There then followed a hiatus when Anne took up an assistantship at her old school, teaching modern languages, in which she had obtained her first degree, but she soon enrolled at the Belfast Municipal Technical Institute, which became known as the Belfast School of Art, and was then situated in College Square in the City centre. A certificate, which has survived for more than 100 years, declares that "Anne Acheson was awarded First Prize for Celtic Panels" during the academic year (1904-5) at the BMTI; and she also, apparently, won a further prize for her anatomical drawing in that same academic year. In her final year Anne emerged with a first class degree in three subjects, drawing in light and shade, modelling from antique and painting still life, while she obtained a second class in modelling design. She also walked off with a Fitzpatrick prize for drawing and painting. It was from the Belfast Municipal Technical Institute in 1906 that Anne won a free studentship to the Royal College of Art in South Kensington, enrolling in the autumn of that year. This free studentship was worth twenty five shillings (£1.25) per week, a sum not to be sneezed at, at the time. She was one of two students from Belfast School of Art to win a free studentship, the other being John Smiley, the Honorary Treasurer of the Students' Union BSA, of which Anne was Hon. Assistant Secretary. In all a dozen people were awarded free studentships by the Board of Education in South Kensington.

It was, by all accounts, a demanding and very full curriculum that Anne pursued at the Royal College of Art. Initially she studied Architecture and Modelling. In the case of the latter discipline she came under the tutelage of Edouard Lanteri, the France-born Professor of

Modelling, who had studied under Rodin, and once more she covered herself in glory. Anne also took the RCA's literary course, which included the history of European Civilisation and Art, Greek and Roman mythology, as well as English Language and Italian. In addition she enrolled in the Methods of Teaching Course, which dealt specifically with the teaching of drawing in primary and secondary schools, something which was to stand her in good stead for the rest of her life.

Clues as to her extra curricular activities are scant, although in one edition of The Budget – the family's round robin news letter to which each recipient would attach a letter with their news before sending it on to the next on the list – which can be dated to 1908 because of the reference to a J M Barrie play, she does reveal how she went roller skating at Earl's Court rink with her brother James, Jess Lawson (a fellow art student, who would eventually emigrate to California after marrying Howard Peacey, who worked for the Canadian Bank of Commerce) and Dick Thomas, a friend of James, before returning to her flat in Sedlescombe Road for tea. She continues: "We parked about Charing Cross and as we felt it would be too dull after our frivolling we two went to see Barrie's 'What Every Woman Knows'. It is splendid and we enjoyed it immensely."

It is a rare break from student activities for this very private person, but she did not stop there. "Yesterday we frivolled slightly again for one of the girls had a birthday and took us all to Piccadilly for tea. We presented her at teatime with a teddy bear and christened it Adolphus."

In the same Budget Anne also reveals her involvement with the College's social activities when she wrote: "... I have been busy rehearsing a silly play for the Christmas Social. I am a landlady."

It was during her first year at the Royal College of Art that Anne learned of her oldest sister Emily's engagement, which caused something of a stir among the family and especially among the siblings. Already Anne had entered a different world from that which she had left behind in Ireland, and to mark the change she had dropped the name of Annie, preferring her given name of Anne, although the student fashion of the time dictated that everyone was known either by their surname or a diminutive of it. In Anne's second term at the Royal College of Art her youngest sister Hazel, known then as 'Harrie' wrote to her, to inform Anne of Emily's forthcoming nuptials. Emily, according to family lore, was regarded as "the naughty one" and certainly the announcement of her engagement, while in itself no big thing, certainly had an element of the shocking to it. That might explain why there is a breathless, schoolgirl-like feel to the language of the letter as the message is imparted. "Darling Nan," wrote Harrie in a letter dated March 15th 1907, "I am sure you would like a little more information about this paralysing event!" The adjective smacks a little of hyperbole, with overtones of girlish gasps of disbelief, but perhaps understandably so. Although Emily was by then a mature 29, the proposal of marriage to her by the Reverend John Irwin had obviously had a seismic effect on the Acheson household because he was fully 25 years older than Emily. Thereafter Harrie's letter reads not unlike an extract from a Jane Austen novel, as the 'baby' of the family explains: "... finally he was invited to dinner on Tuesday on his way to Newry. He asked Emily that afternoon and she did not give a definite answer as the whole affair was a surprise in great measure. He wrote again several times and ... was accepted." Harrie assured Anne that she was the first to know after Harrie.

After two and a half years study at the Royal College of Art Anne Acheson was awarded her diploma in sculpture, and became an Associate of the college, which entitled her to the letters ARCA after her BA Hons. But that was not to be the end of her days as a student at the RCA; a letter from her father, dated May 18th 1909, ensured that she would stay on. "Your mother and I ... have been talking about your prospects and have come to the conclusion that you should have another year at Kensington. Business is better and prospects are better than I have ever known, and I cannot see how there can be any disappointment."

Her father's letter continued: "I will go over to London I expect next month and I hope you, Lawson and Waring will give me a good time." As a PS John Acheson, clearly an occasional correspondent, wrote, rather dryly: "Frame this."

Thus at the start of the 1909-1910 academic year Anne entered the school of design, simultaneously attending evening life classes, having by then already picked up the necessary skills of wood carving, metal work, enamelling and embroidery.

It was during her years as a student at the RCA that Anne met someone who was to become her lifelong friend, Amy K Browning, who attended the RCA herself between 1899 and 1904, and then lived in Chelsea. Browning was born in March 1881, and was therefore close in age to Anne. Browning, then apparently known as Katharine, was a sympathiser with the Suffragettes. Anne, however, was still independent enough, and perhaps cautious enough, to eschew militancy, which would have contradicted her whole ethos on life and would also possibly have been an affront to her spirituality, as well as to her religious upbringing as a Presbyterian. Nevertheless the liberalism of her parents meant a great deal to her and she certainly believed in women's rights, and presumably equality of the sexes, therefore the more moderate, middle class Suffragists, led by Millicent Fawcett, would have held more appeal for her.

It was in The Budget that Anne admitted: "I am on nearly every committee in college." She was clearly eager to throw herself full tilt at all the student activities. At the time she was sharing a flat at 42, Sedlescombe Road in West Brompton, some way north of Fulham Road and even further from King's Road, with some other students – it is likely that she had been at this address since starting her college course in 1906. Unfortunately she only gives the full name of one of the students with whom she was living in her final year, 1909-1910, Jess Lawson, known, as was customary by the progressives at the Royal College of Art in those days, as Lawson; her other flatmate is referred to merely as Maisie.

In this her final year, Anne describes how she and fellow members of the Christian Union at the Royal College of Art, held a party for 'Freshers', "girls only, in Waring's flat .... There were 30 of us. All of us who owned sets of cups brought them.

"I went from College early and cut the bread and butter and laid the table *and* dusted the room. It was rather fun arranging someone else's place while they were out. There was just room for all of us, half sitting on the floor. It was great fun."

But their own place is little better and Anne is quite scathing about Sedlescombe Road, writing in the Budget in October 1909: "Our flat is still unsettled. Anyhow we leave here on Saturday week. It is too noisy and we hate the district generally."

It would appear that the new flat, at No 8 Kensington Crescent, was originally going to include a conservatory, which would have made an ideal studio for Anne and her flatmates. However she explains: "We tried to get the flat cheaper, but we can't so we are going to do without the conservatory downstairs that was to be our studio and we are going to do our own housework. It won't be much since we have almost no carpets and no furniture. We shall take midday dinners at College, so we won't have much cooking. We'll have no kitchen, but a huge bathroom and we can sit out on the roof in the summer. The rooms are all newly papered and painted, and we shall have a bedroom each."

They had their business heads screwed on as well, because during the long summer holidays that they would enjoy they planned to make the flat pay for itself while they went off and did different things. "... the flat will be let furnished during July, August and September, and Mrs Raynor would give attendance and cooking if required.

"We shall have to pay rent all year round so naturally we want to let it, but we are not taking it by the year so if it does not work we can give it up any time." At first there were just three of them sharing the new place, Anne, Lawson and Maisie.

Anne was also in the sketch club and describes at length the annual exhibition that they had to lay on. "On Saturday there was the Private View, which meant tea for 200-300 people. The first visitors had arrived before the girls on the committee, who had been cutting bread and butter etc, had had lunch or gone home to dress. Waring had spent hours buying yellow muslin of the correct shade for the table centre and doing other things which should have been done the day before. However everything went off all right.

"I was secretary for a dance the same day, so I spent all morning cutting sandwiches and helped at the Sketch Club when mine was done, then rushed home to dress (I have got a new mole-coloured dress) rushed back to pour tea and feed folk till 5 o'clock, dressed for the dance and danced till 11.45pm. Mine was a record dance supper. It was so punctual that ... no coffee was spilled and there was no scramble for food, as there generally is."

The Sketch Club was quite a social focal point for Anne and her fellow students, and it was also somewhere they could try out their talents and be judged by their peers. Anne wrote: "Lawson got the embroidery prize at the Sketch Club, and I got Honourable Mention for a badly cast little medallion I faked up at the last moment. To my great joy I beat a very 'swanky' fellow who had two large elaborate reliefs in and who exhibits at the Academy, has scholarships and has now gone to the Academy School."

In this Budget she is very excited because they are on the brink of moving to Kensington Crescent. "We move into the flat on Saturday. I wish we were there. Mrs Raynor is lending Maisie a bed and us a table and curtains and a carpet, also two dressing table-chest of drawers till we get our own."

She revelled especially in the joys of seeking out secondhand furniture for her new home. "We are haunting secondhand furniture shops and auction rooms." And they certainly enjoyed some success in their quest to make their home in their unfurnished flat. "We bought a seat – cushioned – that holds three, for two shillings (10 pence), and we have three chairs already so we are able, from the start, to entertain three visitors, if they sit close."

Like Maisie, Anne needed a bed, but unlike Maisie she wanted to purchase her own. "I am going to buy a bed like our wooden one, but smaller," she informs the family. "That and my share of a stove will be my only big expense just now."

A matter of days later and Anne and her flatmates are ensconced in their new home. "Here we are settled down, most respectable," she wrote on October 31st. "We had a surprise party today ... they all brought presents, a kettle, soap strainer, tinned fruit, stair brush, cakes, nuts, fresh figs, hot water jug, dates, chestnuts and hearth brush. Luckily we were not provided with any of these things."

All this time Anne was keeping a strict account of where her parent's money was going. "I have spent 37 shillings (£1.85) so far on furnishing. Mrs Raynor has supplied bits of carpet, two dressing tables, and our common room table.

"Our great joy and pride is a beautiful divan, genuine, springs all over and wire mattress, on castors, six feet by two feet, with a nice wool mattress on top and a chintz cover. It was secondhand, but had just arrived from a decent house, so it seems quite clean. We are getting the chintz cover laundered. It cost eight shillings (40 pence). It will do beautifully as an extra bed for visitors."

Household duties were to be shared on a weekly rota. "I am cook this week, so I have my first experience of clearing a grate this morning. We have a beautiful oil stove, to take the place of a kitchen. It cost 20 shillings (£1), has an oven and boils a kettle and a saucepan at one time as well, and is supposed to cost, when fully on, about one penny (less than half a pence in modern currency) for four hours of oil."

What with Sunday dinner for 9d (4p), cooked by Mrs Raynor, it could not have been a nicer home. "The flat is delightful as regards airiness and quiet and space after Sedlescombe Road."

Anne was still full of praise for Kensington Crescent when, six months later, she informed her fellow Budgeteers in a missive in late April 1910: "The roof of the flat is much appreciated now. I have some nasturtium seeds in flower pots up there and I go up every hour or so to see if they are coming up."

The rooftop access – "Ours is the only house with a proper door and staircase to the roof." – sparked a little adventure for her two flatmates, which Anne describes and even illustrated with a simple diagram of a series of up-ended Vs. "Lawson and Maisie went for a stroll, or rather climb to the end of the crescent the other day. Their path was like this" [she then breaks off from her narrative to insert her diagram of the jagged roofline] "and very dirty."

Aside from her modelling class Anne was also studying a bit of calligraphy. "I was at the Writing and Illuminating class again yesterday and am progressing. If anyone has a pet poem, or prose passage, they would like written à la Illuminated Addresses, but in a sort of little book, they might send me it immediately." Then, recalling her brother's love of poetry, she continues: "Perhaps Jim could suggest something." And in a rare display of humour , Anne adds: "Of course it will be much superior to the Book of Kells."

By now she was beginning to think beyond the end of the academic year. In the previous October Anne had applied for a post in Twickenham, although she wrote that she had little hope of getting it. And she didn't.

Then in that Budget of April 1910 we learn that Anne has been doing some sort of part-time work for the London County Council, presumably teaching, perhaps on supply. The LCC job came to light because she also talks of a teaching post in Wallasey, Cheshire.

"I had notice of a post in Wallasey High School ... Miss Limebeer, the principal [and a former pupil of Victoria College, Belfast], wanted specially to hear from me. I applied formally, and also wrote to Miss Limebeer saying practically that I did not want it unless there was a jolly big salary. It would be a rise in life of course, and easier work than the LCC, but if the LCC take me full-time I should get £140 a year and London is so much better than Cheshire to live in and keep up art work."

Miss Limebeer responded to Anne's letter, inviting her for interview and a lunch. "I could get the Wallasey post, but she does not advise me to leave London. It was jolly to see her again."

But turning down the Wallasey job was no bad thing. Ever the pragmatist Anne knew there would be something in London that would suit her, although it was becoming clear that teaching was going to be merely a means to an end. Her ambition was to become a professional sculptress.

2

... and a Model Teacher

A nne Acheson was a natural teacher, as indeed was Grace, who went on to become principal of Victoria College, Belfast and a distinguished educationist, eventually being elected to sit on the senate of Queen's University Belfast in her later years. Anne's pedagogic potential had been spotted by Anna Matier, one of Grace Faris's predecessors, early in Anne's school life. As a result when she had completed her foundation art course in the Municipal Technical Institute in Belfast – emerging with a clutch of prizes and distinctions – Miss Matier snapped her up and invited Anne to try her hand at teaching in Victoria College, which she did, taking up the post of an assistant teacher. The upshot was a glowing reference some years later from Miss Matier when Anne applied for the role of part-time art teacher at The County Secondary School, Putney in South West London.

"As an Assistant Mistress in Victoria College," wrote Miss Matier, "she was most satisfactory. She is a clever, painstaking and enthusiastic teacher ...." And there was a wistful note to the testimonial when Miss Matier added: " ... when she decided to give up teaching for a time in order to continue her art studies in London, we accepted her resignation with great regret. It has given me much pleasure to speak of this side of Miss Acheson's worth, with which I am best acquainted and I can heartily congratulate any college that may have the good fortune to secure her services."

Augustus Spencer, the principal of the Royal College of Art, was equally impressed when he too was invited to supply a reference for the same job, and he happily listed her achievements at the Royal College of Art. In his letter of reference dated November 25th 1909 Spencer concludes: "Miss Acheson is an enthusiastic student, and to each branch of study pursued by her she has brought the same industry and interest to bear so that she has worked her way to a forward place in each class. She is moreover possessed of those qualities, sympathy and tact, which in a teacher are indispensable."

Her aptitude as a teacher must have shone out like a beacon, because her modelling guru Professor Edouard Lanteri also supplied her with a glowing reference when she applied for the teaching position in Putney. Lanteri, who had been an assistant to Joseph Edgar Boehm from 1872 to 1890, before going on to teach at what was then known as the South Kensington Art Schools (later the Royal College of Art), wrote: "[Anne Acheson] has been for some years under my instruction in the Modelling School of the Royal College of Art and has made very good studies from ... life, and designs for sculpture applied to architecture. I am convinced that her experience in every branch of sculpture as well as her serious and conscientious method of study will make her a desirable and successful teacher of modelling."

She did not disappoint. In 1910 she completed her studies at the Royal College of Art and thanks to those testimonials secured, initially, the part-time post at The County Secondary School, Putney.

But before she could start work there were the summer holidays to consider. Anne and Grace had decided to travel to Italy together. They would conduct their own 'Grand Tour' rather as the young ladies of the 19th Century were wont to do. Anne decided to keep a journal of the trip and although the beginning and end are missing enough has survived to suggest they had a fine old time, especially Anne once they had arrived in Florence, where she noted all the famous works of art that she managed to see.

They set off on their great adventure from London at the end of July 1910, but the real travelling began in Paris, where the pair got off on the wrong foot through a misunderstanding. The journal picks up at the Gare de Lyon in Paris at a point where a French railway worker, presumably a porter who had helped carry on their bags, makes it clear he is not happy with the 60 centime tip the young ladies had given him. "He demanded a franc," wrote Anne, "Grace thought he was worth it, he had such a grand manner."

Then another hiccup. "We did not know that we should have reserved seats, so we had an awful rush when the train did come in, but we managed all right to get middle seats. We might have been worse off as there was supposed to be room for four where we had three."

Anne remarked that their immediate travelling companions comprised "a nice Frenchman, with his mountain climbing apparatus, and his mother, and two men." Conditions on board, however were not ideal, and they got worse. "The train was hot when we got in, but when they closed up every window we were fairly baked, and one of the men wrapped himself up in a huge blanket coat."

Even taking a nap was not that easy, the heat and seating position rendering it all but impossible as Anne noted: "It was not very comfortable to sleep in such heat sitting upright, however we got up now and then and stood at the window in the corridor."

Anne loved the scenery the train passed through on its way to Modane, the flatlands around Dijon and on into the more mountainous countryside from Aix-les-Bains. "We had no map, but we believe we had the river Iser beside us all the way from there to Modane. We went by gorges, mountainsides and tunnels, with the rushing, waterfally river beside us all the way."

When their train pulled into Chambéry there was finally some relief from the energy-sapping heat on the train, because three of their fellow passengers got out there and the two sisters wasted no time. "We got all the windows open."

It was still better to view the scenery from the corridor of the train. "We could see the scenery in front and behind better than in the carriage," explains Anne in her journal. "There was generally snow on some of the mountains."

Modane saw the customs officers board the train and there was a delay of some 45 minutes while the baggage was inspected. Anne and Grace caused a little consternation among the officials because of one item of their luggage. "They opened our green portmanteau to my surprise," wrote Anne, "... when the Customs people had gone, the man in the train with us told us that they had found on the Brussels train a trunk of that size full of Brussels lace and a wire had come about one trunk which had escaped and was supposed to be on our train."

Turin was the first stop, a city which left both sisters singularly unimpressed with what little scenery they had time to take in. "There was not much to be seen near the station, and it was very hot." They went cold on returning to the station, however, when they discovered that their train was no longer to be seen. " ... we had left all our possessions on it," wrote Anne. "Luckily a porter, who had not understood what I asked him before we had gone out had said something about Platform Number One in Italian in reply ... I remembered that and we found our train there in good time."

It was still not ideal, however, because they then found out there would be no reviving cup of tea. "Our Wagon Restaurant had left us at Turin, so we could get no tea, which we had counted when we had not taken a proper lunch. To make matters worse, there was more unendurable heat on the way to the next stop in Genoa: "We were absolutely baked in a tunnel for about five minutes and were glad to get to Genoa at 6.20pm."

Remarkably Anne reported their mood as "fairly happy" despite the fact that the two of them had been travelling now for some 32 hours. "We went to bed after dinner and meant to get up and do sightseeing early this morning ...." But their fatigue was not satisfied by a good night's sleep and the two of them eschewed the opportunity for a whistlestop wander around Genoa first thing the next morning. Instead they repaired to their carriage and "saw what the town was like from the train," when their journey was resumed.

The train then took them along Italy's Mediterranean coast – "With short tunnels every five minutes," recorded Anne, in a tone bordering on frustration.

Finally they arrived in Rome, their first real stop. They were staying in a family-run *pensione* "... on the third storey and the stairs up to it are primitive, going up the side of a courtyard at the back of the house. We go up a flight inside the wall then along a sort of balcony, then up another flight – all stone." Anne has even drawn a diagram to illustrate the way the stairs run.

They led to the accommodation. "Our bedroom is quite grand, lofty with good furniture, three large mirrors, polished red, white and black-tiled floor."

The food sounded good, if a trifle basic and monotonous. "The family Suquet do the cooking and attending ... we have coffee and a roll for breakfast, soup and meat balls at 1 o'clock and at 8 o'clock, the latter in a real roof garden, in which grow oleanders and peaches, latticed all over with wisteria ...."

They did the real tourist thing, purchasing a map of Rome and a copy of Baedeker's travel guide to the City. Then the sightseeing began. "... we found a train to St Peter's and did it.... The trains go nearly everywhere and are cheap and cool except when they are crowded."

But the girls were ever mindful of the climate and Anne wrote: "We always come home before 1 o'clock and go out again after three to avoid the heat. It is delightfully cool after five."

That first day, Saturday July 24th, they not only 'did' St Peter's, but they also took in the Forum, and the Carcer Mamertine, also known as the Tullianum, the ancient prison where Peter was incarcerated prior to being martyred and where, legend has it, that he converted his warders and baptised them before they too were martyred. But the highlight of their ambling around the Eternal City appeared to be something more prosaic than archaic. Anne described how they rounded off their first full day. "Then we went to a discovery of our own, a delightful Tearoom, where tea and cakes, both good, came to 4½d (2p) each." Suitably refreshed, Anne added: "After that we went to San Giovanni and saw near it the 28 steps to the cross where you get nine years' indulgence for each step you go up on your knees. There was one good Catholic going up in that fashion when we saw it."

Sunday was somewhat repetitious of the day before, with Anne reporting: "We heard a musical service in St Peter's, walked around the Forum, attended Vespers in the American Church, or rather in its Minister's drawing room. Sermon on Protestant Missions in Italy."

On the Monday they managed to see something that the majority tourists apparently did not. They had taken a couple of "grand carriage drives" which took them to look at the ancient city walls, St Paul's and the pyramid of Gestus/Cestus then came the scoop. "...saw St Peter's actual chains (only shown at festivals, but the casket was being cleaned)."

They saw various palaces, the Coliseum, the Casino Farnese and the Hippodrome among other tourist attractions, then on the Tuesday, it was back to the Vatican to see the Sistine Chapel. They got there nice and promptly. "At Sistine Chapel 9.00am," wrote Anne, "find it closed ...."

Their disappointment was somewhat assuaged by a visit to the adjoining Vatican Museum, where Anne was able to study at first hand the stunning Laocoon Group of statues, dating from the Hellenistic Period in the First Century BC. They also visited the Museo delle Terme (the National Museum of Rome) where Anne was able to study the Discobolus, the famous statue of a discus thrower.

On the Tuesday of that week their tour moved off to Assisi. At this point Anne appeared to lose interest in maintaining the entries in her journal; instead of a narrative she treated the reader to a list of the touristy things that they did, leaving Grace to fill in the gaps.

One building fascinated both of them. "The double church of St Francis (who was the founder of the Franciscan Order)," wrote Grace in a letter to her mother on the headed notepaper of the Moderne Hotel 'Giotto' et Pension Belle Vue, Assisi on Saturday July 30th 1910, "is one complete church on top of another, while beneath the lower is a huge vault containing the tomb of St Francis, so there are really three storeys. In the *chiesa superiore* are frescoes by Giotto, illustrating incidents in the life of the saint."

Having visited the double church on the Wednesday, they then attended a service on the Thursday. The original plan according to Grace's letter, had been to head for Florence on the Friday, however, for some unrecorded reason, they stayed on an extra day.

Anne just wanted to make a list of the great works that she and her sister saw. It is impressive. They began their viewing on the Monday, in the Uffizi Gallery, naturally, taking in Botticelli's Madonna and ditto Michelangelo's. The Pitti Galleries were Tuesday's target, where they were able to tick off Titian's Bella Donna. Wednesday saw a trip to see Fra Angelico's frescoes and the Cells of Savonarola. Thursday found them in the Academia gazing at Michelangelo's David and Botticelli's Spring among other works. On the Friday: "Michelangelo's house – nice old Italian panelled rooms with inlaid work ...."

While in Florence they were given Italian lessons by a Signorina Bianchi, the final one on the Saturday morning of the day of their departure for Venice, after that it was back for one last visit to the Uffizi Gallery where the focus was on Titian's Madonna and Child with St John and St Joseph. On their way to the Uffizi, according to Anne: "American boy in train makes friends ...."

Then it was back on the road, destination Venice via Bologna. "Train to Venice," wrote Anne in a staccato style, "lots of hot tunnels and unpleasant fellow passengers. Bologna change to clean carriage, cross the Po, sunset, level plain, lightning flashes in big cloud."

Anne and Grace enjoyed a little bit of fun at the expense of what she described as a "Naval gentleman" and his ignorance of Italian. In fact it highlights the characteristic of the English attitude to foreign languages. Dryly she wrote, still in that abbreviated style: "Naval gentleman's mistake about train or ticket causes much excitement to crowd of businessmen from Bologna. All give different advice at once and call collector. Englishman says he is NOT going to VENEZIA, but to VENICE."

Their approach to Venice was accompanied by a thunderstorm and Anne describes the view: " ... continual distant lightning showing up the water and the buildings in flashes. Porter hails a gondola and after a little delay waiting for our turn on the steps, we start. 10.00pm. It has been raining, dark canal, few lights showing windows all shuttered. We take a short cut through small canals ...." and there, disappointingly, the journal ends, but the women had planned to stay in Venice until Wednesday August 10th, take a train to Lausanne, then on to Dieppe for the overnight boat to Newhaven, then London, on to Greenock and returning to Belfast on Saturday August 13th.

That gave Anne a couple of weeks to begin preparations for her new job. Once back in London she got stuck into work from the outset. Her first task was to devise her own art course, a syllabus for the whole school. The piece of paper on which she mapped it out has survived for the best part of a century.

It is written in Anne's habitually neat handwriting and has been divided across the top into key elements of art, which go under the general heading of 'The training of: Hand and Eye; Observation; Judgement and Imagination'. These elements are then applied to the various academic years of which she has charge.

Under 'Training of Hand and Eye' she begins, in forms II and III, with brush drawing from nature, and clay modelling; Observation involves the second formers in drawing of simple or flat objects. Memory drawing of objects already modelled or seen daily. The fifth and sixth forms move on to plant studies under Hand and Eye, to a study of the history of drawing styles under judgement and imagination. The range of topics was impressive, Anne's course included drawing, colour, design, lettering, clay modelling, cardboard and basketwork. There is no doubt that she took her duties seriously.

A visit from a schools inspector to the County Secondary School in Putney in 1910 praised Anne's preparation and teaching and the syllabus, which she had devised for the whole of the school, was described by the inspector as having been a " ... well planned comprehensive course of work", and also that it was "being very ably carried out."

The inspector also noted that Anne was perfectly willing to involve herself with extra-curricular activities, in this instance: " ... she has on three occasions on Saturday mornings met a small number of pupils at the Victoria and Albert Museum for the purpose of interesting them in art work."

The report concluded that: "Miss Acheson has proved herself a very able, competent and enthusiastic teacher."

Anne was certainly kept busy as she informed the family via a Budget just before Christmas, at the end of her first term in her new role: "This week's events with me have been signing of reports (nearly 300) at school; a school Christmas party last night, which was a dance; a visit to Mrs Lane (an Old Girl of Victoria College), one and a quarter hours journey from here to North London; several drenchings and three visits to the dentist."

This last sounded truly unpleasant. Anne let her fellow Budgeteers know in no uncertain terms how often it is that pride goeth before the fall. "I boasted not long ago," she wrote, "about my teeth, and now I have an "unget-at-able" abscess in a front one."

She was becoming a bit of a hit at the school, and they obviously wanted to get as much out of her as they could. She added: "I have promised to work ten hours a week next term on an altar frontal for the coronation – embroidery of course."

And then the big news: "I shall probably be a full-time teacher in Putney next year (September), which is sad in some ways as I don't get extra pay quite in proportion to the time. However it will be £160 per year with pension ... for four and a half days' work a week. I would get one free afternoon from one o'clock and Saturdays."

Anne's meticulously planned curriculum, and her assiduous approach to everything she did at the school also elicited unstinting praise from the principal of the school, the headmistress Kate Fanner. She wrote in June

1913, by which time Anne had been teaching there for three and a half years: "Miss A Acheson is the best art teacher I have met. She is herself an artist and a craftsman of distinction and has exhibited statuettes in the Royal Academy for the last three years, and is now giving up her post here in order to devote more time to original work."

It is probable that Anne needed the testimonial to persuade the parents of private pupils that she knew what she was doing and was qualified to do so. Kate Fanner certainly laid it on, and continued by saying: " ... Miss Acheson ... has had entire charge of the art teaching." This effectively made her the head of a department of a subject, one which, to judge from Mrs Fanner's explanation, had been neglected, or perhaps even overlooked, since Anne had to devise a curriculum for the whole school in Putney, prior to her arrival. Mrs Fanner continues: "... and has drawn up the scheme for fine and applied art and for handwork for the whole school. She has shown that she knows how to grade work according to the age and ability of her pupils, and she not only has perfect command over all her classes, but she knows how to make them enthusiastic and to bring out whatever originality they possess."

The testimonial then moved on to Anne's personal attributes. "Miss Acheson's personality, her wit and her dramatic gifts, have made her extremely popular on the staff and she will be a delightful acquisition to any institution that is fortunate enough to secure her services. ... I shall always be pleased to answer any questions about her."

That was Anne's last year in Putney, but by then there was no doubt that she had proved a source of inspiration to the pupils. The school magazine, produced a month after the headmistress's testimonial, in July 1913, not only saluted Anne, paying tribute to the departing art teacher's legacy, but it also carried a composition by one of the pupils which had been inspired by Anne's sculptures, because by this time she had actually had pieces accepted for exhibition by the Royal Academy.

There was also a report from Anne on 'The Sketch Club'. "The bad weather of last summer discouraged the faint-hearted Sketch Club members so much that there was not enough work brought in after the holidays to make an exhibition.

"At our first meeting this Summer Term we learnt to despise the weather, and on a day too cool for sitting out of doors we turned out the best set of sketches so far by trying views from the school windows.

"The subject of our first competition this season is a portrait of any girl in the school. The exhibition at the end of term will include the best of these, with last summer's holiday work and this term's sketches. There will probably be two Saturday excursions and six afternoon meetings this term."

The stinging start in which she accused club members of being faint-hearted was in keeping with the way Anne was to approach life. Her philosophy was clearly that when the going gets tough, you had to get going. The fact that she was then able to persuade the girls to sketch the outside from indoors shows the teacher at work, adapting and maintaining the interest of the pupils.

Teaching must have been very close to her heart and she may well have felt torn between that and her career as a professional sculptress as she debated in her mind whether or not to take the plunge into the full-time world of the professional artist. Although she did give up full-time teaching, nevertheless, throughout her life, she kept her hand in at that profession taking on a string of private pupils, as well as becoming involved with the examining board in Northern Ireland, where she was an examiner in drawing, from the 1940s on.

Should anyone have had any lingering doubts about Anne's pedagogic bent, then Mrs Fanner's valedictory words should carry even more weight. "Each year when we have heard that Miss Acheson's statuettes have been accepted for exhibition at The Royal Academy, and when we have gone to see them there, we have felt a thrill of pride, accompanied by a thrill of fear, for we realised that those who have genius and can do creative work, ought to give all their time to it, and that we could not hope to keep Miss Acheson on our staff.

"We shall always rejoice that for nearly four years our artistic efforts have been guided by her, and that the designs for our book plate, our magazine, our hat-band, and the lettering for our leaving certificates, have all been due to her and her teaching.

"We are glad that Miss Acheson means to spend part of each year in London, and we shall look forward to many visits from her."

The reference to Anne spending "... part of each year in London ...." suggests a plan that Anne had not made known to many others, certainly there is no hint of such a strategy in any of her or her siblings' writings, but she did revisit the school in early October 1913, when she wrote in

The Budget: "I went to an afternoon tea party at Putney yesterday. The staff there are going to make a garden for themselves. It is to be a formal garden, probably with the centre sunk and a pond. They have £14 to start with and the ground free and are going to do their own digging." What she doesn't say is whether, as a professional sculptress by now, she had been commissioned by her former colleagues to create a centre piece for the pond.

Around this time she let the family know that she had taken her first tentative steps at learning the 'Tango', the dance that, having originated in Argentina, had gone on to take the world by storm after first being introduced in Paris in 1907.

Mao Zedong, the former Chinese Communist leader, in his Little Red Book, stated that "The journey of a thousand miles begins with a single step"; while she may have been learning various dance steps in 1913, more importantly for Anne, by handing in her notice at Putney, she had also just taken the first step on what was to become a long and rewarding journey as a professional sculptress.

3

The Bronze Age

~~~☙~~~

Perhaps it would be more accurate to describe that 'first' step as the 'final' one in her journey, because the first steps had been laid years before, with those naive sketches and drawings of her childhood; the direction in which she was heading had been reinforced in Belfast when she had enrolled in the foundation art course at the City's Municipal Technical Institute; finally there was the voyage across the Irish Sea and her enrolment at the Royal College of Art in South Kensington.

It had almost certainly always been in her mind ultimately to submit work to the Royal Academy, but perhaps she had intended to do so only once she had become a full-time sculptress. As it happened though, her first submission to the bastion of the art establishment was made when she was a full-time teacher in Putney.

The Royal Academy, which is based in Burlington House in London's Piccadilly (it was granted a 999-year lease in 1867, by the government who had purchased it 13 years earlier in 1854), was founded in 1768 during the reign of George III, and considering its eminent position in the art world almost two and a half centuries later, it would suggest that perhaps His Majesty was not so mad as all that after all. The aim of this regal institution was to promote and to educate the nation in the visual arts and to set before the world the finest examples of contemporary art, artists and architecture. It incorporated an art school and almost from the outset it has held a selling exhibition every year, uninterrupted since 1769. According to the Royal Academy the 'Summer Exhibition' as it is now known was open "to all artists of distinguished merit". According to the latest figures the 'Summer Exhibition' attracts 10,000 entries for inclusion these days, leaving the panel of eminent Academicians and their president to sort out the worthiest works.

In Anne Acheson's day there were even more submissions, 13,000 according to Mark Pomeroy, the Royal Academy's present-day archivist. Of those 13,000 submissions just 1,500 were hung or displayed, and with some 300 of those emanating from members of the Academy, it left 1,200 from non-members such as Anne and her student friends, so her chances of getting an exhibit hung were around one in ten; the point of these figures is to demonstrate just how good Anne's work must have been.

Anne's close friend Amy K Browning had first exhibited in The Royal Academy in the summer of 1906. Then, some five years later, Anne 'sat' for Browning for another of her Royal Academy exhibits, which went on show in the 1912 summer exhibition. It was a painting entitled 'The Red Shawl', which depicts a young woman with long dark hair pulled over her left shoulder, while she is gazing over to her right. The model is wearing a long white gown, possibly of silk, while, just sliding off her right shoulder, is the eponymous red shawl, which reaches down to the back of the tall figure's right knee, which itself is covered by the shoulder-to-floor length white gown.

In Joanna Dunham's biography "Amy K Browning – An Impressionist in the Women's Movement", the author, herself the great niece of Browning, is able to draw on a later interview with her subject for her memories of 'The Red Shawl'. "I had done this painting of Acheson, who was dark, with long hair, and she's put on a false curl," recalled Browning. "She wore her mother's wedding dress, which really was very nice – beautiful corded silk with bows all down the front.

"I bought some white wallpaper, and stuck it on the wall. It was striped white. I wanted to hire a white bear rug, so I went to a fur shop, and they wouldn't let me have one. I was quite willing to pay. So, not wanting to be done I asked Tommy to go in. Course, he got it all right – he was a man!

"The painting was all white tone. I can remember it, a nice picture.

She looked about ten feet tall, but never mind. She had a brilliant vermilion embroidered sort of shawl, which was the period of the dress.

"Oh yes! The picture fell off the wall of the studio, and the corner of the table went through it. I stuck a bit of linoleum on the back, and sent it to the Salon in Paris, and they bought it! God knows what has happened to it now."

In fact Joanna Dunham managed to track it down recently, discovering it in the collection of the Baron Gerard Museum in Bayeux, and apparently the piece of linoleum patchwork is still in place. But at some time in the intervening years, between the Royal Academy in 1912 and the present day 'The Red Shawl' was also hung for a while in the Kelvingrove Art Gallery in Glasgow.

Browning was not alone among Anne's friends and contemporaries in having had work accepted for exhibiting by The Royal Academy. In the Spring of 1910 Anne was able to report some good news in a letter that pre-empted the latest Budget.

By then she was ensconced in Kensington Crescent. She wrote: "Here I am actually writing before The Budget arrives. Our great news is that Canada, Dick and Lawson have all had their work accepted by the Academy. None of the men in the modelling school had any luck, but something like 15 in the etching class have got things in."

Then came the first hint that she was preparing something for submission for the following year, 1911. She wrote: "... this morning I have made half my bedroom into a studio by putting the dressing table in the middle, for a wall, and have started a little figure."

This 'little figure' was her first offering to the Royal Academy, The Pixie, a 12 inch high piece that was cast in bronze. This was the version which appeared in the Royal Academy selling exhibition in the summer of 1911. There is a *pro forma* from the Academy notifying Anne of a sale. It is on headed notepaper, Royal Academy of Arts printed in an elaborate script. It is dated May 1st 1911.

It begins with a handwritten: "Madam," before continuing, "I have to inform you that your work No. 1864 in the catalogue of the Royal Academy for the present year, entitled The Pixie, and priced at £7.7.0, has been selected for purchase by Mr J W Birnbaum, 21 Avenue Road, Regent's Park, NW.

"As the Royal Academy only undertakes to register the selection of works, it is left to the Artist to communicate with the Purchaser in reference to the payment and delivery of the work at the close of the Exhibition. I am, Your obedient Servant, Fred. A Eaton, Secretary."

A trifle stiff in tone perhaps, with just a whiff of stuffiness about it, but nevertheless the missive must have thrilled Anne, even if the only bits of handwriting were the number assigned to her figure, the name of the piece, the price for which it sold, and the address of the purchaser, the rest of the document having been pre-printed.

Anne had already accepted a full-time post at Putney for the following academic year, so she had to fulfil that contractual obligation. However, she had proved that it was possible to produce a figure to a more than acceptable professional standard while holding down a full-time job, so she decided to have another go at getting a piece accepted for the Academy's selling exhibition.

Her second offering, 'Will o' the Wisp', was another bronze. On May 3rd 1912 Anne let Grace know: "Lawson, Maisie and I all got in to the Academy." Quite an achievement that all three inhabitants of No8 Kensington Crescent should have had work accepted for the 1912 exhibition. Anne was scheduled to make another appearance there as well, as she told Grace: "Browning's portrait of me is ... in the first room. Her bathroom one is on the line in the gem room." This is a reference to 'The Red Shawl'.

Once more she received formal notification of the sale of the piece, again it went to someone in same area of North West London, a Captain J Audley Harvey of Elsworthy Road, for the not insubstantial sum of £16.0s.0d.

By the time Will o' the Wisp was sold, Grace had married the Reverend George Faris, a Presbyterian minister at Caledon in Co. Tyrone. Grace and her mother Harriet had spent a couple of weeks in London in mid-February that year, seeking Anne's help to choose a suitable wedding gown.

Harriet Acheson kept her husband John apprised of how the shopping for things nuptial were going in a couple of letters bearing the Kensington Crescent address, which were written on 23rd and 24th of February 1912. "We are just going out to meet Anne at the dressmaker's," she wrote in the first letter.

The second one carries some good news: "We got Grace's wedding dress fitted on yesterday afternoon, met Anne at the dressmaker's and she made several corrections in it. Her costume will be sent home, and, I think, the bill. Today we got her a hat and paid for it."

Just to underline the family's liberal background and their sympathy for the Women's Movement, her mother wrote in the same letter: "Last night [February 23rd 1912] I took Miss Lawson to the Women's Suffrage meeting in the Albert Hall, and heard Lloyd George speak. The Suffragettes and some men were most insulting to him. It was a great entertainment for me ...."

There was another treat in store for Harriet. A friend had managed to obtain tickets to visit the House of Commons; they arranged to meet up "in the Central Hall at 2.30pm ... that will be my biggest treat." Harriet concluded: "I think we have had a very good and satisfactory visit ...."

In the letter there was a reference to John Acheson's most recent acquisition: "I am glad the car is doing well ...." Perhaps there was just the faintest hint of irony in the remark, in that Harriet referred to the vehicle almost as if it were a person, but it must have meant something to John and family lore has it that he was among the first ten people in Ulster to own an automobile.

The car itself featured in a disturbing incident in the Spring of 1914, a very short time before John Acheson's death. According to researches carried out by Professor John Faris and his wife Mary, the Acheson family received a visit from the then Royal Irish Constabulary. Around this time the Ulster Volunteer Force was active and among its many operations it was moving arms clandestinely around the country as it prepared to oppose the government's Ireland Bill. Apparently there had been some recent gun-running activity in Portadown and the police arrived at Dunavon demanding to know where the family car had taken the guns. There was no doubt they were wide of the mark; violence was not something John Acheson would have espoused, and anyway by then he was on his deathbed, and therefore would not have been able to have driven it anywhere, so his younger son Edgar was quickly able to persuade the officers of the car's innocence.

Back to 1912, and during the summer of that year Anne received another cheque for £16.0.0. for the sale of a figure, which could only have been Will o' the Wisp; this time it was a corporate sale, the figure having been purchased by a firm in Galashiels, Scotland.

The reason Anne was able to sell more than one Will o' the Wisp was because she made it a principle that she would produce a plaster master and from that, a limited edition of between half a dozen and ten reproductions.

As things turned out 1913 was quite a year for Anne. In addition to choosing to become a full-time artist she also became an Aunt for the first time when, in March of that year, Grace gave birth to John Faris – 'Johneen' as the women referred to the future distinguished Professor of Logic and Metaphysics at Queen's University Belfast – and for months thereafter there was invariably one mention or another of the baby's progress. In Autumn 1913 Grace reported in one Budget that: "Johneen is flourishing and he can now sit up, I mean raise himself to a sitting position when lying on his back. He learnt to roll a few weeks ago and has practised it assiduously ever since. He is very good with strangers, but doesn't laugh as much for them as he is too busy staring at them, his eyes as big as saucers. His latest accomplishment is waving his hand when taking farewell. He is very proud of this achievement." And even brother Jim, all the way from India, made reference to 'Johneen' cutting his first teeth in one letter home, referring to the baby as "his toothfulness".

Anne's 'Echo Mocking', her third bronze statuette, was also deemed worthy of exhibiting at the Royal Academy in the summer of 1913. Henceforward submissions to the Royal Academy would be by Anne Acheson, professional sculptress.

It was in this capacity that she also starting looking further afield and was accepted as a member of the Union Internationale des Beaux-Arts et des Lettres in Paris. This body had been founded in 1905 under patronage of the sculptor Auguste Rodin, the writer Paul Adam and the composer Vincent d'Indy, and its stated aim was to make freely available to the public the works of artists, writers and musicians, in order to allow the general populace to become familiar with contemporary art, music and literature. To this end the Union Internationale des Beaux-Arts et des Lettres staged an important exhibition every year of the latest art works, so from Anne's point of view membership of it was important, and she wasted little time in contacting the committee of this avant-garde body. She was rewarded for her efficiency in being accepted for membership in the summer of 1913. She subsequently exhibited regularly in the Paris Salon.

She still found time to get out a bit though, and in one edition of The Budget that year she reported that she and a friend, Anna Bailey, who was

based in Watford at that time, went to see the distinguished actor Charles
Hawtrey, who was later knighted in 1922, starring in a West End play
entitled 'Never Say Die'. Hawtrey, no relation to the comic actor of the
same name who appeared in so many Carry On films, is reputed to have
been a guide and guru for Noel Coward in his early days in the theatre.
The young women, wrote Anne, also "... did the National Gallery
cursorily" before going on to visit the Ideal Home exhibition.

Early in her professional career there entered into Anne's otherwise
orderly life a moment of drama – the theft of one of her works of art. It
was an incident which, if it did nothing else at least proved that what Anne
was producing was highly desirable, even in 1913, before she was properly
launched on her professional career.

It transpires that Anne had decided to exhibit a bronze figure in the
Walker Art Gallery in Liverpool, which houses significant works of pre-
Raphaelite art, including Millais' 1849 work Lorenzo and Isabella; it also
boasts a fine collection of sculptures.

After the Royal Academy this was a key place for Anne to send any of
her work. Unfortunately her first offering suffered a sad fate. While no letter
from Anne exists that speaks of the incident, there is one surviving
document, in the form of a letter from the curator of the Walker Art Gallery;
it is dated December 2nd 1913, and at least manages to tell most of the sad
story of the theft of her statuette, only failing to identify the piece.

It is addressed to Anne, who was still living at No 8 Kensington
Crescent: "Thanks for your letter. We have heard nothing yet in regard to
your stolen statuette, although, as you are probably aware, we have done
everything in our power to overtake the thief. As soon as the plaster copy
arrived I had it placed where the bronze had been previously, with a notice
underneath in regard to the reward of £10 offered by my committee for
the recovery of it. We are, by our regulations, not liable in any way for loss
or damage to exhibits, but my committee felt that it was due to themselves
to offer this reward, and they would gladly pay it to recover the statuette.
The thief must have been an expert one, supplied with the requisite tool,
as the statuette was firmly wired down."

Inquiries to the Walker Gallery almost a century later have
subsequently revealed that the 'victim' of this crime was Anne's Royal
Academy offering that year 'Echo Mocking'. There is no mention of
whether the statuette was eventually recovered.

Later that same year Harriet Acheson fell ill with a heart problem. There had been a reference to Harriet not being well in a Budget dated October 2nd 1913, when Molly informed the rest of the family via this practical news medium: "Mamma is still going on very quietly. She did her own Weekly Irish Times puzzle today for the first time ... Hazel is looking after Mamma now, while I write ...."

Sadly the illness was eventually to prove terminal, but an optimistic Anne and brother Jim, together with their father, accompanied the ailing Harriet to Blackpool for some specialist treatment and convalescence. A letter from Anne to new mum Grace, sounded one or two alarms. It was written shortly before Harriet was due to be discharged, Anne wrote: "I am sure Mammy won't be fit to go on Tuesday, though she is improving steadily. Papa hopes for Wednesday, but even that is exceedingly doubtful. Dr Molloy has gone for a fortnight, his assistant called Finlay, a Scotsman, reigns in his stead. He seems more cautious about when Mammy is to go home."

At least Harriet was well enough to enjoy some photographs of her grandson John that had been sent over to her by Grace. "Mammy is glad to get the photos, she does not think they flatter him. She thinks one of those with nurse is best. Also note that the hat has been seen please and take one without the hat, preferably with the mother."

In the same letter Anne made her excuses about not having given her nephew a present yet. "I have been meaning to send his Highness a present, which I intended to embroider, but it has not come off, and now Mammy has told me of all his presents there does not seem much left to give, but I will get a shortening frock when I get back to London."

Harriet had another visitor to her bedside in Blackpool, this one was from outside the family. Anne reported: "Lucy Plant came yesterday and is staying here with Jim. We are rejoicing because it makes things more lively for Jim, who has been doing a lot of nursing." But before Grace had the chance to conclude that Anne was not pulling her weight in the sick room, Anne added: "Of course I have relieved him of attendance in Mammy's room."

If time weighed heavily upon the younger ones there was the odd distraction to entertain them. "There was a dance in the hotel on Saturday evening, which Jim and Plant and I enjoyed." However, she confessed: "We are all dying to get home, but we don't think it wise to hurry Mammy. She had a tiny walk in the corridor today and was none the worse."

Harriet was not the only member of the family who was ill. In the same letter Anne passed on to her sister news of another of their brothers-in-law, the Reverend John Irwin, who had married their sister Emily. "John Irwin is improving slowly. He has a cough still."

Surprisingly in the face of such illness Anne was able to finish her letter with the line: "Pappy seems to enjoy Blackpool, in a mild way ..."

By a quirk of fate John Acheson pre-deceased his wife, Anne's father succumbing to pneumonia and concomitant heart failure at the age of 68 on April 13th 1914. They had been such a close family and John Acheson's standing in Portadown was no less important. He had been elected to the Town Commission in 1889 and served on it until his death in 1914, by which time it had become an Urban District Council.

The obituaries were fulsome in their praise of him, and genuine in the grief at his premature death. One newspaper, 'The Witness', stated: "Very sincere regret has been occasioned in Portadown and district by the announcement of the death of Mr John Acheson JP ... Mr Acheson was the principal of the firm of Achesons Ltd, owners of the Bannview and Parkside Weaving Factories.... he came to Portadown in early life and has for many years occupied a prominent place in the business and public life of that busy and prosperous town. He was a leading member of the First Presbyterian Church and one of the most generous contributors to its funds. In the work of the District Nursing Society and other charitable institutions he took a keen practical interest, and no appeal ever was made to him in behalf of a deserving object to which he did not liberally respond." The paper also drew its readers' attention to Harriet's own poor state of health. "His sudden and unexpected death will be lamented by a wide circle of friends and acquaintances throughout Ulster and their regret will be intensified by the fact that Mrs Acheson has been lying seriously ill for some considerable time."

An appreciation in the 'Ulster Guardian' reported: "No stauncher son of Liberalism, no man of freer or more open mind ever walked the soil of Ulster than the late John Acheson of Portadown.... You could not spend ten minutes in his company without feeling the brighter and happier for it. He had something good to say about his bitterest enemy, if he ever had one."

Tragically Harriet followed him three months later on July 24th 1914, aged 62. The cause of death again heart failure. Altogether 1914 was a year filled with sadness, not only for Anne and her siblings, but also for most of Europe, when, not long after her whimsically entitled 1914 Royal Academy exhibit, 'Thirteen o'clock' – Anne's first work as a full-time sculptress – had appeared in the summer exhibition, Britain declared war on Germany early in August. The only consolation, poor as it might be, was that Anne's parents had been spared all the human misery and horrors which the First World War was to inflict upon Europe.

There was another important showing for Anne in 1914, when she exhibited 'The Leprechaun' at the Royal Hibernian Academy in Dublin. Then came a change of address. By late 1914 Anne had left Kensington Crescent, moving into No12 Redcliffe Road, which was just off Fulham Road, where she was to live until sometime in 1916.

Anne's brother James wrote to her from the United Service Club in Lucknow, Uttar Pradesh, where he was temporarily based and from what he wrote, she was clearly happy with her new base. "Your studio sounds charming, but aren't laurel branches rather gloomy things to have about?" It would seem that the garden at No 12 was filled with the evergreen shrub.

James Acheson also alluded in the letter to the death of their mother, Harriet: "I think I will distribute my weekly letters in future, as it's not of the same importance now for them to reach Dunavon punctually, as when poor wee Mammy was expecting them."

Initially the war did not appear to touch Anne's professional pursuits and she was able to produce another exhibit for the 1915 Royal Academy Summer Exhibition at Burlington House. This particular figure was recorded in the Royal Academy archives as 'A Small Conceit – statuette.' Oddly, a year later, by which time Anne had virtually suspended her professional career in order to concentrate her voluntary work, 'A Small Conceit' was exhibited again, this time though it was listed not merely as a statuette, as it had been the previous summer, but also as a 'bronze'. It proved to be 'a little earner', because, among Anne's papers is an acknowledgement of receipt of the statuette, a missive which also included a cheque for 15 guineas (£15.75).

4

A Small Corner of England

~~~∿∿∿~~~

In the summer of 1915 Lord Kitchener's famous recruitment campaign was in full swing. The finger-pointing peer's imperious statement 'Your Country Needs YOU!', was eventually to pull in around two and a half million men by the end of the campaign in March 1916.

The exodus of men inevitably left behind a raft of job vacancies in pretty well every walk of life. Initially no one had woken up to the fact that there were any able bodied persons left in this country to fill those vacancies. However the authorities had conveniently, and in the eyes of some, insultingly, overlooked the presence of a few million able-bodied people – the country's women.

When Britain entered the 'Great War' women still did not have the vote and the Women's Suffrage movement was in full swing. The main bodies in the movement were the National Union of Women's Suffrage Societies (NUWSS), which came into being in early 1897 and was presided over by Millicent Fawcett; the other, based in the north, was the more militant Women's Social and Political Union (WSPU), which set up by Emmeline Pankhurst and her daughter Christabel, coming into being in 1903, and they coined the motto, 'Deeds, not words', which effectively defined the two organisations and highlighted their differences.

Fawcett's NUWSS, with which Anne was a sympathiser, pursued peaceful tactics, sending petitions to Parliament to try to persuade MPs to change the law to enable women to vote, but they failed to attract much attention or sympathy and therefore did not drum up much support.

Direct action was Pankhurst's way. Emmeline Pankhurst's supporters were called 'suffragettes', while the adherents of Millicent Fawcett's non-militant organisation were called 'suffragists'.

In July 1915 the powers-that-be were finally disabused of the notion that there was no one left in the country able or willing to do something for their country when Christabel Pankhurst led her final demonstration, 30,000 women marching down Whitehall carrying banners bearing the slogan: "We demand the right to serve".

And serve they most certainly did, because the upshot of that march was that close to 200,000 women were employed in government departments, a further half a million took up clerical posts in private businesses, while a quarter of a million went to work on the land, others became conductresses on trams and omnibuses, but it was engineering which attracted the highest number. In the year following the Whitehall march more than 770,000 found their way into engineering works.

A contemporary newspaper report trumpets the abilities of women in these less familiar fields. "Women have taken their place as emphatically in the laboratory, as in the industrial world," begins an article focusing on the work done by women during the war years. The article goes on to talk about the inventions of women from "death-dealing gases" to "life-saving splints", this last a clear reference to the work of a voluntary organisation known as the Surgical Requisites Association. Interestingly, while women poured into these traditional male enclaves, they also left domestic service in their droves, some 400,000 housekeepers, maids and cooks quitting in that same period of time. Women's suffrage was a movement which did much to change women's place and role in society, and, indeed, changed society dramatically as well. It is now widely recognised that the Suffrage movement won the first leg of its crusade, when it proved that women could do 'a man's work' during the First World War. It finally brought home to opponents of women's suffrage that women were the equal of men and so, in February 1918, the government decreed that women aged

30 and over, who "occupied premises of a yearly value of not less than £5", were granted the right to vote; but another decade was to pass before the voting age for women would be lowered to 21 – in those days the age of majority for everyone, male and female.

Among the million or so women who wanted to do their bit in 1915 was Anne Acheson. In the Autumn of that year she signed up to do her duty with the Surgical Requisites Association and, as things turned out, was to play a key role in the organisation.

The SRA, which was to have a significant impact on the life of Anne Acheson and others, had been set up by Mrs Edith Stokes in June 1915, under the auspices of Queen Mary's Needlework Guild, which had been founded in 1882, coincidentally the year of Anne Acheson's birth. It had its beginnings as The London Guild and was started after the matron of an orphanage asked a Lady Wolverton if she could supply two dozen pairs of hand knitted socks and a dozen jerseys for the children. This prompted Lady Wolverton to form a small guild, comprising her friends, with a commitment from each member that they would provide no fewer than two garments per annum; in addition they pledged to help other charities as well. A year later it boasted 460 members with other 'unions' being formed up and down the country and around the world. In 1885 Princess Mary, Duchess of Teck, became patroness, taking over as president four years later when it was renamed the London Needlework Guild.

On her death in 1897 her daughter, HRH The Duchess of York, later to become Queen Mary, took over the mantle of patron of what was said to be her favourite charity and one for which she had worked during her youth. By the outbreak of World War One, Queen Mary's London Needlework Guild as it was now known, had developed a distribution network to hospitals and charities all over London; it continues its good offices today under the title of Queen Mary's Clothing Guild, with HRH Princess Alexandra, the Hon. Lady Ogilvy, as its patron.

In 1914 the Surgical Requisites Association was founded as an adjunct of the Guild. Early on the small band of volunteers was concerned solely with the rolling of bandages, the creation of antiseptic swabs, and antiseptic dressings, some of which required the inclusion of sphagnum moss.

They were based in a modern detached house in Chelsea, at No 17, Mulberry Walk, London SW3, a quiet residential part of Chelsea, off Old Church Street and within hailing distance of the King's Road. The unprepossessing building, which had been constructed a short while before the start of the Great War, belonged to a Major, later Colonel, Edward Randolph Armstrong of the Indian Medical service. He had handed over the property to be used by the SRA for the duration of the war. For a detached residence it was a modestly-sized house comprising five rooms, all of which were allocated to various tasks. The largest room was concerned with the making of pneumonia jackets and stretcher quilts. Outside there was a flagstone courtyard in which grew a horse chestnut tree. The Association relied heavily on goodwill, volunteers and a contribution of one shilling (5 pence) per worker per week.

It was an organisation which attracted a lot of aristocratic ladies. Its president was a Lady Crutchley, vice president was Lady Mary Howard, while the committee boasted Adele, Countess Cadogan, Lady Douglas Dawson and a Lady Riddell. Leaflets were sent out regularly explaining the aims and the achievements of the Association, and it invited people to visit the premises and its many workshops. "A guide will be glad to show you the wonders of these Surgical Aids Studios, and you will feel proud at this further example of what our women are doing for our wounded men." Gradually, as more and more artists and sculptors arrived, bringing with them their specialist skills, so the output from Mulberry Walk became more ambitious, to the point where they were even designing and making bespoke medical and surgical furniture.

The need for an organisation such as the SRA was never more urgent than in 1915, the year of some of the bloodiest fighting on the Western Front, at Ypres, Neuve Chapelle, Aisne and Loos; the casualties, Kitchener's volunteers, kept coming. And it was into this maelstrom of voluntary activity that Anne entered in the autumn of 1915.

The civilian volunteers all wore starched white uniforms, with matching white coiffes binding their hair, which all added to the formal, antiseptic, clinical appearance of a hospital.

A contemporary newspaper article, contained the following description of the goings-on at No17 Mulberry Walk. "It is the calmest and cheeriest of places. The pretty house ... is a new one ... white and light within ... and the workers, in their white overalls and caps, look as peaceful and purposeful as a flock of nuns."

In fact the volunteers were far removed from nuns or nurses; they were more akin to precision engineers, while the house in Mulberry Walk, with its light, airy rooms, was not so much a hospital as a laboratory-cum-factory, where experimentation led ultimately to a production line in bespoke surgical appliances. The same article in The Daily Sketch continued: "Not until one goes to a bench and watches the work in hand does one realise that here is war work of the grimmest sort, that the white house and the white clad women at their white-covered benches are closely connected with the pain and mutilation which war brings in its train."

Sculpture certainly embraces elements of the discipline of engineering – you only have to view metal sculptures to appreciate that the artist has to have an understanding of the laws of physics, dynamics, structural engineering, articulation of surfaces, as well as possessing a more than rudimentary knowledge of more prosaic processes such as welding. Add to this a need to know how to cast in metal – eg bronze, lead and iron. An understanding of the application of all these elements in sculpture, coupled with their manual dexterity, meant they were ideally suited to this sort of work. Anne would be joining another young sculptress called Elinor Hallé, who also wanted to apply her artistic skills to more pragmatic projects. Miss Hallé's speciality was working in metal, and this pair was joined by a third key member of the team, a Mrs Sannyer Atkins, an accomplished wood carver according to contemporary reports and someone who had also designed several different kinds of splints over the years.

Another dimension to their artistic skills was their anatomical exactitude so it is little wonder that Anne and her fellow artists were to prove so useful as they applied their studio skills to something far more practical, far more in keeping with the troubled times and far more altruistic and far more worthwhile. Here were people who had been enjoying success professionally, making a good living and one which could have continued throughout the war years, yet they eschewed potential earnings, and for the next four years as things turned, to help others. It is a recurring theme throughout Anne's life. She was one of life's givers.

So, later in the year of its founding, Anne Acheson enlisted with the SRA. She wrote: "In Autumn 1915 I joined the Surgical Requisites Association and undertook to help in making in my studio parts of the arm cradles designed by Miss Elinor Hallé."

Papier maché was being used before Anne's arrival at Mulberry Walk, but Elinor Hallé, who had decided to try this out was applying the papier maché mix to softened cardboard. Elinor was herself a sculptress, and indeed by an odd quirk had designed the insignia for the Order of the British Empire. Like Anne she too was subsequently appointed CBE, although in her case the accolade had come six months earlier than Anne's, in June 1918.

Elinor had joined the SRA some three months after its founding and a few weeks later Mrs Lawes Webb, the buyer for the Association brought an arm cradle to Elinor at No17. It was covered with cloth and lined with red flannel and had cost 11/6 (57.5p) – no small sum in those days. Elinor was charged with producing something similar that would support a broken limb that had been splinted with wood and bandages. What was required of Elinor was that her version of the cradle should cost a fraction of the cloth apparatus.

By chance some months earlier Elinor had learned of a doll maker who made papier maché and so she paid a visit to Westminster to learn about the simple process.

After the war Elinor wrote: "I first thought of papier maché for surgical splints when I was asked by the Director of Mulberry Walk in 1915, shortly after the department was started, whether I could possibly make arm-cradles which would be less prohibitive in price than those on the market, as great numbers were required.

"The process of papier maché is extremely simple; it consists of tearing rough paper into small pieces, soaking them in paste, and pressing them firmly into a mould."

But Miss Hallé found that trying to make the whole cradle in papier maché was a long and laborious process. In fact the Misses Acheson and Hallé were eventually to discover that the best material for papier maché was sugar bags, and to that end, besides accepting donations from grocers, there were endless appeals throughout the war for people to send their empty, blue bags to No 17 Mulberry Walk.

Once there the bags' fate was sealed; the volunteers turned them into papier maché according to a 'recipe' of Elinor's, which also required bill sticker's paste, a sloppy concoction which softened and rendered pulpy the sugar bags. In the first instance the papier maché was used simply for the arm cradles to support the inadequately splinted limbs, but it was to come into its own after Anne Acheson 'joined up'.

It was a laborious process, the papier maché having to be built up layer by layer. The first one, the 'coat', used 'best' paper. The next half dozen layers comprised sugar paper, but each layer had to be a different colour from the previous one. The seventh layer comprised cotton "cut on the cross" in strips two inches wide. The eighth coat reverted to sugar bags; the ninth was best paper again "to match the first". When the whole thing had dried off, the outside, *and inside*, of the cradle were buffed to a shiny smooth surface using dry stocking darner. The result was a greeny-blue appliance.

If it sounds simple, it wasn't. That basic 'recipe' was complemented by a far more detailed description of how to apply each layer and ensure that they did not simply peel away from the plaster cast.

The process needed to be streamlined and Elinor Hallé describes how she accomplished that. "... this process," she wrote, "is rather a lengthy one, very many layers of paper being necessary before a sufficient thickness is obtained for strength." And despite certain limitations in the process, Miss Hallé adds: "... for simple shapes such as cradles etc, I found that a foundation of cardboard, dampened and pressed into shape and strengthened with fewer layers of papier maché was a much more expeditious method."

After practising and polishing the technique for a few days in her Chelsea studio Miss Hallé was able to take along to No17 Mulberry Walk a completed papier maché cradle that had been covered in khaki material and finished in leather, neatly lined and wadded. And the beauty of it was that the whole thing had cost less than sixpence (2.5p).

Elinor Hallé added: "With only a few workers we found we could turn out about twenty cradles a week and they cost less than a tenth of what we had paid for the original model." A further refinement to the original 11/6 model was that the team at the SRA shifted the weight bearing of the cradle from the neck by passing a sling over the shoulders and across the back, which proved a boon to the patients.

For a few weeks Miss Hallé had had to work alone on the cradles, with one helper to machine the linings and the slings, then Anne signed up. At first Anne was unable to attend Mulberry Walk on a regular basis, however she was able to hold evening classes in her studio, where the papier maché cradles were made, before they were taken along to this small corner of England to be covered, lined and finished.

It was a modest beginning from which great things would grow. Anne had joined an enthusiastic and talented band of volunteers all prepared to offer their skills in the design, preparation and construction of practical, surgical appliances for those casualties of 'the war to end all wars'.

5

Superintendent of the Baths

————✺————

T he house in Mulberry Walk was less than half a minute's stroll from the fashionable King's Road in Chelsea, and this unprepossessing dwelling was to become, under the thoughtful leadership of Anne Acheson and Elinor Hallé *inter alia*, the front-line for an innovative string of surgical inventions. It was the centre where all manner of bespoke surgical appliances would be fashioned to help heal the broken bones and battered bodies of the many soldiers and sailors, as well as the airmen from the Army's Royal Flying Corps and the Royal Naval Air Service, which two branches of the aforementioned services were combined in April 1918, before the end of the Great War, to form the Royal Air Force.

And Mulberry Walk was where Anne Acheson, sculptress, really came into her own. Although she did not commence full-time work for the SRA until the New Year of 1916, once she did she followed the same hours as the other volunteer workers, turning up at 10.00am most weekdays, and working through to 6.00pm on weekdays. However, Saturdays were shorter, with work winding up at 1.00pm.

Besides possessing a sound knowledge of anatomy – in fact Anne had shone in anatomical drawing while a student – and having considerable manual dexterity, Anne and her artist colleagues had another quality which was to prove vital to solving the problems that were presented, virtually on a daily basis, to the Surgical Requisites Association, and that quality was imagination; in fact so bright were they, so quick-witted, that the SRA very quickly set up an Inventions Department at Mulberry Walk, as work went way beyond the production of arm cradles, sphagnum moss dressings and the rolling of bandages.

One of the first things to which Anne addressed herself was the arm cradles. The only problem with Miss Hallé's creations was that their use was limited, they were found to be suited only to certain curved and flat planes. It was Anne who saw their potential to be turned into splints, as Elinor Hallé acknowledged: "Papier maché is admirable for producing rounded forms, and was adapted the following year [1916] by Miss Anne Acheson when she began her orthopaedic work ..."

All sorts of materials have been used down the centuries to provide stiffened bandages to immobilise a limb at the site of a fracture: starch, egg whites, flour, animal fats, sea shells mixed with egg white, and in the 16th Century casts were constructed from wax, cardboard, cloth and parchment. By the Twentieth Century things had moved on somewhat, as the team at Mulberry Walk was to demonstrate.

Anne showed how the paste and paper combination could be shaped to a patient's anatomical contours to form, once it had 'gone off', a comfortable, sturdy, yet light and practical, splint; moreover Anne's splints were 'patient friendly'.

A contemporary newspaper article acknowledged the efficacy of papier maché as a material for splints. The feature in The Times Educational Supplement in November 1917, which looked back at the achievements of Anne and the team at No17, stated: "Rigid support must be provided for some kinds of damage to bone, muscle, nerve. Weight is intolerable, hardness or roughness acute torture.... A material of extraordinary lightness that can be moulded to the exact form shown by a plaster cast ... was the ideal..."

These splints were a far cry from the crude, wooden, one-size-fits-all, clumsy and heavy contraptions, with which patients and medical staff had traditionally had to struggle; what is more, it was not unusual for the traditional splints to result in bad deformities as the fractures healed, because the ends of bone had not quite been married, or the limb had not been properly immobilised during the healing process and that resulted frequently in joints ending up painfully distorted.

As the number of volunteers grew, the consequent increase in production finally dictated that the 'papier maché' department be given its own, albeit small, room at the top of No17 Mulberry Walk in which to work.

In addition to the patients who could come to Mulberry Walk and have the papier maché splints applied directly onto their injured limbs Anne decided that it would be sensible to take plaster casts of the limbs of patients who were hospitalised. She wrote: "I ... tried to get permission to take plaster moulds from the limbs of patients, but the doctors, naturally enough, did not like the idea of allowing amateurs to take casts."

However, after a Captain Hort of the Military Hospital at Millbank paid a visit to Anne and her team in Chelsea he was so impressed with the potential of the various and ingenious papier maché contraptions that were being produced almost on demand by the innovative and imaginative members of the SRA, that he taught Anne how to take casts of patients' limbs using Plaster of Paris, from which could be made the papier maché splints. And this opened the door to Anne and her helpers. Thanks to Capt Hort they were no longer regarded as 'amateurs' by the surgical fraternity, but rather, were invited to the hospitals, taken on to the wards and shown the various ways of taking casts from the bed-ridden; she for her part revealed to the members of the surgical department the processes involved in making the papier maché splints and ultimately waterproofing them.

A newspaper article latched on to this. "Miss Acheson herself goes to the hospitals and takes moulds of the distorted limb or broken hand and there is a collection of pity-stirring casts hanging round her little workshop – here a twisted set of fingers – there a bulging, bandaged frost-bitten foot."

Later Anne herself wrote: "We went to hospitals when the patients could not come to us to take the moulds. On the casts made from the moulds we put two layers of paper, dipped in cupro-ammonium solution of cotton wool, then the ordinary papier maché, then a final, waterproofed layer and binding. We found there were many difficulties to contend with, for example the difference between the fleshy and bony surfaces in treating with a non-padded splint." They also had to try to prevent adverse reactions from patients' skin when in contact with the cast."

As if trying to underline the painlessness of the process, she added:

"In taking the plaster moulds our patients sometimes fall asleep. One laughed so much he cracked the mould. So our process is not painful."

Anne also began to receive her first patients from Millbank at Mulberry Walk, and it was from these patients that she took plaster casts in order to make improved versions of the SRA's bespoke splints, thus replacing the painstaking building up of papier maché on the injured limb.

The bespoke splints were welcomed by the patients. Anne was quoted in one article which appeared in the Daily Sketch in January 1917 as saying: "That man," pointing to one of the biggest moulds of an injured limb that was to be seen hanging on a wall of the plastics department, "was in terrible pain when we took the cast, but the day after he got his splint they sent word from the hospital that he could scarcely be kept in order, he was so pleased and relieved."

That same Daily Sketch article singles out Anne's work: "Still more wonderful splints are made in another department of Mulberry Walk, and these too have been devised by a woman, Miss Acheson, who is there working on them herself – a young woman with the keen clear eyes and clever-looking hands of the artist."

Over the ensuing months the appliances elicited unstinting praise from a legion of surgical and medical staff. "We have been using the splints for drop-wrist and drop-foot for many months and find them of the greatest value, as they act very efficiently and are, at the same time, comfortable for the patient," wrote Dr Emma Gill at the Military Hospital in Endell Street in Central London. "The workmanship is excellent. We have also found great benefit from the papier maché splints made especially for the more abnormal cases, these fit perfectly, wear well and are very comfortable."

There was more praise from other professional bodies, as an edition of The British Journal of Nursing in February 1917 bears testimony. It casts a closely critical eye over these 'amateurs' in ancillary medicine, and approves. "The labour is voluntary ... the room where the splints are moulded on to the models is very workmanlike. The papier maché splint, which is at the same time perfectly rigid and beautifully light, is manufactured from old sugar bags applied in very small pieces, in order to secure perfect fitting, as any wrinkle or bubble is fatal to its success." And one source of supply of the precious sugar bags is revealed when the writer in the Journal adds: "...the sugar paper is collected by Boy Scouts from neighbouring grocery firms, so that the cost is very small."

By now the SRA in this corner of West London was devising and producing all manner of apparatus and appliances, from cradles and splints, to hand supports of various descriptions. And every Wednesday morning, as regular as clockwork, a Royal luggage van would be sent from St James's Palace, under the aegis of Queen Mary's Needlework Guild to collect the products of the previous seven days. The items were then taken back to Friary Court, St James, to be sorted, packed and despatched either to the front or to the various hospitals around the country that had requisitioned specific items.

Steadily this weekly despatch increased to anything between 15,000 and 20,000 items, unsurprisingly since, through 1916, the battles on the Western Front had increased, casualties had arrived from Verdun, the Somme and Ancre, the Allies had also evacuated Gallipoli, and the Battle of Jutland had taken place.

Some of the injuries sounded horrific, and beyond repair. One newspaper article spells out just how damaged some of the patients were and just how brilliant were the workers at the SRA. Anne, as ever, is singled out for special mention: "Much credit is due to the woman sculptor whose skill in plaster modelling has been, and is, devoted to the work. Imagine the case of a man severely wounded in the shoulder and upper arm. Flesh and muscle being shot away from the top of the shoulder, all that remained sagged downwards, and the torture of the damaged nerves made sleep impossible, except under constantly increased doses of drugs..." The piece explains how the mould-taking works on this badly injured soldier. "The flesh was firmly pressed upwards and held, and the arm held also while a cast was taken, and even as the plaster set came relief from the pain. The plaster was used to mould the papier maché splints for arm and side ... the patient can now enjoy a dance."

Anne was well aware of what was happening on the front. Not only did she follow the progress in the newspapers, but she also had her younger brother Edgar's correspondence to study as well. He had arrived in France as a lieutenant with the 11th Kings Liverpool Regiment in May 1916 and he informed his sister of the strange pattern of life they had been forced to adopt on the front line. "We lead a funny life here, down in the ground all day and coming up to work in the night-time. We have breakfast at

1.00pm, tea at 5-6.00pm and dinner at about 2.30am. It feels very funny to go up for a wash in the morning and find the mist has gone and the sun right overhead. I am living with another officer in a dug-out about 400 yards from my Company, as my platoon is detached. We live in the ground and walk about the trenches except when Fritz is drowsy in the afternoon when we can lie out on the grass. The chief danger here is from anti-aircraft shells, but as we are warned of aeroplanes overhead we can generally get cover. So far I haven't had to dodge shell fire, but we have them going over all the time."

There is an element of humour when Edgar adds: "Our machine-gunners enliven the night with 'tum-tiddly-um-tum, hush, tum-tum at frequent intervals, and of course Fritz barks occasionally too, but altogether peace reigns here in the trenches."

Edgar had married Nora Brodie a year earlier, in 1915, and as things turned out they were to have four children, John, Billy, Harriet and Forrest.

Shortly after his previous letter Edgar informed the family: "Our dug-out is comfortable, but damp. ... We live under shell fire and within rifle range of the Boche .... Bath night is our rest night. It comes as a rule, once a fortnight ...."

There was a major piece of expansion late on in 1916 when the Surgical Requisites Association admitted that its original premises in Mulberry Walk could not cope with the enormous output. It was apparent that the work of the SRA had obeyed Parkinson's Law and had expanded to fill time and space, so much so that a couple of rooms in a larger house in Old Church Street, which was just around the corner from 17, Mulberry Walk, had also had to be requisitioned by the SRA, and simultaneously a hut had been erected at the Mulberry Walk premises.

It was no modest garden shed either, but rather it was a capacious construction capable of housing 200 of the white-uniformed figures, who daily busied themselves in this non-profit-making factory. The extra space was all needed. And while the Western Front had seen an upsurge in savage fighting and ever mounting casualties as it moved inexorably towards the fourth year of hostilities, those who had remained at home were not safe either, courtesy of the increased intensity of Zeppelin raids on the country.

One of the SRA team's many successes was the splint used for drop-wrist. Certain basic tenets had to be established. Anne listed them thus: "First: Does surgeon want wrist up rigidly, or with movement? – if no instructions give latter unless it hurts. Second: Are fingers and thumb to be extended; or are fingers to be free; or fingers and thumb to be free?"

Her concern for accuracy, her attention to detail, is highlighted even more sharply under some further clinical notes by Anne. It was headed "Complications with wrist drops" and proceeded to outline to the uninitiated what to look for. "Contraction of fingers – loss of power of extensors; generally cannot spread sideways and sometimes twist." There then followed the instructions: "To cast, press on slab and get orderlies to hold in best position, and don't forget the thumb."

No detail was too trivial for Anne, and not surprisingly, since precision could mean the difference between an injury healing completely, while overlooking a detail could leave the patient with a chronic disability and, in the worst cases, perhaps incapacitate completely the injured limb. She continued: "Very bad cases should have wax casts at once. Wires should go between the fingers on splint to prevent twisting and to hold down knuckles. If thumb is to be extended, find position required. Ideal is metal projecting from wrist with sling round thumb attached to it by a spring – allowing flexors to bring thumb in front of palm, downwards or outwards. In this case make little lip round thumb crease and cut good hole for thumb."

There were other ingenious devices emerging from Mulberry Walk, one of which was the Hallé Boot. A request was made in March 1916 for something to help an officer who was suffering from drop-foot. That same day, when the request was made, Elinor Hallé made a prototype in wood and cardboard, and 24 hours later she produced the first papier maché boot.

The object of the boot was to provide firm support at the heel to keep the foot right angles to the leg; to achieve this Elinor Hallé inserted steels or whale bones, depending on which was in plentiful supply, under the papier maché, then holding up the toe end of the boot with strong straps attached to the leg on both sides. The boot was also made so as to slip easily over bandages when necessary.

Initially the heeling and soling was done by professional workers in Wright's Lane in Kensington, but it was felt that the standard of finish was not as high as might be achieved by SRA members, so the more experienced workers at Mulberry Walk taught themselves to add the soles to the boots. An article in The British Journal of Nursing records: "They are made with an adjustable foot piece, which enables the foot to be screwed up to the proper angle.... The boots are covered with leather (from gifts of old motor coats), stitched, soled and heeled ... they have proved such a comfort that, owing to the men refusing to part with them at night, she has invented a light canvas night boot."

Perhaps the most significant piece of work carried out by the Surgical Requisites Association and Anne Acheson around this time came about as a result of an exploratory visit from a doctor in the Royal Army Medical Corps based at Millbank Military Hospital in Chelsea.

In addition to the splints, which were forever in demand, the SRA's papier maché team was informed that there was a desperate need for baths, in particular arm baths, in which injured limbs could be soaked for a period of time, in saline and other solutions, which was regarded by the surgeons as a vital aid in the healing process.

Since tin baths had become prohibitively expensive, and porcelain ones were also out of the question for the same reason, once more the SRA was asked to apply its ingenuity and skill to construct baths, out of a material that was far more readily available and of course a lot cheaper, for immersion of the injured limbs. At first sight papier maché appeared to be out of the question, and for fairly obvious reasons.

In a treatise shortly after the end of the war Elinor Hallé wrote: "Necessity is the mother of invention and the need was great, metal baths were almost unobtainable, and the dearth of baths in hospitals was pitiable. Cardboard, sugar paper and paste did not seem very promising materials as a substitute for tin, but we persevered until we had produced a sufficiently strong and solid bath." She made it sound more of a foothill than the mountainous challenge that it in fact was.

Anne Acheson takes up the tale. "I experimented in making rubber baths with cardboard foundations and reported to the Surgical Requisites Association who had my attempts tested and who also made experiments. This method was not a success."

It took them quite some time to crack the problem. A matter of months as things turned out, because of course producing something that looked like a bath was one thing, the Mulberry Walk workforce naturally had no problem with that, but producing something that behaved like a bath was another. The baths had to hold a saline solution into which the injured limb could be placed for up to 24 hours at a time. The problem, therefore, was how to render the baths waterproof, without resorting to commercial procedures in which papier maché was made using immense hydraulic pressure, an impractical solution for the Mulberry Walk workers, since the machinery was far too cumbersome, and of course, way beyond the SRA budget; in addition it would have occupied far too much precious room in the crowded premises.

Three principal people, Anne, Miss Hallé and another Chelsea-based artist Miss Freda Stanhope all set about trying to produce papier maché baths capable of withstanding sterilisation through scalding, holding saline solutions for long periods and which would prove resistant to various acids and alkalis used in other treatments. According to a contemporary, anonymous report of the deeds of the SRA, there was something of a friendly rivalry among the three artists to see who could produce the first waterproof bath.

The trio experimented with every conceivable varnish and wax available at that time, but the results were far from satisfactory; waterproofing with jaconet and inserting India rubber linings proved far too expensive. One bath, which was constructed by Miss Hallé at Mulberry Walk, did hold water overnight, but then collapsed the following day.

In the end it was Anne Acheson who made the breakthrough, as acknowledged by Elinor Hallé. "The problem of making them waterproof was solved by Miss Acheson," she wrote. Anne, she explained, had received a 'recipe' for waterproofing, but the application of it was not as straightforward as it might have seemed. The waterproof arm bath would need a little more time before it could be described as the finished product.

Anne had heard from a scientist of her acquaintance, Sir William Tilden, that copper dissolved in a solution of ammonia and water with a current of air passing through would waterproof paper, and she was given an introduction to a professor at the Royal College of Science who would teach her the process. Strangely the professor was rather vague about the quantities needed to make up the correct strength of solution, but he gave her a bottle of the formula, leaving Anne to discover the correct proportions of the ingredients. She did so, but only after much trial and error; she then had to discover for herself how best to apply the solution, because she quickly found that merely painting it on simply meant that it peeled off when dry.

Anne wrote: "Sir William Tilden suggested painting it with a cupro-ammonium solution of cotton wool. This peeled off, but after some experimenting I found that by using the solution instead of paste for the final layers of the papier maché, and then rubbing on more solution, a satisfactory waterproofing could be obtained and the first arm bath passed tests, at St Thomas's Hospital, early in 1916."

She expanded her account of the development of the waterproofing in the latest edition of The Budget. "My arm bath has succeeded beyond my expectations. It is an improvement on the usual kind because it keeps the water hotter. I am to set up an apparatus in the studio to make the copper solution myself. It is all done by a running tap which works a suction air pump and sends the air through the ammonia and dissolves the copper. After that I dissolve cotton wool in it.

"I have more helpers – three very good ones – who have been working at the arm cradles in Mulberry Walk (headquarters). We have got a present from a paper manufacturer of lots of rough paper, which makes an excellent basis for the sugar paper we use for papier maché and which I use soaked in the solution.

"This waterproofing is hard physical labour as it has to be pressed very tight and has to be done very quickly as the stuff sets in a funny way in a few moments. I have a helper or two in every morning."

By this time Anne had become Superintendent of the Baths, and it was in that capacity that she was responsible for the testing of the finished products. She wrote: "I then taught some of the Surgical Requisites Association workers how to make these baths and several started in various places, but finding it difficult to keep up the standard of the waterproofing in scattered centres, the Surgical Requisites Association gave us rooms and the Bath Department was started, where I was able to supervise and test all the baths myself."

Given the toxic nature of the chemicals used there must have been an element of discomfort, and even to a certain extent danger, involved, however slight, but still it was important that the testing procedures were thorough, and that all possible safeguards were taken, Anne explained in The Budget: "I am getting used to the ammonia fumes and don't weep over it now."

During this period Freda Stanhope had worked out a more reliable method of moulding baths on wooden blocks. Initially the baths were

made by teams of workers in the studios of Anne Acheson and Freda
Stanhope and a third studio, which had been lent to the SRA, which was
situated in Upper Cheyne Row. It was not ideal and eventually all the bath
makers were moved back to Mulberry Walk.

The baths were in great demand in hospitals at home as well as by
those at the 'front' – little wonder, since the SRA's baths cost a mere 2/6
(12.5 pence) as compared with the 30 shillings (£1.50) a similar limb bath
in porcelain would cost. Lady Lawley CBE took the first consignment to
the front herself and reported that she could hardly get through with them
they were so eagerly seized upon by the surgeons and matrons. Indeed so
coveted were they by medical and nursing staff that they became the
subject of an attempted robbery. It seems that a doctor turned up at the
Upper Cheyne Row premises, ostensibly to examine the baths with a view
to purchasing some, but he went away empty-handed. However the
cunning quack slipped back in the dark of the evening, after the workers
had called it a day and helped himself to seven baths. The hue and cry was
raised the following morning and he was quickly run to earth and made
to hand them back, which was just as well since they had not yet actually
been tested for clinical use.

All this industry was being carried out on an extremely professional
basis and inevitably the question of applying for patents arose. Anne refers
to it in her contribution to The Budget the following year, but it must
have been a subject for discussion for some months by then. Her words
reveal just how alien to her the concept of profiteering was. She had pretty
well given up professional sculpting in order to work at the SRA, work
which she clearly enjoyed to the hilt, and there was never any doubt either
that she would take all the credit for what was being achieved. Nor would
she take any money. There was a deep-seated vein of charity running
through Anne Acheson as the following reveals. "The SRA are very
excited over the arm baths because doctors are so keen about them. The
materials cost between sixpence (2.5p) and ninepence (4p) a bath. The
SRA talked of patenting them to prevent any trade firm doing so and
keeping us from making them, and then they found that as my sample had
been in use in St Thomas's hospital for a week no one could prevent us
doing so.

"However a Major Stokes (I think that is his name) says they should
be patented – there <u>may</u> [Anne's underlining] be money in it – and Major

Stokes is paying for doing it in my name. If there is money I can't have it because these science folk helped me – but I can pass it on to Disabled Soldiers fund or something of that sort. There won't be any till after the war. Probably never." She was right as it turned out.

Throughout her time with the Surgical Requisites Association Anne had kept in touch with the friends she had made in her student days at The Royal College of Art in Chelsea. One such to whom she was particularly close was T C 'Tom' Dugdale, who was to become a renowned portrait painter, and was himself half Irish.

In 1916 Dugdale, as Anne and her circle addressed him, found himself in the military and based in Ireland. He sent Anne a diffident letter from Dublin in August of that year in which he referred to a visit to Anne by her younger brother Edgar. "So glad you have had your brother over for two days – beastly short leave, but better than none – and I hope the shell shock won't have any permanent ill-effects."

Dugdale, who had married Anne's great friend Amy K Browning that same year, added: "The first hand news you've had from Hazel – about the portraits – has probably found your conscience at rest now. I hear from AK otherwise B that the two pictures are liked ... I'm glad. What does Hazel herself think of them? How's my 'herself' looking just now? I fear she is rushing about rather like a shuttle on a loom just at present and I guess it won't do her worlds of good – and my soothing (and restraining) hand is too far away, also the hand is not at this moment over-clean, but that is by the way."

Here he starts to let his eye and his mind wander for a moment before returning to his musings with a rather sad and even frustrated look at his life right then: "I keep looking at the Wicklow Hills, and wishing I were out of the d——— army, daily, nay hourly, and at times begin to feel despair, and there are no Turks to relieve my fury on. I tell you Ach, life in barracks is enough to drive me mad! I prefer the trenches. Of course it's safe here and I pat myself on the back and call myself lucky when I think of that, and that helps me to carry on for another few days.

"I daresay when this war is over – say 1930 or thereabouts – if we are still on this earth we'll all be able to foregather and think of these strange experiences and laugh, but now, tut-tut!"

The impression from Dugdale's easy, relaxed prose, is of a languid, ascetic figure. But he is also someone who does not enjoy the inaction.

"Things go dull as ever here in your country," he wrote, making it very clear that half Irish or not he is English, "no risings – not even meetings – and the rains have begun ... I'm thinking of indenting for my oilskins, sea boots and sou'wester." His laconic sense of humour further reinforces the impression of a dry wit and a keen observer of humankind and indeed the world, prerequisites of all artists of course.

Then he injects an element of the wistful, it borders on some gentle flirting, when he adds: "One day perchance you'll spoil this soldier (?) again and write to him and tell him about yourself and what you are tiring yourself with. I know it's not really long since you wrote but it seems long, as the man said about being married – (not endorsed by me however!).

"Anyway Ach, keep fit, don't overwork and pray that the Austrians chuck in soon, Best of luck and love, yours very sincerely..." He then tacks on a whimsical postscript: "The Barrack clock striketh nine. A dark and stormy night!"

It was in 1916 that Anne took time off from the Surgical Requisites Association to pay a visit to to Browning's family home, accompanied by Hazel, Anne's youngest sister who was living with her in London.

Amy was the daughter of James Browning, a farmer in Bedfordshire and one of eight children, similar to Anne's family background. The Brownings were evidently comfortably off, to judge by what Anne reports about the weekend in an undated edition of The Budget. "They live in the country, 13 miles from Bedford and about the same from Luton. Mr Browning met us with a trap on Friday night at Flitwick, their nearest station."

Browning's family lived in Kitchen End Farm, near Silsoe, which was not far from Ampthill, in Bedfordshire. "Browning's sister and brother-in-law motored over from Luton and he took us to Bedford where we had tea. The roads are glorious there, a sort of asphalt.

"We spent a good deal of time wandering around the garden, inspecting valuable horses and pigs, took walks across huge fields, rather muddy. The farm is 400 acres, it was 900, but the married sons have parts now. The house is very old."

There was, of course, ample time for some art and Anne reports to the family that she 'sat' for her friend. "Browning did a little pencil and water colour sketch of me which I sent to Jim instead of a letter. I told him it would do to express my feelings."

The trip over, the Acheson sisters returned to London. Hazel had decided to do her bit for the war and had volunteered her services as a nurse with the Red Cross. She had already been living with her sister for a few months while attending Chelsea Polytechnic School of Art, the pair of them initially sharing a flat at Number 12, Redcliffe Road in South Kensington, before moving on to Number 18, Beaufort Mansions in Beaufort Street, Chelsea.

Hazel was to work for the Red Cross from January 1916 to the end of July 1918. Once she had been trained, the bulk of Hazel's voluntary work was done at Mitcham Medical Hospital in South London; she began working there as a nursing orderly in December 1916, and was still there when she wound up her duties with the Red Cross.

But while the two girls were clearly happy in their voluntary roles it was not so for their brother James. Indeed there was a sense of frustration for him, because he was working for the Indian Government, but he clearly wanted to do his bit for his country as well, as a letter dated August 1915 had revealed. "We do our bit of soldiering too and every man would be of some little use in the case of a row," James Acheson's euphemism for the hostilities. "He would have arms and an organisation even though the Light Horse man or volunteer is not particularly well trained. Not that there is any prospect of a row thank goodness. The relations between Europeans and Indians here are splendid."

In a further letter, written in 1916 James, still in Lucknow, wrote on the headed notepaper of the United Services Club there, expressing his desire to apply for a commission. "I have good qualifications, Higher Standard in Urdu, Hindi, a year's efficiency in the OTC (Officer Training Corps), member of the Uttar Pradesh Light Horse, passed as first class shot in musketry tests the other day.... Everyone in the services out here is trying to get a go at the Germans."

Back in Blighty, for Anne and her fellow team members the work continued. The Mulberry Walk workers were forever turning their minds and their hands to some new demand, some new contraption that would make life easier for the stream of injured soldiers, sailors and airmen who were being shipped back in their thousands from the bloody frontlines.

6

The Presiding Genius

From those modest beginnings at No 17, Mulberry Walk the Surgical Requisites Association grew rapidly, with branches opening around the country. And Anne Acheson did not remain Superintendent of the Baths for long. Once the taking of plaster casts had been mastered by Anne and a couple of her helpers she wrote: "On seeing what we did for Captain Hort, other surgeons immediately made use of us and the Plastics Department was started. I then gave over the 'Baths Department' to Miss Mure, one of my assistants."

Inevitably, after so much success she was appointed head of the Plastics Department and it was from here over the next few months that she and her fellow workers made even greater strides in the construction of surgical appliances, including harnessing the properties of Plaster of Paris to make the first mass produced PoP splints.

In 1917, the same year that the Allied Forces found themselves subjected to the mustard gas at Ypres, the feats of the Surgical Requisites Association began to attract the attention of the press. One feature, from an unidentifiable newspaper, bearing the headline "The Ladies of Mulberry Walk" – a description which did have a rather unfortunate, salacious double meaning attached to it – with a sub-heading 'A

Wonderful War Industry', focuses on something quite the opposite to what was implied in the headline. The article goes into some detail, recording the activities at No17 and in its 'hut' out the back, and sets down in more detail the process of making a waterproof splint.

The reporter describes how there were tables around and over which the workers huddled, bent on their specific task, while from the walls of the hut hung the various moulds and other contraptions which had been produced there over the previous 18 months.

"At one table in the hut a woman is at work on the plaster cast of a shoulder and an arm, which will have to be put in a splint to support the arm at a certain angle. The cast is covered with a yellow wax, and on this she lays little bits of ... paper, which have been steeped in the waterproofing solution and have turned a beautiful blue. She overlaps them like the scales of a fish and smooths them down. This part is done with leather-gloved hands for the preparation is poisonous to the skin. Now comes the messiest job imaginable. The waterproof lining is covered with layer on layer of ... paper scales, each scrap of paper having been dipped in paste before being applied. There are eight or nine layers, and then the outer layer of waterproofing is applied."

The splints were not confined to limbs. An article in The Times marvelled at a jaw splint which had been fitted perfectly to the face of the patient and had been attached to a crochet cap that covered the head.

Anne's limb baths also came in for praise in the same article in 'The Thunderer', the writer commenting on how light the items were in each case.

The SRA's appliances were not simply constructed from papier maché, though, sometimes they incorporated metalwork, where leverage or articulation might be required during rehabilitation.

Anne later wrote: "From our simple, rigid splints for feet and hands we gradually developed flexible sided splints, and splints with metal supports, then with joints, with springs, or with screws for flexion and extension, the chief advantage being that by moulding the splint from the individual, a large amount of pressure be brought to bear without causing pain or re-fracture because of the even distribution of pressure.

"Our 'blued' splints are transparent to X-rays, sterilisable and non-inflammable. Their greatest disadvantage is the amount of careful labour involved in making them, so we aimed at developing quicker methods."

They resorted to using standard proprietary brands, as Anne revealed.

"Varnishing with 'Pinchin and Johnson's' specially prepared varnish, stowed in a gas oven saved the trying blueing method, but could only be used for shapes not likely to warp."

A doctor also devised a 'pulp' method using waste products from batteries, Anne explaining that "ordinary paper pulp is too fine, so is too brittle for machine pressure." The splints made from pulp turned out to be slightly heavier and not quite so durable as the original ones."

The original trickle of patients into Mulberry Walk had long since turned into a torrent, and the plastics department had to expand quickly, so the SRA eventually decided that Anne and her department needed to be given a couple of rooms in the 'annexe' at No 111, Old Church Street, which was just around the corner from Mulberry Walk.

It was here that Anne intensified her efforts to expand her specialist team of workers; she taught them casting and certain elements of metalwork, in addition to showing them how to create the papier maché splints and the method used for waterproofing them. But so large did the Plastics department become that they even outgrew the annexe and had to be moved again, this time into the garden of the Church Street premises. Anne records: " ... for a while we shared Miss Hallé's hut, where arm cradles and foot-drop boots were being made, finally we had to build a large hut of our own." The hut was apparently paid for thanks to some hard work on Anne's part in raising the necessary cash.

Then came the big step, sometime late in 1917. There was no moment of epiphany. No yelling of Eureka! But for some time now Anne had been working with Plaster of Paris and she eventually came to realise that the plaster casts themselves made ideal splints, possessing the qualities of papier maché, in that they were light, comfortable yet strong, and like papier maché also allowed X-rays to be taken without having to be removed from the injured limb. Anne further reasoned that, since they were made *in situ*, this meant that the patient was less distressed, because the process of splinting a fractured limb had been reduced from three stages to one; it avoided the need to move patients around, from military hospital to Mulberry Walk and back; it also saved the Plastics Department staff a lot of time and energy, as well as saving on the materials needed for papier maché, so that they could be used on other contrivances that Anne's co-workers needed to fashion. Furthermore these Plaster of Paris splints were non-inflammable and could be easily rendered waterproof, usually by the application of wax, so there was no need for toxic agents to be applied to them. "I had already found that the same materials were useful for splinting, my first case being a splint for use in a bath. I made several for special cases," she wrote.

Plaster of Paris casts were not an invention of Anne Acheson. As long ago as 1852 a Dutch surgeon Antonius Mathijsen had devised a method of rubbing bandages with dry Plaster of Paris (gypsum) and then moistening the bandages with a wet cloth when they were applied to the site of the fracture. Then, around 1860, the Plaster of Paris casts were rendered waterproof by the application of shellac dissolved in alcohol. However it was not universally accepted and there were problems with the early casts, because of the side effects of, effectively, sealing the wound from the air. Patients would develop dermatitis, ulceration of the skin and other problems due to contact with the Plaster of Paris. But towards the end of the First World War Plaster of Paris was viewed as a huge advance in the treatment of fractured limbs and a vast improvement on the papier maché splints. So credit for the more widespread use of Plaster of Paris must go to Anne Acheson and her team, whose pioneering work with papier maché splints had ensured that the traditional problems of sealing a wound from the air had been solved.

In a post-war talk given to the Chartered Society of Massage and Medical Gymnastics in November 1920 Anne and a colleague described how the versatility of the Plaster of Paris casts had made them very popular with orthopaedic surgeons, as they were to remain throughout the 20th Century and into the 21st. The splints could remain rigid, or be articulated where necessary and where desired, and they lent themselves readily to the treatment of some of the more straightforward injuries such as Colles fractures.

It is little wonder that one newspaper article of the time described Anne as "The Presiding Genius" at Mulberry Walk. No description could have been more accurate. She had certainly brought something to the team there.

In late 1917 many of the Surgical Requisites Association's inventions were put on display in an exhibition organised for the Royal College of Surgeons at the Grafton Galleries, as much a fund-raising exercise as a chance to show off all they had achieved. Anne found herself on the organising committee of the exhibition, which ran from November 17th to 20th and was as much a vehicle for recruiting more workers as it was for raising funds – there were stalls selling goods and sideshows offering entertainment. The SRA described it as "A Frivolous Fair and a Serious Exhibition". An article in a December edition of The British Journal of Nursing recounts: "The Exhibition was opened ... by Sir Francis Treherne KCMG, the Surgeon-General, who spoke with enthusiasm of the talented ladies who had made such a splendid contribution to the needs of their country.

"The Serious Exhibition consisted of samples of the wonderful inventive genius and the extraordinarily clever workmanship of the men and women who have given the best of their talent, brain and fingers, to elaborate existing instruments and invent new devices for the surgical relief of our wounded and disabled men.

"The 'Frivolous Fair' ... was well furnished .... All kinds of fancy and useful articles were displayed.... There was an oyster bar, a stall for game and poultry, one for vegetables and another for cakes. An auction was held for the sale of autographs among which was one of the late Lord Kitchener."

Across the English Channel the battles still raged on the Front, and for the Acheson family there was some alarming news. A War Office missive in April 1918, reported that Edgar, who had obviously not suffered any long term ill-effects from his 'shell-shock' of two years earlier and had returned to the Front, was wounded and missing in action. A memorandum stated: "On the morning of Thursday 21st March the 11th Battn. K.L.R. was in position ... south of St Quentin near Bonay, between that village and Essigny le Grand. ... At about 4.00am Lieut Acheson went out towards the strong point with his platoon. The enemy were sending over a strong barrage fire of all sorts and many of the men were struck as they advanced. ... Lieut Acheson, who was in the leading platoon, was reported as wounded, well up towards the strong point. The men searched for him, but did not find him. The enemy fire continued up to about noon. About that time the Germans came over and the part of the Company who were at the billets ... retreated. ... Private Knight thinks that he may probably be in the hands of Germans, who in his case, he being an officer, would probably treat him as well as the circumstances would allow."

Edgar had indeed been taken prisoner. The nature of his wound is not known, but he wrote from his prison billet in Rastatt near Baden in a letter dated April 20th 1918 but not received by his wife Nora until mid-June of that year, that he was fine, although leading an "aimless life". He reassured them he was keeping fit and just looking forward to the end of the war when he could return home and start running his father's linen business in Portadown once more.

Plaster of Paris and papier maché were no longer the 'sole stars' of the show at Mulberry Walk. Metal also had its place at No17, as Anne wrote: "Out of our plastic department has grown the Surgical Requisites Association metal department ... to supply the need for specially designed metal splints, or moulded aluminium, or with various mechanical contrivances."

Gradually the SRA, was able to send out competent, trained personnel to work in a specialist splint room set up by one of the doctors from Millbank, and other depots sent out workers to train new people all over the country.

By the Spring of 1918 the SRA was able to report that up to April of that year "almost 3,000,000 articles of various kinds have been made by the Association and forwarded to St James's Palace for immediate despatch to hospitals at home and abroad." The catalogue lists, among other contrivances, the jaw splint, the shoulder splint (named after Anne Acheson), a head splint, a splint for crooked toes, an appendicitis belt and an abdominal belt. The Association also makes it clear that it was the first to produce the moulded and waterproofed appliances for foot and wrist drop. By that point the SRA was also able to list more than 40 depots countrywide, which the catalogue describes as "flourishing".

All the time that the SRA was expanding in Chelsea – the Polytechnic had lent large rooms to the association in Manresa Road where crutches, bed tables and wooden splints were turned out by amateur carpenters – its inventions were reaching out everywhere, and not just the length and breadth of Britain, but also abroad, in Italy and France. Anne and another member of the SRA, Mrs Lawes Webb, had eventually travelled across the Channel, in 1917, to help set up an SRA depot in Paris and then, travelling via Marseilles to set up another one in Nice, the pair travelled first class on the continent courtesy of the French Red Cross, who had a base in Knightsbridge. The setting up of these outposts also involved training, which Anne undertook with gusto. While she and her colleague were in Paris that year her brother-in-law George, presumably on leave, visited the French capital briefly, and in a postcard to his wife Grace dated July 5th 1917, stated: "I intend to look out for Anne this afternoon but may not see her, though I know my way to her street." It is not known whether they managed their rendez-vous.

Given all the expertise at its disposal, unsurprisingly the SRA eventually set up a three-month training course for willing volunteers, who would then return whence they came and set up similar courses around the country and in Europe. The word (and the skills) was spreading.

Elinor Hallé wrote of the depots set up in Marseilles and on The Riviera, as well as in Pau in South West France. "Still more gratifying," she added, "was the pioneer work of two of my pupils, who went to Italy a few months after we had made our first boot. They started the work in Rome, and then, going different ways, they established workrooms in all of the principal towns in Italy – Milan, Turin, Florence, Naples etc, in every place being welcomed with the greatest courtesy and gratitude by the surgeons."

Word of the SRA's good works was doing the rounds. There was even a letter from the Inspector of Military Orthopaedics, a Mr Robert Jones, based in Liverpool, who acknowledged the contribution to the war effort made by the Surgical Requisites Association when he wrote to Mrs Stokes in the summer of 1918: " ... I think very highly of the most excellent work you are doing. I was very much impressed by every department I visited. The work was up to a high professional standard, and showed very little evidence of the amateur. ... An institution such as yours is of the greatest service to the War Office ...." And in an earlier letter Mr Jones had written: "No praise can be too great for the work which has been affected by the Surgical Requisites Association. It has been an inspiration, Mulberry Walk has sheltered some of the best workers of the war, and many hospitals all over the Country owe them a deep debt of gratitude."

Even after the war the work continued, which was the wish of the SRA volunteers. Elinor Hallé wrote that surgeons, at home and abroad: "... have expressed a wish that the technical skills acquired by the SRA workers should not be lost now that the immediate cause , the care of the wounded, is coming to an end, but that the expert work of these ladies should be retained permanently in aid of the civil hospitals and especially to help crippled children. Various schemes have been suggested towards this end, and it is hoped that soon something definite may be settled.

Nothing would be a greater reward to those who started this work, than to see it permanently established."

The legacy of the likes of Elinor Hallé, who gave her name to appliances such as the Hallé Glove and the Hallé Boot, and Anne Acheson, after whom is named the Acheson Supination Arm Splint, the Acheson Shoulder Splint, and the Adjustable Acheson Splint among others, is immeasurable and it is fitting that their efforts were acknowledged when they were appointed CBE.

Indeed it was for this very reason that the Order had been created, to reward ordinary citizens for extraordinary service for their country. Prior to this, awards of this nature were generally the preserve of Royalty, or confined to the political and military spheres. However, when it was realised just how many civilians were making significant contributions to the common weal, and more often than not in a voluntary capacity, it was felt proper to introduce a new award. So The Most Excellent Order of the British Empire was inaugurated in June 1917 and gazetted in August of that year. Britain was already in the thick of the war and there was no immediate prospect of a cessation to hostilities, so there were tens of thousands of volunteers working flat out every day of the week with little or nothing to show for their incredible, unselfish effort.

The second Supplement to the London Gazette, dated Friday 24 August 1917, carried the following message from the Crown Office. "The King has been pleased, by Letters Patent under the Great Seal, to create and institute an Order of Knighthood to be styled 'The Most Excellent Order of the British Empire.'"

Under the ordinances it was decreed that "... the persons to be admitted to this Order shall be such persons, male or female, as may have rendered, or shall hereafter render, important services to Our Empire...."

To underline the high regard in which the Order of the British Empire was held, a statute ordained "... this order shall rank next to and immediately after Our Royal Victorian Order, and before Our Distinguished Service Order ...."

Doubtless when Anne arrived at Buckingham Place on that chilly February morning in 1919 she was buzzing with the excitement of it all, and it took her some time to get over it to judge by the delay in writing about the day to her sister Emily.

"The investiture was very interesting," she wrote in her neat, upright, cursive script. "Knights, one dame and about six women and five men CBEs had a nice drawing room, with interesting paintings, to wait in."

These were the higher awards and the recipients were separated from the more numerous and less exalted Members and Officers of the order.

Anne then described how the equerries instructed the recipients as to the correct form and protocol. "The knights were told where to kneel etc. We were then marched in file in order of rank and alphabetically through many corridors to the ballroom, or whatever it is."

She has sketched out, on the sheet of writing paper, the lay-out of the room showing the dais where His Majesty King George V awaited them all. Anne pointed out how the usher directed them into the centre of the room where the Master of Ceremonies indicated that they should turn to face His Majesty, before, in Anne's case, dropping into a curtsey, before straightening up and approaching the dais to be inducted into the Order and receive the insignia.

"I came next after the knights, being 'A' and was told to wait till the footstool they kneeled on was cleared away, then curtsey, then go up to the King. Downstairs someone had pinned a little hook on my coat for the King to hang the insignia on."

She then became a trifle vague, when she added: "He [King George] said a word or two of congratulation or something, and I curtseyed and went out. In the lobby an official or lackey took off the insignia and hook and put the former in a case. Then Boy Scouts with notebooks showing where people were sitting, found me and Hazel and the seat she had reserved for me."

"We were not allowed to leave till the King had finished hundreds of OBEs and MBEs. About ten of the Surgical Requisites Association workers were waiting outside in the cold and we were snapshotted by about six press photographers all at once. One was in Wednesday's Daily Graphic."

However, it is quite probable that, while hugely appreciative of the great honour bestowed upon her by His Majesty, Anne would have felt deeply moved by a letter sent to her shortly after her award had been gazetted. The letter, which she took the trouble to keep safe among her papers for the rest of her life, was from a Surgeon Major Alan Todd, who had worked in a hospital in Lewisham in South East London during the war and had therefore known at first hand the work undertaken by Anne Acheson and the team at the SRA.

In a letter dated 10 January 1919, Major Todd wrote (and the underlining is his): "I am so very glad to see that the very valuable work that you have done for the wounded has been appreciated in the bestowal of the Order of the British Empire. Quite apart from what you have actually <u>done</u> yourself, the immense amount that you have initiated represents a huge total of suffering saved."

He goes on to urge Anne not to stop her work, writing: "Now let me earnestly urge this upon you: Don't let your work lapse when peace is signed. Keep it up as long as pensioners need appliances, and meanwhile write a book and teach all mankind all that you know about splints and things – how to use them, how to make them, how to design them and so on. Your things are so far ahead of anything that our stupid instrument-makers ever devised that your accumulated knowledge must be preserved to the world."

The sentiments expressed in that letter certainly helped to underline the extent of what Anne Acheson, Elinor Hallé and the rest of workers at the SRA had achieved in their time together. As it was Anne did not carry out Major Todd's wish and write what would have been the definitive book on all she and the SRA had accomplished; instead she and the raft of volunteers at the SRA returned to their day jobs, knowing that they had still achieved something special over the previous four and a half years, something that would outlive them all.

However, she did write: "We have treated about 1,000 special cases and sent out thousands of standard splints made on the same method on casts taken from the human form." It was quite an achievement for this group of volunteers to look back on.

But something else had also been achieved by these remarkable people at the SRA. They had become a team, forging a special relationship among themselves, and their relationship with Anne was all too evident when reading in her letter of February 28th 1919 what transpired after the pomp, ceremony and 'snapshotting' was all over. Then it was time for celebrating as Anne revealed: "Some of my oldest workers gave me lunch at The Berkeley. Very hilarious. A special menu had been printed and all items had reference to the Plastic Department, eg Hors d'oeuvre plastique, and poulet en eclisse (splint)."

This celebration meal was as clear an indication as anyone could have of the regard in which Anne had been held by her fellow volunteers, an impression reinforced when she added the following: "Today they made me a presentation of a sort of illuminated address – or rather a list of names – and a cheque for £37. They had asked me what I would like and I did not know (not knowing how much money they had) so they asked me would I take a cheque and buy myself something. I will get a Chesterfield. Dugdale will want the one I have which belongs to him, and we have no really comfortable chairs."

So, finally, it was back to her day job. But at least by the time Anne returned to 'Civvy Street' it was to a world which had finally recognised the role of women in society. After the rejoicing of the signing of the Treaty of Versailles and the absolute end of the 'Great War' came an important moment in the suffrage movement when Nancy, Lady Astor, became the first female politician in the House of Commons, after being elected as Member of Parliament for Plymouth Sutton in 1919. Nancy Astor took up the cause of the women's movement with great vigour, once she had established herself in Westminster.

The only sad aspect of 1919 was that the previous five and a half years of hostility and slaughter were soon to become known as the *First* World War. There was a lot of fight left in Europe and the rest of the world it would seem.

7

The Roaring Twenties

~~~~~ɷɷɷ~~~~~

It is little wonder that the Americans termed the new decade The Roaring Twenties, there was so much going on. And it was no different for Anne Acheson CBE who roared into what would be a whirl of a decade for herself. First by obtaining a licence "to keep a motor bicycle or tricycle" at her address. Not that there is any documentary reference to, or proof of, purchase of any machine, whether two-wheeled or three-wheeled, at least for herself; but had she bought one then she certainly would have been one of the country's earliest female 'bikers'. The licence was issued to her at No 18, Beaufort Mansions, Beaufort Street, Chelsea, where she was still living with Hazel, and it is far more likely that the motorcycle, or perhaps a motorised bicycle, would have belonged to Anne's younger sister. Hazel was a medical student at The Royal Free Hospital and independent transport would have been a boon for her when she had to work long into the night, for the return journey between King's Cross and Chelsea. The local council would have demanded a licence as the motorcycle probably had to be kept on the pavement outside the front of the block of flats in which the sisters were living.

Anne also roared into the new decade by establishing herself as a popular designer of car mascots, which were all the rage at the time.

Initially they had been mounted on radiator caps, when car radiators were outside the bonnet, at the front, rather in the fashion of a ship's figurehead. But when radiators disappeared under the bonnets of cars the mascots hung around, adorning luxury motors in the main. They could be representative of the manufacturer, Peugeot's lion rampant, Rolls Royce's Spirit of Ecstasy, the crouching big cat on Jaguar cars for example, but they could also be bespoke. Many well known sculptors and artists designed car mascots, which were generally cast in bronze or brass or zinc then plated with either chrome or nickel. However the best known designer of car mascots, the Frenchman Rene Lalique, made his in crystal and in various colours.

Mascots certainly caught Anne's imagination and she designed a number of them. Among her best known is 'Shoo', a figure of a young girl with hair flowing behind her in the wind and her hands in front of her mouth as if calling out a warning to pedestrians ahead of the car. A report in The Auto Motor Journal early in the decade examines the 1920s fad going on to praise the fact that "... not a few well known artists turn their attention to mascots." It singles out Anne as one of those "well known artists" claiming: "... a charming little mascot 'Shoo' ... is an expression of individual taste, and as we still believe that tenderness and beauty are left, even after the War, we feel sure that many users of cars will be attracted by it. We understand it is quite moderate in price. This is but one example of Miss Acheson's work; she has designed quite a large number, some of them more ambitious, as for instance, 'Speed', a charming nymph which may be seen on some large cars of the expensive type in the fashionable part of London." Photographs of both mascots – the only photographs used – accompanied the feature. According to research by Martyn Anglesea BA MLitt, 'Shoo' was exhibited at the Society of Women Artists.

It is understood that Anne also submitted an entry when Rolls Royce invited sculptors to produce a suitable bonnet mascot. The winner was Charles Sykes, art editor of the magazine Car Illustrated, with his 'Spirit of Ecstasy', which depicts a woman with her finger to her lips as if she is instructing others to keep a secret.

Anne also produced car mascots of a goat in a particularly active pose as well as a more prosaic pig. This latter was for a lady who ran a pig farm and a contemporary article in an unknown magazine explains: "One good lady, running a pig farm, insisted that it should be the effigy of a pig that should adorn her car, and a very lovable pig indeed did Miss Acheson make for her, the while the pig sat, or rather ran for its portrait.

"Sometimes it is a patron's child that she is asked to immortalise in this fashion, sometimes the weird beast from a coat of arms."

That the mascots were popular among car owners is demonstrated by her brother Jim, who added a note, at the top of one letter to her, in 1920: "Am taking the Angus Sanderson car ordered by Edgar when I come home – hereby place an order with you for Mascot for same! Jim."

This was a state of the art motor car, unsurprisingly therefore, just months after its first appearance on Britain's roads, Jim was after one. The Angus Sanderson, whose 2.3 litre sidevalve engine knocked out 14 horsepower, had originally been conceived as a vehicle ideal for mass production, however in the end only around 3,000 rolled off the production line between 1919 and 1927, at a cost to the consumer of a hefty (for those days) £575.

Anne had resumed her Royal Academy exhibiting at the start of the decade, but she was also undertaking private commissions, including one for a member of the family. It was a bust of Lady Crawford, her aunt Anne C Crawford, who wrote an effusive letter of thanks in October 1921: "My Dearest Anne, The head is now unpacked and looks beautiful. You are indeed clever. Thank you ever so much for taking so much pains with it. We waited till J [her husband John] came home. He arrived home from America yesterday morning. We have not yet put it where it is to stay, I think it would look best at the angle of the staircase. And now will you kindly let us know what we owe you, I should indeed have asked you this when the bust arrived. So please let me know about it as soon as possible. Emily tells me you are making lead figures now. I am sure they are lovely."

One of those lead figures, 'The Imp' was accepted for the Royal Academy's exhibition the following year. A remittance advice to Anne from the RA in the summer of 1922 informs Anne that the figure had been sold to "The Lord Swaythling, 28 Kensington Court". It fetched £30.

The whole family proved to be diligent correspondents, and there was certainly plenty for them to write about in the new decade. If the 1920s heralded enormous change and great strides in science and engineering, they also contained not a little excitement and drama, at least for a couple of Anne's siblings, Molly in Cork, and Jim, on a visit to Ireland.

It is debatable which of the two, Molly or Jim, had the closer shave, although Molly's experience of the violence of the times was frightening enough, according to her description of a couple of harrowing incidents at the height of the troubles in 1921 involving the notorious Black and Tans.

The Black and Tans (so called because, owing to an initial shortage of RIC uniforms; their garb was invariably made up of a combination of brown army trousers and RIC dark jackets) were volunteers, recruited on the British mainland, and comprising, chiefly, former servicemen, who were eager to help out the Royal Irish Constabulary in their travails against the newly named Irish Republican Army.

The War of Independence, as this period between 1919 and 1921 became known, was particularly intense in the south and centred among other places on Cork. The Black and Tans were ill-disciplined and ruthless, perfectly prepared apparently to resort to violence.

Molly's eye witness account of her brush with the Black and Tans and her reports of a couple of other incidents in Cork serves to underline the perils of living in the City in those troubled times.

She wrote to Anne on January 17th, 1921: "Cork is a lively place at present. I had to rush my tea on Saturday evening in a cafe in town so as to let the waitresses clear up to get home. We saw no firing ourselves, but people rushed into the place for fear of it. We went home quite quietly.

"I went through gunfire to church last night. The Black and Tans fired shots to stop our tram and yelled something. I was on top with about half a dozen and we all came down inside. We were allowed to crawl on for 50 yards or so. Then we were boarded and had all to put our 'hands up' while the men were searched by the most excited man I have ever seen, not drunk at all, but mad with excitement. Then, when he got out, he, or someone, fired two shots and we proceeded."

A couple of days later there were more disturbing happenings. Molly reported: "We were awakened about four last night by firing. An attack on a police barracks near the office, I believe that was, and since I began this letter I have heard several rifle shots, but they are probably nothing.

"Annie, my maid, saw a man fall on Saturday night and her friends saw a man killed. One of them ran for a priest, who gave him the final rites of the church while unconscious. He was a Protestant."

Unsurprisingly she confessed to Anne: "I was a bit nervy last night, but am quite all right again. It was just having to sit still in church that was rather much, but the walk home put me all right, I just managed to get through the service without coming out."

At the other end of the country Anne's brother James and his wife Vio were on a few months leave from India and were staying at Ballycastle in Co. Antrim, when they too found themselves involuntary witnesses to 'The Troubles'. In his two volume autobiography 'An Indian Chequerboard' James wrote: "One evening Vio and I were out fishing the evening rise on a local stream a few miles out of Ballycastle. We caught a few small trout for breakfast and had turned the car and driven about half a mile homewards when there was a muffled roar behind us. The bridge had gone up. The rebels must have been watching us as we fished and very considerately waited until we had moved out of danger before pressing the plunger."

Life in mainland Britain during this time was not quite so dramatic or violent, at least not for one member of the Acheson family; indeed the 1920s represented Anne's most successful period with the Royal Academy. She exhibited in seven of the ten years, and was not confined to just one exhibit per year; for example in 1926 she had three entries accepted and the following year saw another multiple exhibition by Anne.

Anne had entered the decade with her first Royal Academy offering for four years, a bronze bust of a Mrs Wingate. However, she then missed out the following year, before the next three summers saw her bounce back with a trio of exhibitions. 'The Imp' proved a big hit, following up the 1922 Royal Academy exhibition with a successful appearance at the Victoria and Albert Museum, where it was described by a critic as one of the most beautiful pieces of work in the Industrial Art Exhibition.

In 1922 she had also produced what she described as a 'portrait sketch' of her friend Tommy Dugdale; the bronze head shows a good-looking man, short hair parted high on the left side of his head. He is clean shaven and sporting a bow tie. The mouth looks as if it is on the point of breaking into a smile. The eyes are watchful, keen and seem to follow the observer. Given Anne's gift for reproducing lifelike studies of people this can be trusted to be a very good likeness of the man who was later to become knighted and reach prominent status nationally and internationally in the art world.

But it was in the following year through her figure of 'Sally' which was exhibited at the Royal Academy's 1923 exhibition, that Anne really started hitting the headlines. The figure initially caught the eye of some Scottish art officials, and so impressed were they, that Anne was invited to exhibit in the Glasgow Gallery.

The figure of 'Sally' had also captivated art critics and gardening experts alike, and sparked a new fashion for owners of formal gardens, the 'garden baby'. In a magazine called The Gentlewoman, the writer was full of praise: "Miss Anne Acheson's lead garden figure 'Sally' is yet another work in which tradition is delightfully observed in the quaint and chubby naturalism of the baby figure. This robust little earthling is of the proper type to dare the open and accumulate patina without demanding our pity – an admirably conceived and executed figure for the garden."

Another article in the society magazine 'The Queen' was effusive. The author, Marion Cran, herself a prominent writer on gardens and an influential figure throughout society, gushing: "... lately a visit to the Royal Academy introduced me to 'Sally', and I became aware that there are other laughing hands ... in the world at work ... to make sweet moments for our gardens.

"Sally is a darling. She is a life-sized nude baby in lead, holding her fat little sides with dimpled hands and glancing up and along with such a rogue's glance as made me wish exceedingly to take her away then and there and live with her forever. Sally is a gourmet, I feel it in that padded paunch of hers, in the light Friar Tuck gesture of her hands, and that little laughing twinkling greedy eye.

"I have always liked my kitchen garden to look beautiful with borders of sweet herbs and flowers to all the paths, and a pretty design for the utilitarian beds of it ... and suddenly I knew where Sally should be ... in a paved centre place, on a seemly pedestal, laughing deliciously over the strawberries and the asparagus and the peas and beans and all and all!"

The writer continues: "Having found out the author of 'Sally', it was not long before I saw more work by the same gay hands. A jolly little lad in lead, sliding down the steep bank of a pond to the water's edge, where his toes thrust forward into the crowding mimulus and forget-me-not at the water lip. A merry lad laughing in his reckless descent at the shivering lass away by the steps of the lake, curling her feet up from the touch of the clear water that wimples below ..."

At last the writer named 'the author'. "Miss Anne Acheson is less exclusive than that other sculptor though not by any means easy, either;

she limits her replicas to six." This other sculptor was a reference to Fergus Scott Hurd-Wood, who was a noted garden sculptor, but produced only one of each design, and had not, when this article was written in the summer of 1923, produced a garden figure for ten years. He also happened to be married to Marion Cran at the time the article was written.

Unsurprisingly Marion Cran purchased a 'Sally' for her own much-written about garden at her house 'Coggers', on the outskirts of the village of Benenden in Kent. Writing in 'The Women's Magazine' Mrs Cran advised those of her readers who would like, and could afford to acquire, a lead garden figure such as the ones produced by Anne Acheson: "The garden baby, if it is decided to have one, should be chosen with the utmost deliberation and care. It is not a matter over which to hurry, nor one in which price should be grudged; it is better to wait and save up for a real work of art than to try and live with some vulgarity of incredibly bad taste in imitation stone. The nicer garden figures are generally found in lead, and cost anything from £10 to £100."

Having found an artist, and selected the garden figure, Mrs Cran continued: "At the time of buying the figure it is best to ask ... the artist ... to give a rough sketch of the height, material and design of the pedestal on which it is to be mounted." There was also the question of where in one's garden the statue should be placed, which, according to Mrs Cran was an enjoyable experience as well. Once the figure has arrived, she wrote: "... there is the fun of taking it from place to place in the garden to be absolutely certain that it will be finally set in the perfect spot."

Mrs Cran herself did not bother to ask Anne Acheson to make any sketches. She decided to invite the artist to her home to help decide where to place the figure in her garden. "I was lucky enough to inveigle [Anne Acheson] to my home for a weekend to decide this momentous matter on the spot."

This entailed a train journey for Anne from Chelsea to Charing Cross and thence to Paddock Wood, where she would have changed trains to get on the Hawkhurst branch line – closed down by Dr Beeching in the early 1960s – and she would have alighted at the appositely named Cranbrook Station, which lay between the town of that name and Hawkhurst, finally, unless Marion Cran or her husband met her, she would have taken a taxi or a bus to travel the remaining four miles to Benenden.

Mrs Cran continued: "Like all these garden babies of Miss Acheson's, 'Sally' is life-size. We found a wooden box of the right height, and moved it hither and yon till at last we found Sally's place, studying her in all the lights of morning, noon and sunset, and from far and near, to see how she fitted into the garden design. Then I was given a rough sketch for the pedestal; it must be of old red brick to match the roof of ancient hand-made tiles, I was told – square to chime with the simple line of the old house, and 'stepped back' in ample line proportion. That was all. But I needed her eye and her knowledge to tell me how to get that harmony. I was lucky enough to find a pile of very old mellow bricks, made in the half-thickness of their day, which gave the little pedestal both character and charm."

Anne must have repeated her journey to Kent becuse a photograph shows her in the garden at Coggers. She is facing the house and on the left alongside her is the figure of Sally, just a few yards short of the pond.

Marion Cran was obsessive about Sally, waxing maternal about the lifelike lead figure. "I have grown to love Sally almost like a living creature … those fortunates who achieve their 'Sally' will know that five other people on this round globe have also a naughty whimsical Sally laughing in their gardens. And I am not perfectly sure that I do not rather like the idea of sharing the rogue's glance with a select few…. We might have a Sally Club and pay each other visits to see how we severally thought fit to mount and display her."

And once Sally was *in situ* Marion Cran continued: "I cannot tell the times that I have found 'Sally' peering up at me, when I was depressed or troubled, with her whimsical intelligent, questioning baby-face; and laughed at her, losing the black clouds … put my arm around her fat little shoulders, loving the beautiful modelling of her dimpled infantile shapelessness, and gone back to my study strengthened by her sweet nonsense, refreshed by a trickle of laughter. These garden babies … come to us from the seeing hands of a warm and gifted woman."

The one thing Anne never had in these frantic years was a proper garden of her own. Indeed in 1923, the same year she created 'Sally', she left Wentworth Studios which she had rented while living in Beaufort Mansions for yet another gardenless base. She did not make the move alone. Hazel went with her, the pair of them abandoning their shared flat in Beaufort Mansions for the new place at No 1, King's House Studios.

These were purpose-built and incorporated living accommodation. The entrance, as indicated on the letterhead was behind No 394, King's Road. Anne's niece Harriet remembers the place well. "When I first stayed in her studio at King's House, off the King's Road at the age of ten it seemed to me a very exciting place," said Harriet, "with a permanent smell of wet clay and wooden plinths all over the place bearing figures shrouded in dust sheets, looking a bit like small ghosts." Anne was to spend a total of twelve years there.

8

Leading Light

～～ⅢⅢ～～

With the success of 'Sally' behind her it was also in 1923 that there came a more significant happening in Anne's professional life. In October of that year she was elected an Associate of the Royal British Society of Sculptors. At the time of her election it was known as the Royal Society of British Sculptors and was based in Queen Square in Central London. It had been founded in 1904 and was granted a Royal Charter in 1911. These days it is a registered charity, retaining its original aims to promote and support sculpture, but from its base in Old Brompton Road, where it moved in 1982.

Anne's proposer in 1923 was none other than Sir William Reynolds-Stephens, who was president of the society at the time. Sir William was a distinguished sculptor and painter of the late 19th and early 20th Century, and a founder member of the RBS. Anne was seconded by Phyllis Stabler, who had herself been granted an Associateship earlier that year, so, together with Christine Gregory and Flora Kendrick (1922) – Lady Feodora Gleichen had also been elected as an Associate, but posthumously, in 1922 – as well as her old student friends Mary Morton and Jess Lawson-Peacey (both in 1923) Anne Acheson had become one of the first women members of the RBS.

In 1924 Anne also entered 'Sally' in the British Empire Exhibition in Wembley and there was another more modest landmark in Anne's professional life that year when she had her first fountain figure accepted for the Royal Academy exhibition. Again the figure was in lead, entitled 'Boy with hose-pipe'.

By the middle of the decade Anne's work was well enough known and widely enough enjoyed that she warranted yet another full page feature, this time in The Lady. It was entitled 'The Art of Anne Acheson – Adorning the Family Garden with Lead and Bronze Statuary'. The writer, Margot Hirons, praised Anne's astuteness in creating a fashion for reproducing lead figures of a patron's child or children in the wonderful chubby, 'age of innocence' of the toddler. Anne's accuracy and eye for detail included every dimple and roll of 'puppy fat' on the child.

Ms Hirons introduced her feature thus: "Wherever there are discerning people – men and women of taste – a gentle purr of praise goes up for the child statuary of Miss Anne Acheson .... These babies in lead and bronze are real babies, gurgling with laughter, bubbling over with high spirits, or, like the 'Child with a Hosepipe' solemnly immersed in mischievous endeavour." Not for nothing was Anne Acheson known as the 'Children's Sculptor'.

While it cannot be claimed that Anne was the only sculptress accepting these sort of commissions, nevertheless the entry in the 'Dictionary of Irish Artists', By Theo Snoddy (Wolfhound Press 1996) suggests that this fashion of immortalising one's children or grandchildren as garden figures in lead or bronze was originated by Anne. There is no doubt at all that she was the foremost exponent of this type of garden statuary, and it is to Anne Acheson that Ms Hirons referred: "During the last few years a novel idea has occurred to several modern parents who are the lucky possessors of both babies and gardens. They have had their children modelled by Miss Acheson, and now, in lead they adorn the garden. To crystallise the fleeting beauties of childhood is always a happy scheme. And the notion of being able to hoard up your own baby's loveliest moment – to let her play for ever in her own garden so to speak – is an inspiration so full of fragrant charm that there is little wonder that it is becoming popular. It is a delightful idea ...."

Marion Cran also applauded the concept of portrait statues. In an article in The Queen in September 1925 Anne's greatest fan wrote:

"Fountains are another garden feature which seem difficult to acquire in satisfactory form. Anne Acheson, the sculptor (whose beguiling 'Sally' took every heart by storm when it was seen at the Royal Academy two years ago), has made a pretty portrait group in lead for the rose garden at Olivers [a house in Painswick, in the Cotswolds], and the idea is a very delightful one for those garden lovers who would like to keep their dimpled babies for ever among the flowers. Children grow up .... It is a pretty idea to keep them modelled in the garden – better than photographs, which fade and soil."

That was reinforced in an interview with the Daily Mail in February of the following year, when Anne herself wrote: "Not many people have so far considered the possibility of letting their garden statuary commemorate their children's youth. One of the most interesting pieces of statuary I have done was a portrait group for a fountain .... These two – a boy of three and a girl a little older – were modelled for their grandmother's garden in the Cotswolds, the girl seated and her brother squeezing a ball to form the mouth of the fountain."

The article in The Lady gave an insight into how Anne went about capturing these 'moments of childhood', Ms Hirons continued: "It has been said that genius is a long patience. It is this quality which Miss Acheson brings to bear upon her tiny models, and this is the secret of her success. A sort of professional aunt, Miss Acheson spends hours playing with her baby models (for the time being the studio is turned into a lively bear garden), and having snatched rapid sketches of innumerable, lovely poses – babies, like kittens, find it impossible to be ungraceful – she is able with exquisite skill and sympathy, to interpret childhood in all its moods."

In the Daily Mail interview Anne expanded on her methods: "Children are my favourite subjects, though they can never ... be persuaded to 'sit'. I usually play with my child subjects, noticing their characteristic natural attitudes and expressions and model them afterwards."

In another unidentifiable magazine, with no author's name either, the writer pointed out how difficult it is to get any child, especially under-10s to sit still long enough to study them, and wrote: "[Anne Acheson] is obliged to devise such games for them as will bring the desired movements into being as frequently as possible, and while appearing to enter into those games, to memorise carefully the necessary points – an arduous business.

"The little girl playing with her kitten, and named Rags from the piece of chiffon that she is tempting him with, was, for example, distracted by little lumps of potter's clay, placed high up on a wall mirror. To fetch these down with a stick, the child was obliged to lift her arm continually above her head. The while Miss Acheson studied the little hollows and dimples that she has portrayed so exquisitely.... the figure made one of the most charming exhibits in the sculpture room of the Royal Academy of 1926."

Mrs Cran joined in with: "Miss Acheson models in clay from living children, and the little monkeys are anything but easy to work from; they hate sitting still, and she has to be quick and very clever to catch the vagrant expression which desires to fix at last eternally in lead or bronze; practice has given her a marvellous dexterity in this difficult modelling and also a measureless loving patience with her jolly little models. They are often the children of friends, and she will spend an hour playing with one of them to get a few priceless moments of the special pose and expression she is trying to catch."

Given Anne Acheson's diffidence, even reluctance, to promote her own works – this is perfectly in character with someone who displayed a natural modesty and humility in everything she did throughout her life – Marion Cran's enthusiasm would have gone a long way to help to sell the garden figures, and indeed Anne Acheson, to her faithful readership.

In The Women's Magazine, she explained to the readers just who, and how good, Anne Acheson really was. "Perhaps the best known artist of lead garden babies is Miss Anne Acheson, who exhibits them at the Royal Academy, the Grosvenor Galleries and many special exhibitions of decorative art. Those who are fortunate enough to acquire one have something of eternal beauty to add to their gardens, of which they will never tire and which will increase in value as time goes on and her work becomes more and more famous. I believe her old rule still holds good – of making not more than six replicas of each different model, so that they never become common, but more sought after."

However good Anne was with her 'model' children, she did not always come across as the lovable, amusing aunt, with her own nieces and nephews. Her nieces especially were wary of her.

One of her nieces – in all she had 12 nephews and nieces – Harriet Rhys-Davies (daughter of Grace Faris) remembers: "During seaside holidays she would always take her sketchbook on family picnics and then ask for a volunteer nephew or niece to sit for her. Usually there was a bribe of tuppence per hour, but she was quite strict and an hour would seem a very long time."

Evelyn 'Muffet' Durnford, nee Williams, said: "I don't think Aunt Nan felt entirely comfortable with children, but she was extremely kind to me in a rather brisk way. She would settle me down at a table with a huge lump of clay to model and she would then uncover which ever particular statuary she was working on at that time and proceed to work."

When she was modelling, according to Harriet Rhys-Davies: "... she always wore a long-sleeved overall made of a coarse cotton and usually beige or oatmeal in colour..." an outfit which would have been unfamiliar enough to a child to distance the wearer from the youngster.

Anne just occasionally might have had an edge to her, especially when dealing with Grace's children. Harriet Rhys-Davies again: "When she stayed with us at Rosebank, in Belfast, she would frequently scold us for our common childish misdemeanours. Saying things like: 'Haven't you made your bed yet? When did you last wash your hair? Who put this away without rinsing it? Always wipe the bottom of a tray as well as the top.'"

Another niece, also called Harriet, but known as Harrie, the daughter of Edgar and Nora, remembered: "My earliest thoughts were of a stern lady, and thinking I had better behave. I was always really scared of all my aunts. When we were in the back bedroom at Blairbank there would be a 'tap, 'tap' followed by: 'You girls ought to stop talking and go to sleep.'"

But Professor John Faris, older brother of Harriet Rhys-Davies, recalls: "I don't remember crossness towards myself, but I think she was more indulgent to boys than to girls. Katharine [John's other sister] and Harriet got the cross side."

Perhaps it was as Ms Hirons put it so insightfully, Anne Acheson, the sculptress, was only a "professional aunt", although that is probably being a trifle too harsh on her, particularly since her niece Harriet was the model for one of her garden figures 'Harriet Emily'.

It was in the Daily Mail feature about her that Anne, clearly enthused by the interview, went on to describe the process of producing the statues, albeit she simplified the different stages hugely, but because it was rare for Anne to say anything about the physical processes of her art, it was quite a coup for the Mail reporter. "My models are done in clay, and though I go to the foundry to touch up the finished statues, I do not carry out the process myself. Having gone through it once or twice to make myself familiar with the technicalities involved, I have decided that it is too long, slow, heavy and hot for most women. There is one really thrilling moment – when the molten metal is poured into the hollow mould."

The anonymous author in the unidentified magazine added: "Lead, because of its soft gradations of greys and the pleasant way in which it weathers on exposure, is the medium in which the greater part of Miss Acheson's sculpture is developed. It certainly suits these child studies remarkably well, having neither the chilliness of marble, nor the hard highlights of bronze." And this same writer also made an interesting point, that Anne's garden figures were not merely one dimensional, to be admired from the front only. The writer explained: "It is a feature in Miss Acheson's work that the back of her figures, usually less interesting than the front view in the majority of sculpture, are always as alluring as any other portion; full of beautiful planes and delicate nuances."

There was further endorsement of lead in 'The Lady' when Margot Hirons wrote: "There is something about lead which makes it the ideal medium for garden sculpture, its soft neutral tone merges simply and naturally into the background created by homely English flowers."

Of course Anne could not copyright or patent these 'portrait statues' of people's children, and a couple of years later, when the popularity of garden figures of children was at its height, Margot Hirons, writing in The Daily Telegraph, lamented the inferior attempts by lesser artists hopping on to the Anne Acheson bandwagon. While she conceded that these 'portraits' of people's children were very popular she remarked how few of these figures actually added to the charm of a garden. She described the figures as girls and boys as dull and stodgy, whose chubbiness was their only attraction. She allowed that they were pretty, but that they were also stereotyped. She claimed that only a sculptor who understood the rhythm of babyhood, as well as its anatomy, could possibly hope to create a figure which would compete with the beauties of lawns littered with daffodils, woodlands spotted with snowdrops, lavender patches and rose beds.

She concluded that the perfect garden statuette had to have a personality and cited 'Harriet Emily', with an apple in her hand, a delicious come-hither look in her eyes, and, doubtless under her breath, a chuckle of fat laughter as a perfect example, likening the figure to Eve.

Marion Cran warned in 'The Women's Magazine': "There are not many good garden babies to be found when one comes to look round for them; a great number of bad models cast in cement or composition stone are unfortunately broadcast on an undiscerning public which is attracted by their cheapness, and, urged from within by the desire for a child figure in the garden, buys these meretricious efforts – shocking comments on our national taste."

But Margot Hirons retained a broader perspective of Anne's output, introducing her reading public to other works in her portfolio. "Very charming for interior decoration are Miss Acheson's miniature bronzes." She was also drawn to Anne's pottery figures, "... which are carried out by disabled ex-servicemen at the Ashtead pottery in Surrey."

On the personal front, there was one moving moment for Anne when, in 1925 she helped her sister Hazel prepare to emigrate to India, where she would work for that country's Women's Medical Service. Hazel was headed, in the first instance, to Bannu in the North West Frontier Province, which at that time was still in India. In July that year Anne wrote a letter to a friend called George, possibly more of a friend of Hazel's than of Anne's, since it would appear that she was simply doing her sister a favour by putting pen to paper.

"Hazel meant to write to you before she left, but she had such a rush she had not time, so I said I would write in case she had not time to do it at Birkenhead."

Anne then launched into a detailed description of Hazel's final hours on English soil at least for the next quarter of a century. "We were up to 12 o'clock or two o'clock every night getting her outfit ready. Her inoculation made her ill for one day and she had lots of surgical instruments to buy as well as bedding, camp outfit, solar topee etc.

"I had a wire from her at Birkenhead saying she had the cabin to herself. She left London at 12 midnight and you may have had a letter by now, but I expect she was too exhausted to write. I am very lonely without her.... Tell Grace her last letter arrived after Hazel had sailed."

It was in that same, rather poignant, letter that Anne also revealed: "I am going to Darlington on July 22nd to do a medallion portrait of an old lady." That 'old lady' can only have been Mrs Fanny Spafford, the first principal of Darlington College of Education; that bronze portrait medallion was one of three pieces accepted by the Royal Academy for exhibiting the following year, 1926.

There was sadness for the family in 1925 as well, because not long after Hazel had departed these shores, the Reverend George Faris, husband of Grace, died in September, a victim of pernicious anaemia. By a cruel twist, it was in the following year that it was discovered how beneficial the eating of liver was for sufferers of this debilitating and ultimately (in those days) fatal disease, one that is now easily managed by sufferers taking doses of vitamin B12.

Anne was kept busy thereafter, for in addition to the portrait medallion of Mrs Spafford she also had to work on 'Rags', a garden figure, as well as a statuette entitled 'April' for The Royal Academy exhibition.

Hazel duly arrived in Bannu and wrote a letter to Anne from the Assistant Commissioner's House, her temporary accommodation. "I am now tackling outpatients on my own and, with the aid of an interpreter, who speaks Urdu (not English) Pashtu and Punjabi, I can manage about 25 new patients as well as about 30 old ones – we have about 60 new patients a morning." In this same letter Hazel referred to a rather dramatic change of appearance in her sister, that Anne has obviously spoken of in a previous letter to India. "If you cut your hair you must send a photo – I can't imagine what you'll look like ... I am told that the patients think I am either a man, or of bad character, because of my cut hair, so now I wear a silk hankie on my head. Jim and Vio think it's nonsense and I incline to agree with them." But Hazel's superior, a Dr Matthews (female, of course, because the hospital was exclusively for women), had insisted on her sporting the silk hankie.

A few months after this Anne found herself drawn to warmer climes. Just around the time of the Royal Academy exhibition in 1926, and right at the start of the miners' strike, Anne and Browning, as well as someone named only as Mrs Kirkaldy, presumably a friend of Browning's, since she came from Colchester, took themselves off to Amalfi in Italy. The one surviving letter to Emily, and the first one of the holiday, informed Anne's sister that she and Browning had been bathing and sunning themselves, although it was clear that the purpose of the trip was art. "It is perfectly delightful," wrote Anne. "Hundreds of paintable bits." There is a delicious coincidence in the timing of the writing of the letter, because it is dated May 3rd 1926, the date of the start of the General Strike in Britain and there were Anne and Browning talking of bathing and sunning themselves.

The plan was that the pair of them would be joined by Dugdale, but

Anne explained: "I foresee that we will stay here for more than a month as Dugdale can't come till Whitsuntide and the journey would not be worth his while for a week. It was some journey as well. Anne wrote: "We stayed a night in Rome, and motored from Naples, a four-hour run in the big motor owned by the hotel. The first hour or so was over the worst roads I have ever met, stone-paved with big stones, our luggage broke the grid of the car and we had a long wait in a filthy Naples slum surrounded by horrid children while they roped it on the step and put the big trunk inside the car." Anne's mention of "horrid children" possibly refers to the fact that they might have been begging or had even tried to steal something from the women. It was also in the autumn of 1926 that Anne decided to become more organised and she purchased a small notebook and in capital letters on the first page she wrote "STUDIO RECORDS" it ran until the beginning of 1939, when Anne began a second volume.

As the end of the twenties drew nearer Anne was able to submit two items for the 1927 Royal Academy exhibition, a lead statuette, 'Tangles' and a head of Mrs Dugdale – Browning – for which the subject might well have 'sat' when the two of them were in Amalfi. She sent five items to Sweden for an exhibition, although none of them sold. In this country she submitted pieces for exhibiting to Manchester, Wells, Bradford, Bristol, Darlington, and Plymouth among other places. She also exhibited 'back home' as it were, when she submitted a piece, sadly unidentified, at the British Artists' Exhibition, which was staged at the Belfast Museum and Art Gallery.

She also produced a piece entitled 'Larrikin', which she exhibited at the Society of Women Artists, of which she was secretary. Yet again it was a child, this time one kneeling, short hair blown back by the breeze. She was also producing pottery figures for the Ashtead Pottery in Surrey.

These were possibly the best years of her professional life, when she enjoyed enormous success on the professional front, achieving signal recognition for her talent and her skill. The crowning moment came in November 1927, when, apart from learning that Hazel had passed her first year examination in Urdu, Anne was approached with a commission for an internationally significant piece of work, one that would seal her reputation as one of the era's finest modellers. It was a moment that could probably and properly be described as the apogee of her artistic career.

9

The 'Queen' of Iraq

~~~\m\~~~

The explorer and Middle East expert Gertrude Bell was a celebrity of her time. A romantic, somewhat tragic figure, whose adventures and achievements had done much for the women's movement. So it was a signal honour for Anne to be invited to model a bust in bronze to commemorate the life of this remarkable woman. Miss Bell was renowned throughout the Middle East and the Western World for her work in helping with the creation of Iraq from what was Mesopotamia, following the collapse of the Ottoman Empire. She had also, almost singlehandedly, set up what was to become the Baghdad Archaeological Museum, initially siting it within the confines of the royal palace.

So the fact that the Royal Academy did not want to exhibit any of Anne's works the following year, 1928, might well not have bothered her overly. Pride might have been dented, but she had been rejected before, and would be again; however, she would need as much time as possible to work on the bust of Gertrude Bell, to ensure a high quality product that would match the quality of the woman, whose head she was modelling.

Bell was a charismatic figure, possessed of an enormous intellect, which allowed her to master an impressive number of languages. She was fluent in Arabic, Persian, French and German and could also speak Italian and Turkish.

She was born on July 14 1868, in County Durham, the daughter of the ironmaster Sir Hugh Bell, and the granddaughter of the industrialist Sir Isaac Lowthian Bell, she wound up the early years of her education at the recently founded Queen's College, based in London's Harley Street, before, at the age of 17, going up to Lady Margaret Hall, Oxford. Two years later she graduated with a First Class Honours degree in Modern History – the first woman to achieve a first in the subject at Oxford University.

On leaving Oxford Bell spent three years mixing with high society in London before, in 1892, she made her first visit to the Middle East. In May of that year, at the age of 23 she headed off to join her uncle Sir Frank Lascelles and his wife Mary at their new post in Tehran, where he was British Minister at the time. She had been to the London School of Oriental Languages order to learn Persian as part of her preparation for the visit.

The journey aroused in her a wanderlust and subsequent world tours taking in India, Japan and Korea among other countries followed, as well as jaunts in Europe, including Switzerland. That was where she acquired a love of climbing and gained a reputation as an extremely accomplished Alpinist. She found herself drawn once more to the Middle East in 1899, when she travelled to Jerusalem; there she learned Arabic. She also visited Palestine and Syria in the same year and gradually found herself becoming more interested in archaeology, visiting ruins in the region and recording information and discoveries in cities such as Damascus, Antioch, Beirut and Jerusalem. Her first foray into Mesopotamia came in 1909 when she saw Babylon and the Hittite city of Carchemish, it was when she was based in the latter that she first met T E Lawrence – Lawrence of Arabia as he was to become known. She was building up her knowledge of the Arabs and their culture, and of course of the region, on top of all that she was adding to her linguistic armoury. She also travelled to Asia Minor and helped the British archaeologist Sir William Ramsay excavate early Christian churches. She visited the ancient city of Ha'il in the middle of Arabia, a place few Westerners had ventured. It was there that she was robbed and held captive for a short while before eventually being released, but instead of carrying on to Riyadh as originally planned, she cut her losses and her journey short. By the outbreak of the war she had an impressive knowledge of the deserts of northern Arabia, its ruined cities and its indigenous peoples.

There were echoes of Anne and her voluntary work with the Surgical Requisites Association, when, at the outbreak of the First World War Bell, whose understandable request to work in the Middle East had been denied, volunteered instead to work with the Red Cross in France. The following year though her specialist knowledge of the Middle East, coupled with her fluency in Arabic and Persian, was finally acknowledged and she was summoned to Cairo to work for a branch of Army Intelligence. Her role was that of liaison officer of the newly formed Arab Bureau, in Iraq and as an assistant political officer. It was there that she met up again with T E Lawrence, and together with others they set about analysing data about the location and disposition of various Arab tribes that might be sympathetic to the British cause against the Turks. The information used was invaluable to Lawrence and the British in forming their alliances.

Twelve months later found Bell in Basra, where she became the sole female political officer in the British forces. Some of her work involved drawing maps to help the British Army get safely to Baghdad; she was also the field controller of Harry St John Philby, the father of the spy Kim Philby, who was working at the time for the Colonial Service. In the early 1930s he was to explore the Rub al-khali (the Empty Quarter) he was not the first to do so, but his explorations of the region have endured. He also helped to negotiate the agreement which opened Saudi Arabia to American oil exploration.

Once Baghdad fell in 1917 Bell and Lawrence became part of a group formed by Winston Churchill that was influential and instrumental in getting King Faisal I on to the throne of Iraq. Bell's knowledge of the country meant she was invited to draw up the boundaries for the new country of Iraq, and after compiling a report over ten months in 1919 Bell had concluded, presciently, that Arab leadership was the way forward, which did not endear her to her bosses. Eventually Faisal, who had been advised by Bell since his arrival in Iraq two years previously, was crowned King Faisal I of Iraq in August 1921; it was because of her influence with Faisal, the former King of Syria, whom Bell had advised about the various tribal leaders in the region, that she was dubbed 'The Uncrowned Queen of Iraq.'

Once things had settled down after the coronation Bell devoted her time to setting up the Baghdad Archaeological Museum, which had a home initially within the confines of the royal palace. Bell oversaw all excavations and scrutinised every artefact uncovered and every find. It was at her insistence, and in the face of some stern opposition from various European bodies and leading figures, that all excavated artefacts should remain in the country in which they were discovered; this therefore guaranteed that her museum retained a collection of Iraq's antiquities. And somewhere in the midst of all this activity Bell found time to translate the mystical Sufi poetry of the Hafiz.

Family problems and her own poor health had led Bell to return to Britain in 1925, where she discovered that the family fortune was in decline. On returning to Baghdad she first went down with pleurisy, then on recovering, she learned that her much-loved younger brother Hugo had died of typhoid.

A tribal rebellion against the British-backed regime in the infant country of Iraq a bare month after the opening of the Baghdad Archaeological Museum, in 1926, was yet another distressing event for Bell. Not long afterwards she was found dead in her bed, after apparently overdosing on sleeping tablets, although it could not be established whether the overdose was intentional or accidental. She was buried in the British cemetery in Baghdad.

Gertrude Bell and Anne Acheson never met; however they did have some things in common. Bell, like Anne, was appointed CBE for her war work – she was the only commissioned female officer in the British Army during the First World War. Like Anne she fought against the prejudices and taboos of the day and gained a university degree. Like Anne she was fiercely independent, highly intelligent and mindful of others. Where the two were polarised was in their attitude to women's suffrage. While Anne was a supporter, albeit a moderate suffragist, Bell appeared to have little time for the women's movement. Apparently she believed that if women regarded their domain as being the kitchen and bedroom, then they were not deserving of, and unprepared for, any opportunity to take part, via the vote, in deciding how a nation should be governed. It was a fairly intractable attitude, and that inflexibility, that indomitability of spirit, was captured perfectly by Anne in her bust of Gertrude Bell, which was modelled not from life, but from photographs.

At the beginning of December 1927 an article appeared in The Illustrated London News which recorded the commissioning of Anne Acheson to produce the bust of Gertrude Bell. By all accounts, up to that point it had not been a *fait accompli*; presumably Anne had to undergo some sort of final selection process. However, if the selection panel had read what The Illustrated London News wrote about her and her works it most surely would have been persuaded to choose her immediately. "It is interesting to hear the suggestion that the sculpture of the memorial to Miss Gertrude Bell, which is to be placed in the Museum at Baghdad, and which has been designed by Mr I M Wilson, may be executed by Miss Anne Acheson. The selection of a woman sculptor would certainly be appropriate, though the committee in Baghdad that is arranging for the memorial would not, of course, be influenced by that consideration. Miss Acheson's work, which has been seen at several Royal Academy Exhibitions and at many others, is charming and distinctive, but her portrait medallions and busts are less well known than the delightful leaden child figures she does for gardens."

No doubt Anne still had plenty of private commissions to fulfil in the meantime, and indeed she might not have been invited to exhibit at the Royal Academy, but she was able in 1928, to enhance her reputation internationally, as she wrote that she had been "... invited to show in Brussels, Sweden, Italy, Paris, Toronto, New York, Dublin and Glasgow, as well as at the Victoria and Albert Museum and Lancaster Art Gallery." So it was a hectic time for Anne, since she would have had to organise, with the help of her trusted administrative assistant Bill Baker, the packing and transporting of her various works to these far-flung places.

Yet another article appeared by another of Anne's big fans, Margot Hirons, this time in Home Magazine in which the author wrote about a couple of Anne's Royal Worcester figures. "Delicious whimsicality is expressed by another illustration. Here is a couple designed by Anne Acheson CBE, the famous sculptor, who makes the world's loveliest garden figures. 'Edwin and Angelina' she has called this early Victorian pair; he in a peacock coat, very courtly and gallant, she very attractive in a white frock, striped with blue, and a blue and green paisley shawl. These figures cost a guinea each, but who would divide such a devoted couple, when the two can be bought for 35 shillings [£1.75]?" This would have represented a saving of seven shillings, some 35 pence in modern money, but it was also an extremely good advertisement for Anne since the two figures of Edwin and Angelina are also pictured. It was also further evidence that Anne was being kept busy throughout 1928.

Eventually things calmed down and towards the end of February 1929, she was pictured, deep in concentration, at work on the plaster cast of the striking looking bust of Gertrude Bell. Naturally enough the newspapers carrying this picture were both in the north, one being the Sunday Sun based in Newcastle-upon-Tyne which covered County Durham, the county of her birth, the other The Yorkshire Post, covering the county where Gertrude Bell's father and his second wife eventually settled.

In the summer of 1929 the bust of Gertrude Bell was finally cast in bronze and it was then a matter of putting it on display for a 'showing', and so, to this end, Anne issued invitations to various dignitaries to a viewing at the Forum Club, where she was also a member, in Grosvenor Place, Hyde Park Corner. The invitation read: "Anne Acheson CBE ARBS requests the honour of your presence at a Private View of the Portrait bust of the late Gertrude Lothian Bell CBE and other portions of the Memorial designed by J M Wilson ARIBA to be erected in Baghdad, Irak [sic], in memory of her work in that country." The viewing was to run from Saturday July 6th to Wednesday July 10th, daily from 11.00am to 6.00pm, although it was closed on the Monday.

The completion of the bust was recorded in most newspapers and periodicals that July. In The Times it warranted a single column 'short' of about 200 words, in which the reporter explained that the inscription accompanying the bust would be in English and in Arabic and would be on a wall panel. The article went on to describe the bust as " ... an excellent piece of modelling in the round, being placed on a bracket supported by a scroll between them. The memorial will be so placed, on the wall of a round arched recess, that the head 'tells' against a stone background, upon which is to be carved a semi-circular relief, like a halo, of lotus and rose intertwined, and the effect is very good indeed."

The article revealed that Anne seized the opportunity to promote her other work when the readers were told: "Miss Acheson is best known as a sculptor of garden figures of children, generally carried out in lead, and some charming examples of her work, including four 'Seasons' for a garden in New Zealand, are on view with the memorial."

There was an even more fulsome piece in a periodical called 'The Woman's Leader – And The Common Cause'. "Miss Anne Acheson's portrait bust of Miss Bell was on exhibition at the Forum Club recently, giving those who remember the keen eyes and pointed features so full of vitality, an opportunity of seeing how strikingly these characteristics can be portrayed in bronze. The portrait was a live thing, dominating the room. The memorial is to be a doorway in the courtyard of the Museum which Miss Bell herself founded at Baghdad. The bronze bust and bronze tablet, with its inscription both in English and Arabic, will have a background of yellow Yorkshire stone, which is also being sent out direct from this country."

The Women's Leader quoted the full text of the inscription: "Her memory the Arabs will always hold in reverence and affection. She created this Museum in 1923, being then Honorary Director of Antiquities for Iraq. With wonderful knowledge and devotion she assembled the most precious objects in it and through the heat of the summer worked on them until the day of her death on 12th July, 1926. King Faisal and the Government of Iraq in gratitude for her deeds in this country have ordered that the principal wing shall bear her name and with their permission her friends have erected this tablet."

The same article also revealed: "It will be remembered that Miss Acheson was a member of the important small committee entrusted with the responsibility of inviting and hanging the work at Wembley in the great exhibition of British sculpture."

In 'The Queen' the anonymous 'Art Critic' wrote: "The bust is an excellent portrait of Miss Bell as she appeared after her strenuous post-war work in Arabia.... Miss Acheson has certainly done justice to a difficult subject."

In August 1929 newspapers were reporting that the bust was now packed and ready for shipment to Iraq. However the bust was not to be unveiled until early the following year. When the ceremony took place, appropriately it was King Faisal I of Iraq who did the honours on January 18th 1930, at a ceremony which was attended by members of the Iraqi Cabinet, and diplomatic and consular representatives; the British High Commissioner Sir Francis Humphrys, proffered the work on behalf of the subscribers. King Faisal replied: "I appreciate the spirit of those who have contributed towards the erection of this memorial to the late Miss Bell, whose name will ever remain inscribed on the heart of Iraq. It will be a symbol of her great services to the country, which were more valuable than any material offering could have been."

Anne did not attend the unveiling, but someone had obligingly copied out a report of the unveiling ceremony on to Anne's headed notepaper at King's House Studios. It described a " ... short impressive ceremony at the Baghdad Museum on Saturday..." before going on to list a Who's Who of dignitaries gathered for the ceremony. Interestingly it then made mention of the accuracy of Anne's handiwork, "... all who knew Miss Bell are satisfied that there has been set up in Baghdad a vital likeness of a very vital woman." And in 1959, some thirty years after its creation, in an article in the Belfast Telegraph, Anne's masterful depiction was praised again: "... she achieved what was regarded not only as a fine work, but an excellent likeness."

Since its unveiling of course there has been another World War and two Gulf Wars, leaving the fate of the bust shrouded in mystery. Inquiries to the Middle East department of the British Museum drew a blank, although Dr John Curtis, the keeper of the department of the Middle East said he would be surprised if it had survived. However there are claims in various quarters that the bust was removed from its regular spot and was transferred to the basement of the Museum as a precaution, and that it would gather dust until such time as it was deemed safe enough to put it back on display.

However, a replica of the bust is sited permanently at the Royal Geographical Society in Kensington Gore, in London.

There is nothing in Anne's papers to indicate how much she was paid for the Gertrude Bell commission, although in a letter dated April 30th 1930, when things were clearly none too good on the financial front, she told Grace: "The Gertrude Bell thing will bring me in something in the meantime."

The Spring of 1929 must have been a busy time for Anne, because in addition to finishing off the bust of Gertrude Bell in time for the showing at the Forum Club, she also had to complete and submit two works for the Royal Academy's summer Exhibition. On this occasion her offerings, which were both accepted, were two pieces that were following one of her themes, the months. She chose to show the two months of the year which also mark the summer and winter solstice, thus it was that 'June' and

'December', both of them garden figures in lead made their appearance in prestigious surroundings.

She did then manage a break. Just a couple of months before the unveiling of the bust of Gertrude Bell in Iraq, Anne was staying in Suffolk with Browning in November 1929. The two old friends were based in a rented farmhouse in the hamlet of Iken, which lies between Snape and Aldeburgh, but on the other side of the stretch of water known as Long Reach. Browning and Dugdale had moved to Poplar Farm two years previously in 1927. It was, according to Joanna Dunham's biography of Amy K Browning, a place that the Dugdales fell in love with immediately. However they still retained their London Studio just off the Fulham Road, somewhere that was something of an artistic enclave in Chelsea, and coincidentally, a place that was to feature prominently in Anne's life.

Back in 1929 it is apparent from her letter from deepest Suffolk that Anne was clearly worried about money and work. The Wall Street crash had just happened in the last week of October sending tremors throughout the banking and financial world.

But Anne's letter, dated November 1st 1929, began with matters more mundane than worldly. It was addressed to Grace, who was by then teaching at Victoria Girls' College in Belfast. It was apparent from Anne's reply that the school wanted to stage George Bernard Shaw's play 'St Joan', which had first been produced five years previously in 1924, and Grace had sought Anne's advice for the scenery and back drop etc.

"I think the cathedral might be managed with a curtain (stencilled) between, or behind, two pillars as background. I forget what it was in St Joan." Anne broke off here to sketch a couple of pillars, indicate a curtain and scribbles in three figures, for scale presumably. She then picked up her thoughts again: "I shall try to send you illustrations and measurements of pillars."

There are echoes, most likely, but not necessarily, unintentional, of 'Greensleeves', once thought to have been written by Henry VIII, when she let it be known that she was also prepared to help out her sister with a costume. There was a drawback to this generous gesture, however, as Anne explained: "I can lend my mediaeval green velvet dress, but the sleeves are lost. I think I destroyed my bustle one, but I shall look when I get back." There were invariably occasional outbreaks of dry humour, and it would have been entirely within the bounds of her sense of fun for Anne to have slipped in a gentle joke, given the period design and the colour of her dress.

This break in Suffolk involved Anne in looking after a couple of animals. It has already been seen that she appeared to like cats, she and Hazel having kept a couple a few years back in London. This time though the animals were Browning's, and they proved a nuisance to Anne.

She wrote: "I am still working on the rabbit. He has bitten me once. Browning's small Yorkshire terrier got into the garage and pulled the netting off the nails and had just got into the small hutch which we brought the rabbit in, when we happened to come on the scene. Luckily I got Tibbets (the dog) out quickly, but Cuthbert (the rabbit) was nervous all day after."

She was taking the opportunity of writing the letter to Grace while Browning was out of the house to meet her husband Tommy Dugdale, who was based in London at No 9, Avenue Studios which was just off the Fulham Road, during the week, returning to Poplar Farm at the weekend. "Bill Baker [Anne's administrative assistant] is here for the weekend. He and Browning have just gone to meet Dugdale, who is coming home for the weekend."

She gave a clear idea of the extent and depth of her financial worries when she revealed how much she got for a recent commission. "I have got a cheque for £225 for my four figures going to America – a relief to me as I had no references, and knew nothing about Mrs Manning." But there is no doubt that Anne was feeling the pinch at this time. "Not a word of a job or sale anywhere now."

10

Indian Summers

~~~~~~⚏~~~~~~

While the world was whirling towards depression, the 1930s began rather more promisingly for Anne Acheson. For a start she was made an academician of the Ulster Academy of Arts; she was also represented in an exhibition of Irish art, which was staged in Brussels; then in the wake of her completion of the bust of Gertrude Bell, Anne was given another important commission, by The King's School in Worcester. The headmaster, Cuthbert Creighton, had lost his wife Margaret in 1923 and he wanted to create a garden in memory of her. Thus it was that seven years later, when he was in a position to be able to purchase an acre of land from the Ecclesiastical Commissioners, he subsequently charged Mr Hope Bagenal with the task of designing the garden, and Anne Acheson was asked to produce a suitable figure to sit above the fountain.

The King's School is set on the banks of the River Severn, and Anne's familiarity with the classics and more specifically with Milton's poem Comus, led her to producing a figure 'Sabrina' (the Latin name for the Severn) who is regarded as the mythological goddess or spirit of that river.

That statue's permanent place – it is still to be seen in The School Garden – echoes the following lines from Comus: "May thy lofty head be

crowned/with many a tower and terrace round/And here and there thy
banks upon/with groves of myrrh and cinnamon." As Mrs Caroline
Roslington, the archivist at The King's School, wrote dryly of the setting
for the figure: "I don't think they had myrrh and cinnamon bushes, but
it's a nice idea. There are terraces."

Anne completed the lead figure in late 1930 and the garden, having
been donated to the school by Mr Creighton was formally opened in July
the following year. For her efforts Anne was paid £200.

Fiscally though, it was still a far from satisfactory state of affairs for
Anne, who was feeling the economic pinch. In April 1930 she confided
to Grace that money was tight. Thankfully she was back in the Royal
Academy for the first two years of the new decade. In 1930 she submitted
'March', and 'Leveret', both of which the Royal Academy described as a
"garden group, lead".

Anne also exhibited 'Leveret' at the Society of Women Artists, and
at the Royal Institute in Piccadilly in London in 1931. She was still
secretary of the society and there is a newspaper photograph and caption
which credits her with organising the exhibition. A caption in another
newspaper describes the scene thus: "[Miss Anne Acheson] has got the
smile out of the block of stone in which she has modelled Arabella.
Arabella is a prim Victorian maiden with a bustle and a bonnet and a
blush, and the joke is that she looks far older than her probably short-
skirted grandmother would today."

The following year saw Anne submit two more figures to the RA,
'Annabel Cundall' (head), and 'Josephine G Owen as Puck' – garden
figure, lead. Later in the decade Anne was to visit Dora Owen, the mother
of Josephine, in Chipping Campden, in Gloucestershire, with a view to
selling another garden figure. She also exhibited in Dublin in the summer
of 1932.

Earlier that year an article appeared in the Glasgow Herald, which
focused on 'Women's Topics' and was written by F Marie Imandt, who
paid a visit to The Forum Club in the Capital and gives the reader a
glimpse of what was going on inside. "... No one could pass the open door
of a salon and catch a glimpse of an exhibition of pictures and sculpture
without going in to the room to look round, and on a recent occasion the
two artists gave me a cordial welcome." The two artists in question were
the husband and wife, Tommy Dugdale and Amy K Browning. The writer

reveals that Dugdale had been occupied for the previous seven years in assessing designs and paintings in the "... four central Scottish schools of art – Edinburgh, Glasgow, Dundee and Aberdeen."

The Dugdales were not the only artists to feature in the article; the writer also chatted with Anne, reinforcing the impression that modelling children in lead as an eternal reminder of their cherubic childhood had taken off over the last few years. "... Miss Acheson ... has a long record of important work. She is doing delightful portraits of children just now, which are being used to adorn gardens. The taste for these decorative schemes is growing, and many parents have their children's statuettes among the flowers of their gardens."

However, the depression was having an effect, and people were no longer as willing to put their hands in their pockets and indulge themselves in the purchase of lead statuary, whether it was modelled on their children or not. In those austere times it was, frankly, a luxury, and luxuries were what Anne could not afford either. In the end she was to turn back to something that seemed to come naturally to her and would not cost her anything – teaching.

There was an anxious-sounding letter in early 1931 to her sister Emily in which Anne frets about a prospective purchaser of some figures. "A New Zealand woman is coming to see my figures this morning. She has just rung up." A little later in the same letter her impatience is apparent when she interrupts her narrative about a visit by her nephew John Acheson, to add: "I wish this New Zealand woman would come and put an end to the suspense."

Ever the pessimist Anne was convinced that the visit would produce nothing. "I expect she will fade away when she hears the prices ...." And if the price would not put off the New Zealander Anne, perhaps because she regarded 1930s New Zealand as some kind of social and artistic backwater, supplied a further reason why there would be no interest in her figures: "... because they are nude."

In the event she was proved wrong. In a characteristic postscript squeezed around the narrow margin of the letter, Anne announced to Emily: "New Zealander has come and wants four figures probably, like the Hampton Court ones, so she is taking me there on Monday. Not exactly like, but to go in a garden like Hampton Court, suggested £50 each. It did not seem to stagger her. I hope it will come right."

While Anne was forced to take on private pupils she made it abundantly clear that she regarded them as a necessary evil; the money was welcome, but the time they took up and the fundamental intrusion into her private and professional life were acutely irritating to her. Then Anne heard of a vacancy at The Norland Place School along Holland Park Avenue in West London; she applied for and got it. The vacancy had arisen because the art mistress had taken a sabbatical for a year. It tided her over a rough financial passage and she certainly pleased her employers, if a testimonial by Mrs C E R MacClymont, the Principal of the Norland Place School, is anything to go by.

It was written in February 1932 and in it Mrs MacClymont wrote: "Miss Acheson came to teach advanced modelling to our elder girls during the year our Art Mistress was in America. We have the happiest recollections of the time she spent with us, both from the good work she inspired the girls to do, and from the able manner in which she conducted her classes. She seemed to us a very gifted teacher, and we parted from her with much regret."

These days the school is co-educational for boys aged four to eight and girls aged four to eleven. In Anne Acheson's day it occupied Nos 164-168 Holland Park Avenue, these days its address is Nos 162-166. Unsurprisingly art still features strongly in the school's curriculum in the 21st Century.

Teaching turned out to be just one different source of income for Anne in the early to mid 1930s; she also began producing figures for Royal Worcester as well as creating dolls for Exella. A page from the trade magazine of the time 'Games and Toys' and dated July 1934, carries a full page advertisement for "*The new Exella Dolls – speaking likenesses of typical English characters*", and among Anne's creations were 'Pc Bloggs' a police constable, described in the advert as " ... the genial fellow who helps the children across the road. Dressed in regulation uniform, with silver badge and buttons, white gloves and patent leather boots ... "; another 'character' was 'Jolly Jack' a sailor, sporting white bell bottom trousers and puffing "a cherry wood pipe ..."; 'Jeanette' was a more conventional if more anonymous doll in the same series who wore a party frock "in pink frilled organdie ..."; and finally there was 'Baby Mary' in her "... blue woolly matinée jacket and bonnet and organdie dress."

Amidst all this worry and effort to provide an income for herself

Anne was still open house to members of the family. First there was John Faris, who sat the scholarship examinations for Oxford Colleges, and in December 1931 her nephew landed at his Auntie Nan's doorstep at Number 1, King's House Studios, King's Road. Early in his letter home to his mother, John informed the family that Anne was "... very busy interviewing reporters and so on" presumably because she was, by then, something of a celebrity, although perhaps with a trifle more substance than the celebrities of the modern era.

Then there was her other nephew John, son of Edgar and Nora, obviously younger than John Faris, but someone whose company Anne enjoyed. She had brought him across from Ireland with her and had also volunteered to accompany another youngster, a girl called Dorothy, the 15-year-old daughter of a family friend Mrs Gilbert, who, according to Anne, "... used to stay at Portballintrae every year." And Anne's love and enjoyment of children are patently obvious and she clearly revels in their enjoyment of the long journey from Ireland. "John and Dorothy were thrilled at their first meal on a train," she wrote. "We stayed in the dining car all the way after breakfast, so had a table and lots of room."

John was to spend a couple of weeks with Anne and if there were any doubt about her attitude towards children it was dispelled when she told her sister Emily: "I shall have no trouble amusing young John. He is about the opposite of John Faris in some ways, such as talking, but is also able to amuse himself." Later in the same letter she added: "John A wrote a long letter to his mother last night, telling her all he had seen." And it transpired that John Acheson had seen a lot. Bill Baker, Anne's administrative assistant, had shown up one morning when Anne was suffering with a headache and had offered to take young John out sightseeing. "He is keen on seeing the old engines etc in the science museum, all sorts of working models, so they have gone there .... He has bought a steam engine for 2/- [10p] and expects it to work."

It was also early in 1932 that Anne played hostess to one of her nieces, Katharine Faris, who spent some three months with her aunt, convalescing after an illness. While she was there Anne encouraged Katharine to attend public lectures in modern languages at various educational establishments around the capital in order to sharpen her skills in a field that was to become her niece's speciality.

It wasn't all that easy to find places for her to go, as Anne explained to Grace: "Katharine has difficulty in finding lectures to which the public are admitted, on her courses in German and English this term. There are some later in the year. She has gone to one at the Polytechnic today, in German. We have written all round for lecture programmes." It might have been difficult, but such lectures, to which anyone could just drop in at this or that educational establishment, were not a feature of the modern day.

Katharine also sat an exam during her time in London. "We await Latin exam result anxiously," Anne confided to her sister, "but K has not much time to worry. We had dinner with Vio and Mrs Field [Vio's mother] at their hotel yesterday. K wore her black and white silk, and looked very nice. I let the sleeves down a bit, making it less evening dressy."

Anne also reassured Grace that Katharine was generally enjoying herself, adding that she "... seems quite happy, except about the Latin exam." And in one of her characteristically crushed postscripts up one side of the paper, she scribbled: "K seems less nervy that she was in Portballintrae when I was there."

Despite this constant stream of visitors to her studio, Anne also did her share of staying with relatives, one in particular being Hazel who was in India. And in these troubled times a trip abroad seemed as good a way as any to leave the problems of the Western world behind her. In addition India was the perfect place to inspire artists given the cultural differences, not to mention the quality of the light. Anne did a number of water colours on every trip to the Sub-Continent, even selling some works while she was out there on different visits, as she reported in a brief letter home from one of those trips early in the 1930s: "I sold another sketch at £2 yesterday."

Spring 1932 found her in Jubbulpore. Unfortunately only a couple of letters have survived from that particular visit, but they contain plenty of news, some of it lightweight gossip about the state of Hazel's garden, some of it a little more sad.

It seemed that Hazel had recently acquired a puppy, but Anne had to report: "The puppy died of pneumonia on Sunday night and we all miss it – Hazel was very fond of it." In the other letter, almost by way of a reminder to herself Anne stated: "She must get a new dog this week, before I go."

Her other worry about Hazel was that Anne was not the only one leaving Jubbulpore. "I am sorry to go away now just when most of her friends are leaving the station for the hot weather, or for good."

She explained this last remark more fully later in the letter. "We went to the Jub. Dram Soc's show last night, a crook play, The Crooked Billet. The best amateur show I have ever seen, a real thriller. Date was suddenly made a week earlier as two of the men in it had been wired to join the Everest expedition. They are in the Signals Corps." It is likely that this would have been the 1933 Everest expedition, when, for the first time, and with the help of four members of the Royal Corps of Signals, radio communication was tried out in a Himalayan expedition, with great success.

There was also something of an exodus from Jubbulpore, as Anne recorded: "Yesterday morning the regiment called 'The Frontier Force' now stationed here, got sudden notice to move to Delhi in five days. How would you like to have five days' notice to move your family and goods and try to sell refrigerators and non-movable things?"

In another short letter Anne added: "Her nice neighbours have been ordered to Burma, which is another grief, so she is rather depressed this week and looking very thin again. I am sorry to leave her so soon."

At least Hazel had her garden, which was, apparently a thing of wonder in that climate. "We have had a lot of rain and everything is fresh and cooler," wrote Anne. "Hazel's roses are still magnificent. She has had another dinner party and again had a big bowl of them on the table, a good subject of conversation, not that these folk are silent as a rule.

"The roses are the ones Edgar sent her, and of course cuttings from them. She has good sweet pea and hollyhocks too. We think the reason her roses are better than anyone else's is that she planted them round her pond (a pond the builder made when building the bungalow and which she retained, though it was not meant for *the* pond – a high, built-up affair for irrigation streams) that is the feature of all gardens here. This pond must keep her roses cool at midday we think. The blossoms are enormous."

Anne's brother James, in his autobiography 'An Indian Chequerboard', claimed that she was visiting him early in 1933, when he was the Deputy Commissioner in Peshawar. While the date of Anne's letters would appear to contradict him, placing her on the Sub-Continent later in the year, nevertheless he recounted a bizarre tale about her brief visit to him and his wife Vio.

She was tired when she arrived at the Deputy Commissioner's bungalow, "... a big shady house," as he described it in his book, "with a deep verandah and with an enormous, very old banyan tree with innumerable trunks propagated downwards from the boughs of the parent tree."

The bungalow had been the scene of a brutal murder 80 years previously when Lt Col. Frederick Mackeson, the then Commissioner, was assassinated, stabbed to death, by what Jim Acheson calls a "Ghazi (Muslim fanatic)".

James' narrative continues: "... we were visited by my artist sister Anne, who was touring and sketching in India. It was the beginning of the hot weather and she naturally arrived tired from her journey. We suggested that she should lie down and rest for a while; she agreed, and Vio had a bed made up for her in my dressing room, which gave on the verandah. It was broad daylight and I was busy dealing with case-work and interviews in my home office at the other side of the hall."

It must be emphasised at this point that James was a very straightforward man, highly intelligent, and from what can be gleaned from his correspondence and his autobiography, not a man given to fanciful or dramatic imaginings, so what follows (and he felt it was powerful enough and real enough to be included in the autobiography) gains even more credibility, and certainly throws a new light on his sister.

James continued: "To my surprise Nan presently opened my office door. She seemed upset, and I said, 'Hello Nan, is anything the matter?' She said: 'I'm sorry, but I can't rest in that room – I lay down, but I had to come out.'

"'What troubled you?'

"'Someone was murdered in that room.'

"'You must have gone to sleep and had a bad dream.'

"But she maintained that she had not slept, and that from the moment of entering the room she had an overpowering sense of its having been, at some time, the scene of a murder.

"Nan was an artist, and had certainly the artistic temperament. But she was in no way psychic; on the contrary, she was a level-headed and strongly practical woman. I took her to her own bedroom at once, and she soon slept and was perfectly normal again by tea-time.

"I had never heard of anyone having been murdered in the old house, but on making enquiries I learnt that it was on the threshold, between that dressing room and the verandah that Colonel Mackeson had been murdered many years before. I should add that there had never previously been any talk of the house being haunted, or of any psychic phenomena. Nor was there any after this amazing experience, for which Nan herself could suggest no explanation."

Then, in a protective and brotherly way James added: "We thought it best not to tell her about Colonel Mackeson, and she soon had forgotten the episode ...." Anne made no mention of this incident in any of her letters.

Late the following year Anne revisited the Sub-Continent. Once again she was based with Hazel in Jubbulpore, but this time she ventured a little further afield. This time Jim had decided to give them a tour of the North West Frontier Province, beginning with a visit to the Swat Valley. Again there is precious little correspondence, but at least one closely-written letter to Grace, has survived, dated December 5th 1933. In it Anne described the visit into an area that was the scene of troubles as recently as 2009 when close on two million people fled the Swat Valley while the Pakistan Army battled with the Taleban extremists for control of the region.

However seventy six years ago the only gunfire that could be heard was on the Wali of Swat's duckshoot, to which the Acheson sisters as well as Jim and his wife Vio, had been invited.

Anne opened her letter with: "Here we are back safely after our adventures on the frontier. We had a lovely time. We were ... very far north over the Malakund Pass."

She then went on to explain what the journey was like, and she included a squiggly line to indicate the switchback nature of the road they took by car, before transferring to real horsepower. "... the last bit of the way Hazel and I did on ponies ... We then came to a canal bungalow built like a fort, with a wall for sentries all round, it was on a high rock overlooking the join of the Swat River and the canal."

Anne had obviously done a bit of research into this canal as well because she went into interesting detail about it. "The British made the canal go through the mountain to irrigate the plain on the other side. It is said to be known as one of the wonders of the world in remote parts of China, as pilgrims from China etc come through this way."

The Swat Valley has been described variously as "the Switzerland of Asia", (as recently as 2007 there was a ski resort at Malam Jabba) and "a place of great natural beauty" and even "a paradise". However, as idyllic as The Swat Valley might have appeared, it was still a dangerous place, even in the early 1930s, which explains Anne's next sentence: "We had an armed guard of five or six (as well as Jim's two orderlies and chauffeur with revolvers) at each bungalow, though everyone is friendly there, but the tribes beyond had made war on in these parts in 1930, I think."

The letter is closely written and Anne was certainly gripped as much by the drama of the scenery as by the element of danger that would be threaded through their stay in this remote but beautiful place. She described the setting thus: "A big flat valley, with the huge river in the middle, mountains all round, the higher ones snow covered. The snow on the mountainside is lovely. The mountains are of an almost crimson rock, and there is a pink dried grass about, and small trees lower down."

However there was something of an anti-climax on their first morning as guests of the Wali of Swat. "Next morning was a disappointment as there was three inches of snow at the duck-shooting place. Vio and I, who had meant to lunch or tea at the camp, but not go to the butts, decided it would be too cold." Their 'baby' sister however was clearly made of sterner stuff, Anne wrote: "Hazel went with Jim and brought back a present from the Wali of a Swati blanket, like your Chesterfield cover, for me and one for herself." However, the purpose of the visit, the sport, suffered because of the weather. "The shoot was spoiled by the snow." Although she reported: "Jim shot 14 duck."

What a difference 24 hours can make. "The next day was not so cold. We picnicked on a rock overlooking the river and I sketched ..." Things were, however, far from perfect, because Anne admitted she "...had difficulty owing to the strong sunshine." And irritatingly: "It was too cold to sit in the shade."

Then it was back to Peshawar, where they had made their base for the tour. Here there was more drama on the day after their return from the Swat Valley. Jim went off shooting again, but Hazel's medical skills were called upon, as Anne explained: "... a young officer, who was staying at a ... bungalow nine miles beyond ours with his sister and her fiancé for two days' shooting, arrived to ask advice as his sister was too ill. Hazel had to go up to her and that rather spoilt our day, we were to have spent it sketching."

As it turned out Anne and Vio accompanied Hazel on her 'call' and thus experienced further excitement. "On our way back to our bungalow we were stopped by a wild party of three women and two men and some children, who stood across the road. We had one orderly and the chauffeur with us.

"An apparently mad old woman seized Vio, who was driving, with both hands by the coat collar." Then Anne interjects an aside: "Vio is used to this sort of thing."

The narrative resumed: "The men jumped out to push the women away, but she stopped them and one of the women screamed a long harangue in Pashtu, which Vio is learning, but does not know yet. Two of the old woman's sons were in jail and two were outlawed, and she said there was no one to support the families. Vio, with the orderlies' assistance, told her to get the names written and to report to the bungalow. The whole family awaited us on our return with Jim in the afternoon, and held on to us and made the children hold us, and came and touched Jim's and our shoes, while Jim heard all about it from an aged grandfather. Jim was extremely patient, but evidently asked rather troublesome questions as to why the outlawed sons would not come in for trial.

"It was a case of attempted murder, not Jim's business, but his assistant's. Jim advised them what to do. Next morning the whole crowd were there to 'Salaam' us when we went off. Luckily we got into the car inside the gates, so there was no more shoe touching." Anne added a footnote to the unnerving episode: "They were a well known bad set."

She also furnished Grace with some extraordinary statistics: "There were 380 cases of murder in Jim's district last year, and that was an improvement on other years. Of course there is a big population, 900,000 I think."

Abruptly, Anne interrupted her flow of news with the statement: "This letter is growing too long." However, as things turned out, there was still plenty to tell Grace, after all the tour was not yet over, and so, as a consequence, the letter grew even longer. First Anne had to recount hers and Hazel's journey by train from Peshawar to Delhi, an excursion which was certainly not without the odd 'alarum'.

Anne wrote: "After the first night's journey Hazel hurt her thumb in the window and fainted on her lower berth without my knowing about it. It was dark and I was in the upper berth. A soldier's widow with twins aged three had had to have my lower berth. When Hazel recovered a bit she pulled my rug and I climbed down.

"Just then we got into a station and men rushed in with luggage and more Indian women passengers. It was the end of the Christmas holidays and there was an awful crowd of 'pass-holders', railway clerks and their families. None of us were dressed and there was not much room to dress. Luckily we had iodine within reach."

The sisters' misery deepened. "All day long we were eight women and four children in a compartment labelled 'six seats', with their luggage, our dog and a six-foot bundle of sugar cane."

The children were anything but angels. "The 'bathroom' was flooded by the three ill-behaved, sticky, dirty children."

Things did not improve. At every station the occupants of the over-crowded compartment were like the inhabitants of a besieged castle, repelling all would-be boarders, as Anne explained: " At the very frequent stops Hazel got out, generally with the dog, and prevented more women getting in. I had to hold the door by force occasionally ... unlocking it to let her in."

To make matters worse Anne reported: "There was no restaurant car and no room for trays in the carriage, but we were well supplied with cold food."

The sisters' destination was Nepal, and the city of Lalitpur, or Patan, which is separated from the city of Kathmandu by the Bagmati River, but they had a while to go, including another night on the train. "We reached Delhi about 8.40 and they all cleared out except one nice woman," wrote Anne. "We had got the car sent by rail from Delhi to Lalitpur and discovered it would cost 30 rupees more than we expected. So we had more anxiety as that would leave us short of money for emergencies on our two days' motor drive here. However Hazel phoned a friend in Delhi – we had an hour to wait – and got some more money and we had a peaceful night in the partially cleaned carriage."

Having spent that night sleeping in the train, when they awoke the next morning they were able to pick up the car and drive up the Kathmandu Valley; and Anne revelled in the independent mode of transport and in the sense of freedom, being away from the crowded cities.

"It was lovely to start in the car next morning, we picnicked in a wood, paddled in a mountain stream under trees.... We had a lovely drive yesterday. It is ever so much warmer here than Peshawar."

As for Hazel's injury, that was almost forgotten, Anne just adding, almost as a footnote: "Hazel's thumb is healing all right, but will have a scar, as it should have been stitched."

It is not known how well the rest of the tour progressed, although the sketches and porcelain figures that have survived bear testimony to the inspiration that Anne discovered when she was on the Sub-Continent, and she was certainly fortunate that she had a brother and a sister living over there, thus providing her with a couple of ready-made bases, not to mention a couple of ideal and sympathetic guides, to steer her to places that Anne the artist, as opposed to Anne the tourist, wanted to go. It was also a refreshing and much-needed break for Anne, because she was to find things becoming a little tougher back home from now on.

11

She's a Jolly Good Fellow

The following Spring found Anne Acheson in a slough of despond as revealed in a letter to Grace dated April 30th 1934. True to her selfless nature Anne did at least begin by thanking her sister "for the chocolate cake. I should have replied sooner. I am enjoying it." But then the mood darkened as she revealed: "... have been feeling rather depressed being out of the Royal Academy again." This was the third year in a row that Anne had been overlooked, and although she showed a great deal of professionalism by focusing on preparing a piece for the following year's exhibition in Piccadilly, still she found it tough to accept. Her mood was not helped by the piece she was working on. "Doing the medallion of Mammy makes me sad. I always want to show it to Em." This was because her eldest sister had died two years earlier in 1932, in her mid-fifties, and that had struck a chord with Anne, who, in April 1934, was in her 52nd year. Tackling the medallion of her mother Harriet Acheson had brought to mind other family deaths.

But the medallion meant a great deal to her and she added: "I want to get the medallion of Mammy cast in bronze later on. I could get several casts for very little extra if any of the family want them. If I were wealthy

The Achesons of Portadown, circa 1900. Harriet and John Acheson are seated. Standing at the back, from left to right, Emily, Molly, Edgar, Anne. Grace and Jimmy are seated, and Hazel is between her father's knees.

Alexandra School, Portadown, circa 1895. Anne's sister Grace Acheson is seated in the foreground, her back to the stove and the camera.

'The Red Shawl', by Amy K Browning. Anne Acheson was the model for this painting which was exhibited at the Royal Academy in 1912.

'The Pixie', Anne Acheson's first exhibit at the Royal Academy in the summer of 1911.

TOP LEFT: 'Will o' the Wisp' Anne's second RA offering in 1912.

TOP RIGHT: The hat-trick. 'Echo Mocking' made it three in a row at the Royal Academy in 1913.

LEFT: 'A Small Conceit' the bronze version of the figure which Anne submitted to the Royal Academy in 1916, her final appearance there until the start of the next decade.

Where it all happened for Anne Acheson and her fellow volunteers at the Surgical Requisites Association – Number 17, Mulberry Walk, Chelsea

Inside the shed at the rear of Number 17, where volunteers, male and female, are hard at work.

The uniform look.
Anne in the formal
uniform of the Surgical
Requisites Association.

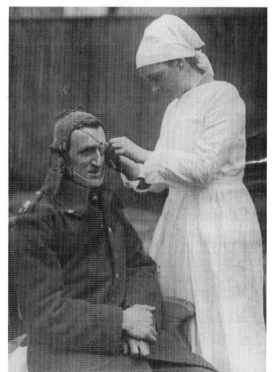

The more clinical look. Anne,
dressed in the SRA's working
garb, which bears more
resemblance to a nurse's
uniform, attending to a
serviceman's eye patch.

'Coggers', the house in the Benenden in Kent where Mrs Marion Cran, Anne Acheson's biggest fan lived. Anne's figure 'Sally' can be discerned between house and pond.

Mission accomplished. Anne Acheson, having decided where her creation 'Sally' should have a permanent place in the garden at Coggers, relaxes on the lawn.

'The Imp' a portrait of an unknown client's child. The figure was exhibited at the Royal Academy in 1922.

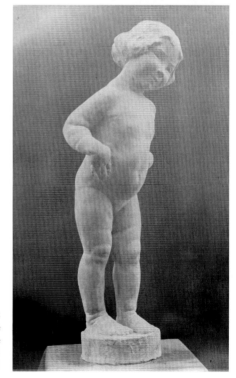

The apple of Marion Cran's eye, 'Sally', who captured the imagination of so many people after being shown at the Royal Academy in 1923

A bust of her friend and fellow artist T C 'Tommy' Dugdale
which was completed in 1922

Motor mascots 'Shoo', left, and 'The Winner' ...
and ...

... 'Sober Ernest', left, and 'Speed'.

King's House Studios tucked away just off the King's Road

A portrait of Anne's youngest sister Harriet Elizabeth 'Hazel' Acheson, when she was a medical student. The artist is Helen Budd, a friend and later neighbour of Anne's.

'Harriet Emily' a lead garden figure modelled by one of the daughters of Anne's sister Grace, in the mid-1920s.

'Rags' another garden figure, which was exhibited at the Royal Academy in 1926.

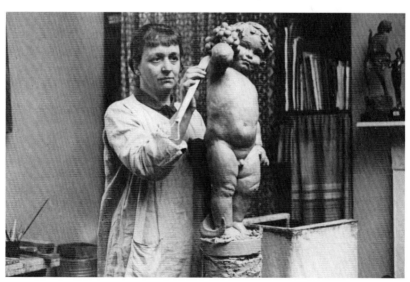

Anne Acheson putting the finishing touches to 'October' in the late 1920s.

Bust of Anne's close friend Amy K Browning, which bore her married name Mrs Dugdale for the purpose of exhibiting it at The Royal Academy in 1927.

The striking bust of Gertrude Bell, the explorer and Arabist, the original of which is in the National Museum in Baghdad, a replica is in the Royal Geographical Society in Kensington, West London.

The end of the ceremony at which the bust of Gertrude Bell was unveiled by King Faisal I of Iraq.

York
Stone

Bronze

Stone

Drawing

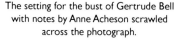

The setting for the bust of Gertrude Bell with notes by Anne Acheson scrawled across the photograph.

The inscription in Arabic and English which sits under the bust of Gertrude Bell.

Fountain group in situ at 'Olivers' in Painswick, Gloucestershire. Anne Acheson wrote an explanatory note at the foot of her working photograph, revealing that the boy squeezes the water up and out through his ball.

Anne's 1931 Royal Academy exhibit 'Puck', modelled by Josephine G Owen. Anne priced the figure at £180 in 1931.

A close-up, right, of 'Sabrina' and then a view of the figure in situ at the King's School, Worcester.

The entrance to Anne Acheson's final base in London, at No 9, Sydney Close, off the Fulham Road.

'Water Baby' which appeared in Burlington House in the RA's summer exhibition.

'The Thief' which was exhibited at the Royal Academy in 1938.

'Mrs Christopher Ironside' – Anne's niece Janey Ironside. This went on show at the Royal Academy in 1944 and five years later Anne had a head of Janey's daughter Virginia on show at the RA, to create an unusual family double.

Still at work in her late 70s. Anne Acheson working on the head of Paul Faris, one of her great nephews in 1959.

I would give one to each grandchild, but that is out of the question nowadays."

For all that, Anne was determined to ride the disappointment of the hat-trick of Royal Academy disappointments and submit the medallion for the following year. "I shall have it to send in to the RA next year," she wrote, "but I feel hopeless about that."

At least she was able to draw some consolation from the fact that four of her friends would be exhibiting at the RA that year. "Browning and Dugdale have done well in the RA, and the Budds are in all right."

Anne was certainly one of those people who, when they are down, decides there is no way back up. She began to see nothing but failure ahead of her. Nothing was going to go right, and her letter took on an even more despairing note. "I don't think I shall ever get a teaching job on account of my age, but I feel I ought to manage some jobs like the dolls job. I could do a lot of good toy designs if I had not Mr Rees to work for." This was a reference to the buyer for the company which had commissioned Anne to design the dolls and whose professional behaviour had clearly upset Anne, to judge by a remark about her business relationship with him and the company Exella in a letter from brother Jim in March 1934.

James wrote: "Evidently the doll-making business is not all gain; I wonder if you can't get the upper hand over that odious buyer [the aforementioned Mr Rees] somehow! I'm afraid not though. Do you really like the work? Does it give you time for your proper work?" The answer to both questions was a resounding 'No', because a month later found Anne writing to Grace and musing on the wisdom of having accepted the commission in the first place. Her brother had got to the heart of the matter with his two telling questions, and it appears that Anne was beginning to see the error she had made.

Certainly the blame for her absence from the 1933 exhibition could be put down to the doll-making commission. Now something over a year down the line she found herself pondering: "I don't know whether the dolls job was worth missing the RA for, but of course I did not know it would take so long, and I thought I could get something done."

When the commissions dried up, as they had been steadily through the depression, Anne's fortitude came to the fore as she looked in other directions for ways to make a living from art. For a couple of years she had been designing and producing masters of figures for Royal Worcester.

According to one letter though, that company was feeling the financial pinch, offering her significantly less for a second commission, as she told Grace: "Worcester have offered me a low price for six or seven of my designs, with a ten per cent royalty. It means £49 anyway, before the royalties start, but it will take me a good while to carry them out. On the former ones I got 20 per cent royalty, but no sum for expenses. They offer £8 for some, £5 for others."

As the decade advanced so the income seemed to dwindle, Anne even mentioned what seems to be a pathetic sum of money that she had agreed for a calendar she had designed; it is highly probable that a pen and ink drawing of Sloane Square at Christmas, which was found among her sketches, was the scene used for the calendar. The original was dated 1934. It is an eye-catching sketch and it is no surprise that it had fired the interest of a buyer at Peter Jones, the department store. But the amount it would earn Anne was risible, even by the standards of the 1930s. "Peter Jones ordered £4.6s.0d (£4.30) worth of calendars," she wrote. And the thing is, Anne was not doing them on her own, "Some of this year's we are not printing by hand, but are mounting them on chintz..." she informed Grace, so that modest sum had to be spread even more thinly, because Anne had to share the income with her co-workers.

It was in the middle of the decade that Anne moved studios for the final time. Tommy Dugdale and Amy Browning relinquished their lease on No 9, Avenue Studios, off Fulham Road, giving Anne first refusal. It was in 1935, and thanks to Tommy's success – this was the year he was made an Associate of the Royal Academy, an elevation which Anne acknowledged in a letter to her niece Harriet early that year in which she wrote: "... Mr Dugdale has been elected to the Royal Academy. Perhaps you have seen his photo in the papers." The Dugdales were able to move to No 58, Glebe Place in Chelsea, still renting, but at a far grander, better appointed and distinctly upmarket address altogether; as a result of their move Anne was able to sub-let King's House Studios for the remainder of her lease on that property while taking up residence at Avenue Studios, where she would remain until the final move of her life, back to Northern Ireland in the early 1950s.

Avenue Studios was an artistic enclave comprising 15 units in total. Originally the second line of the address was given as No 76, Fulham Road, entry was through an archway, which gave out onto what is now known as Sydney Close – the name was changed sometime around, or just before, the start of the Second World War. At the bottom of Sydney Close and to the right, along the bottom edge of the Avenue Studios building, is Sydney Mews. Apart from Anne Acheson's friends the Budds, who lived across from her on the same landing at No10, Avenue Studios, Harriet, her niece, recalls that when she was staying there she used to pass another prominent artist, Dame Laura Knight – the Impressionist painter and the first woman artist to be made a Dame – who also had a studio there. The graphic artist and portrait painter John Gilroy, famous, among other things, for his advertising posters for Guinness from the 1930s to the 1960s and the American portraitist John Singer Sargent were also resident in the complex during Anne's time there.

Anne's nephew Alexander 'Sandy' Faris, has fond recollections of Avenue Studios. "Her own studio had something of the cathedral about it, the first floor being like a wide balcony stretching halfway across the room's width, allowing one to see from the ground floor up and beyond the open staircase to the sloping glass roof, which was designed to give an artist northern light.

"By day Nan would work diligently in the balcony-like studio, in the evenings the figures would stand on a pedestal, shrouded with a damp cloth to keep the clay moist and malleable."

That description was corroborated by Evelyn Durnford, who as Muffet Williams had visited Sydney Close in 1939, and recalls: "Her studio was large with a high vaulted roof and skylights and was filled with partially completed works placed on various tables and pedestals, all covered with wet sheets, it felt and smelt terribly damp, and was bitterly cold if one happened to be there during the Christmas holidays. There was a curtained off alcove where Aunt Nan slept, and kept her clothes. I cannot remember any facilities for cooking or washing, but they must have existed somewhere. I slept on a camp bed amongst the art. It was very primitive but delightfully Bohemian."

It was in the same letter to Harriet that she spoke of the new studio. She had to spend some cash making the odd improvement. "The workmen will be in the bathroom and kitchen of the new studio for a fortnight after I move to it!" she told her niece. "Won't that be comfortable!. However I shall not have to pay any rent while they are there as it should have been done before I move in." Then she added wistfully, almost plaintively: " I hope I can have baths after they go in the evening occasionally."

It appears that Avenue Studios were particularly well-appointed as far as plumbing goes. Anne listed the various basins and sinks available to her. "There are two hand-basins and taps, as well as those in the bathroom and kitchen, so I can manage washing up etc through the day."

She was also able to install a modest luxury. A letter in January 1935 to Grace revealed all. "The electric kettle works beautifully. I paid 4/6 [22.5p] for the fitting. It is exactly the right voltage here – would have been wrong at King's House Studio. Also I have found the bath towel and the fruit knife and pencils *and* the handbag most useful and ornamental. I feel a bit greedy over the loot I brought back." This would have been after having spent Christmas at Rosebank with Grace and the family.

Anne was also preparing for a visit from Hazel, as she told Harriet. "Auntie Hazel arrives on the Strathmore in four weeks from Wednesday. I see that the Strathmore has been delayed on its way to India with engine trouble, but it will make the lost time up before it starts I expect."

In a subsequent letter, this one to Grace and which was written around the same time – she was still in King's House Studios at the time of writing – it was a relieved Anne who announced that: "This studio is let again – I showed it six times to people this weekend. It is not signed yet, but I am sure it is all right this time."

The tenant was described as: "... a new secretary in the German Embassy, very polite and pleasant. He brought a lady to see it before deciding. Luckily I had just washed and darned curtains and put on the best Chesterfield cover – also the sun was shining." She sounds as if she would have made a good estate agent, aware as she was, how important seeing a property in good weather can be when looking to persuade someone to buy or rent a place.

As for the new studio Anne reported: "I have the lease for the other studio seven years, with option to leave at five, and I have to repaint it all some time."

She had also done a little more work for Royal Worcester. She wrote: "Worcester like my two sketches, so that is something." But she had a nagging worry about a private commission. "I cannot get on with the ballet dancer till Mrs Sofio comes to London indefinitely. So I have started a 'band' figure for the Royal Academy, not the cello, but the Russian tuba, or the German brass band instrument that winds around the body." Her uncertainty was obvious and she turned to her musical nephew Sandy for help. "I can't find an illustration of it anywhere, please ask Sandy if he knows where the stops or holes are, or if there are any and how the mouthpiece comes. I believe there is a jazz instrument like it, but can't see one. I have been to the Donaldson museum of musical instruments at the Royal College of Music, but here is nothing like it there. The French horn does not go round the body. I enclose photo."

A postscript then asked Grace: "Please send me the £50. I have an awful lot of big subscriptions to pay. £13 – as well as lawyers' fees for the lease etc."

Finally though Anne was in, and not just in the new studio, the medallion of her mother had been accepted by the Royal Academy, as well as a lead garden figure she called 'Water Baby'. In April Anne had exhibited, under the aegis of the Board of Trade, in Brussels, two figures 'June' and 'March' priced at £50 each, but valued for insurance purposes at a more modest £30 apiece.

The following year saw an improvement in her finances with the taking on of more pupils as well as her having been employed to give a series of lectures, presumably in modelling, once a week. In November 1936 Grace was told: "My new pupil did turn up with a cheque for £16 (for 20 lessons) ...." So Anne had been able to put up her tuition fees as well from half a guinea (52.5 pence) to 16 shillings (80 pence) a lesson.

In addition to that there had been some success at the Forum Club's Handicrafts Show. "I sold Diana, Arabella and two cheap 'Janes' making £7, but the commission comes off that. So this was a good week." So good in fact that Anne postponed a decision that she had made. "I was going to resign from the Forum, but I will not do it this year as this more than covers my subscription and these shows – four each year – keep my name before the right sort of people."

As ever Anne was a willing volunteer for anything and of course she was taken advantage of. In the same letter she bemoaned her lot, explaining how the voluntary work came close to making her late for her regular weekly lecture: "I had an awful day on Tuesday as I had to help place the Feodora Gleichen Scholarship sculpture at the Royal Academy."

Feodora Gleichen was a sculptress and the daughter of Prince Victor of Hohenloe-Langenburg, who was a sculptor and a half nephew of Queen Victoria. When the reforms of the family names of George V were introduced in 1917 she was granted the rank and style of a daughter of a marquess and Lady Feodora Georgina Maud Gleichen lived in a grace and favour apartment in St James's Palace until her death in February 1922. Subsequently she was posthumously elected as the first woman member of The Royal British Society of Sculptors, followed closely by a clutch of young women including Anne Acheson.

Anne's 'awful Tuesday' continued: "I had only promised two hours of my time. The Hon. Sec. asked me to come in the morning, though the sending-in time was not till 3.0pm, with the result that four huge works came in just as I should have been going to get to Notting Hill for those lectures, and I got almost no lunch and had to rush horribly. I had only ten minutes to get the lantern out and change the bulbs etc." (Anne was obviously using magic lantern slides to help illustrate her lectures). It got no better. "It was pouring all day and I had had to fetch, and choose, my slides at Portman Square that morning as my pupil kept me too late here the day before. I usually do the fetching after dark on Monday."

Coincidentally two years later the inaugural Gleichen Memorial Medal, introduced to commemorate the life and achievements of Feodora Gleichen, was won by Anne Acheson for her lead garden figure 'The Thief', which was judged to be the best work by a woman artist in the Royal Academy in 1938.

Anne also managed to get away a little in 1936, and she wrote of a visit she made to the friend of a former client whose grandchildren she had modelled and turned into a lead garden fountain. "I had a nice weekend at Painswick, but not very restful. Miss Odell does not like London traffic so I had to leave here, in pouring rain, by bus with luggage, and meet her at Putney at 9.0am. It is a tourer car and I got terribly rheumatic before we reached Painswick at 1.15pm." It is doubtful whether, at this point in her narrative that Anne would have spotted, let alone enjoyed the irony in the name of the Cotswold town.

Then came a little more torture for the teetotal Anne. "We went to a sherry party, no joy to me, but Lily [Odell] does not know that, where I met Mrs Dent and Peggy Dent, whom I modelled with her little cousin at Olivers years ago. Peggy is now 21. The grandmother and Peggy's mother have died since. Mrs Dent is her aunt. They asked me to come to Olivers next day, so I went for a short time and saw my fountain playing. On Sunday Lily asked the Gambles, who live about half an hour away by car, to come to tea, as she knew I wanted to see them. The Cotswold woods were lovely, mostly beech. Painswick is hilly and very pretty."

There was an abrupt change of subject as Anne reflected on her financial status, as well as that of one or two of her charges. "I think I am paying my way at present. I hope the pupils will continue next term. Miss Dorothy Hilder has three lessons a week now. She is fairly wealthy. I expect she will soon set up her own studio. Gertrude Bigelow might have had more lessons if she had got her school leaving certificate. She failed in science and has to take it all again, so she has not had much time for modelling, though she is terribly keen on it."

Anne had stayed in touch with friends from her student days, no surprise given how close-knit the artistic community was, so there was news of Jess Lawson-Peacey, although Anne, who used to refer to her friend as plain 'Lawson', clearly had no truck with hyphenating names on marriage as can be seen. "I am sharing a pottery stand with Jess Peacey and Stella Crofts (animals) and Miss Seideman (pots) in December at the Applied Arts-Handicrafts Show. I have to pay £3 and share the 'minding' and selling. Bill will do that for me." That was a reference to her assistant Bill Baker to whom she turned a great deal in her life for help. When her young nieces and nephews were staying with her, he was always happy to take them sightseeing around London to keep them out of Anne's hair when she was busy.

Stella Crofts and Anne Acheson had their pottery featured in the May edition of Homes and Gardens the following year in 1937. "Stella R Crofts' birds and animal studies are full of life and character. 'Pollie' the blue-footed Amazon parrot, designed and executed by her, like the 'Goose', with its painted underglaze and stoneware glaze, are modelled in the round, full of understanding of bird life. The Giraffes shown in low relief are equally arresting," says the report.

"More sculpturesque in character is 'The Sacred Bull' in glazed earthenware by Anne Acheson. In cream colour touched with black and brown, it stands just under ten inches in height. The charming figure of 'Diana' with hound on leash is also by this artist. Coloured in green, white and silver on a silver base, this group is slightly larger than 'The Sacred Bull'. It is in pottery but made by the Worcester Royal China Co." The article finishes with a description of a third piece by Anne. "'Arabella' in glazed earthenware by Anne Acheson, a most attractive young lady in the costume of the late seventies [that of course, is the 1870s], stands just over a foot in height." And the writer concludes: "These three potters all pursue an ancient craft, and, in the fashion of the artists of the Middle Ages, use it to express the spirit of today, conscious of the tradition but not trammelled by it."

In that previous December it turned out there was an ulterior motive behind Anne and Jess having a stand at the Applied Arts-Handicrafts Show. "The organisers have invited Jess and me to show two garden figures each, near the platform. So that makes the stand expense more worthwhile. The woman who bought a big bronze last Christmas and a lead the year before, had seen my works at that show four years ago."

But preparations for the Applied Arts-Handicraft Show were not without their problems. "I am having a terrible rush to get things fired in time for the Applied Arts Show. The kiln people only fire when they have enough to fill a kiln, and everything has to be fired twice – once unglazed and once after the painting and glazing. I have one beautiful 'Bull' ready. The best yet."

As with 1936, there was a further rejection by the Royal Academy in 1937 for Anne, and in the letter to Grace at the beginning of February, still more gloom. "It is pouring today and the gutter I asked the builders to see to before Christmas and three weeks ago, and last week, is still leaking and making two great patches on the studio wall."

A couple of months later there was an air of resignation in a letter to Grace. "I am, as I expected, out of the RA. So is Jess Peacey, Morton, the Budds and Watton and her friend Griffin. Browning may have one in." Browning was indeed the only one of the circle to have a painting accepted for exhibiting, it was entitled 'Sun-worshippers'. Rather poignantly Anne quoted one remark: "Jess calls it 'The passing of the old gang'. I blame my failure on 'flu and on pot-boiling work." But she assessed the gamble of concentrating all one's energies on a single piece at the expense of paid commissions. "It is too great a risk spending about six months on an RA work, and the craze in sculpture is a finish in stone, which is costly in labour. If I had enough to live on I would do it."

Not all commissions paid well, if at all, to judge by the following. "I have just been to a cocktail party in Berkeley Square – the Mrs Sofio who let me down over the fountain dancer job. I did not stay long, but thought it politic to go, in case she is reviving her idea of a commission."

She was fairly economically minded and informed Grace: "We had our own model this afternoon, and there were six of us to tea – we have a hurried tea in mugs – with buns to eat in the model's rest (10 minutes). Katharine's cake came in just in time – but we all ate our half buns first so my cake was not devoured, only tested."

Anne was definitely down. "I am exhausted with spring-cleaning. Mrs Smithers has done a little, but her daughter is ill. I have done all the high store places, perched precariously on a very high ladder and not having space to stand upright, very back-breaking. I had the Budds' electric cleaner for part of it. I plunged into this to forget Academy things."

It was around this time that Anne decided to head once more to the Cotswolds. There was a chance of a further commission for a fountain modelled on the grandchildren of Dora Owen, whose daughter Josephine had featured as Puck for one of Anne's 1931 Royal Academy exhibits. Initially it appeared that Anne had been reluctant to make the journey to Chipping Campden, but eventually she relented, although in her letter dated May 13th she told Grace: "I came here after all, but I don't think Mrs Owen will have the figure. There is really no place for it. We have not mentioned it, but she took me to her daughter's house where they are struggling to retrieve a neglected garden and house, and at the moment it would just look silly there."

But Anne was happy to stroll around Chipping Campden, with her artist's eye taking in all the features of the place. "It suits me absolutely to wander about, this is supposed to be the most beautiful village in England, all yellow stone and bulging shop windows." She wrote that she took elevenses and afternoon tea at a hotel in the village, describing it as: "Very spacious and airy clean."

She then charted her movements over the next couple of days. "I go to Painswick tomorrow and to the Gambles on Friday." Whether she made a sale or gained a commission is not known, but she obviously enjoyed herself, because in a subsequent letter to Grace she reported: "I was two nights with Mrs Owen and two with the Bakers and three with the Gambles, with cross country journeys between by car and by bus. Mrs Owen has really not proper room for the figure in her cottage garden, but I'm sure she will not settle there for good. She says she wants the two figures if I can devise a setting with fountain for them. I'll be about 90 years old by the time they are erected and paid for."

Not long after this Anne makes her first foray into becoming an examiner for the Northern Ireland Ministry of Education. She had asked Tommy Dugdale to stand as a referee for her and he did her proud in his letter of reference dated June 8th 1937.

"Miss Anne Acheson CBE ARBS is eminently fitted to act as Examiner in Drawing for the Ministry of Education Northern Ireland. She has had much experience at various times in this kind of work, having, among other duties, served as assessor for the Lady Feodora Gleichen Scholarship, and has well balanced judgement in valuing the varying merits of candidates. Miss Acheson's appointment would, I consider, be of great value to the Ministry." He signed off with an impressive list of credentials, firstly he himself was ARA, but then he added: "Sometime assessor to the Scottish Board of Education in Design and drawing and painting. Member of the Council of the Royal College of Art. Fellow of the Royal Institute of Industrial Art. Member of the Council, Register of Industrial Design."

As things turned out Anne was not to take up the role of art examiner for a couple of years, however there were plenty of other things, professional and personal, to occupy her in 1938.

On the family front, another of her nieces, Janey Ironside, undertook a three-month dress-making course in London and in her autobiography 'Janey' she wrote: "Aunt Nan ... found me a most depressing cheap bed-sitting room in Collingham Gardens, Earl's Court."

Meanwhile Anne's lead garden figure 'The Thief' was accepted by the Royal Academy for the summer exhibition, and it went on, as has been said, to win her the inaugural Gleichen Memorial Medal for being the best work by a woman at the RA. She also exhibited a lead garden figure. 'Harriet Emily' and a figure called 'Madonna' at the Glasgow Empire Exhibition, a bronze replica of the former selling for £55.

But Anne's finest hour arrived on June 13th 1938, when she created a little bit of history by becoming the first woman to be elected a Fellow of the Royal British Society of Sculptors; it was a signal honour and an achievement of which Anne remained justifiably very proud.

However there is no triumphant trumpeting of the honour bestowed upon her. Instead Anne acknowledges her elevation in typical, modest fashion. Her fellowship is by no means the first piece of news which she imparted to Grace. Anne began by reminding Grace that it had been a while since she heard from her sister, then said: "Perhaps it is just that it may be my turn to write."

She went on to inform Grace that she had been busy. "I was teaching on Tuesday and Wednesday, and hanging the Society of Women Artists' show on Wednesday, Thursday and Friday and was a wreck by 4.0 on Friday." That was when she caught a train to Suffolk to visit Browning and Dugdale. Anne confessed: "... I deserted the hanging to catch my train." But that little wave of guilt on her part for seeming to have abandoned others to do her share of the work was obviously dispelled by her break in Suffolk with her closest friend. "I had a lovely weekend and came back in time to teach on Tuesday, and I seem really better this time and have started studio work again. On Thursday Epps came to dinner and we went to see ballet at the Old Vic. Yesterday Janet came to dinner and T C Dugdale phoned to say he had sold my RA Thief ... I reduced the price for him and will make £23 profit when I have had a replica cast."

Her news had taken up almost a full side of the notepaper before Anne eventually ended all these ramblings and finally revealed her wonderful news, although she still played it down. There was an unfussiness, an impersonal tone even in her choice of words and phrases. There was certainly no build-up, making out that she was about to impart something special. On the contrary anyone reading what followed could be excused for believing that something rather mundane was to follow. "Then by post," Anne continued, "I heard that the Royal Society of British Sculptors had elected me a Fellow – a complete surprise for me as I was away at the last meeting and no one had mentioned the election to me, though I had voting papers as an Associate, I think. Clemens, who used to teach in the Modelling School (RCA) phoned me to congratulate me." She was not even sure about the historic impact of her election. "I was the only woman elected (I do not think there were any before). He said it was a popular election and the President Gilbert Bayes has written too saying it should have been done before. I have no intimate friends among the men (Gillick does not belong, he had a row with them and resigned 25 years ago), and there are very few women to vote."

So what did it mean to Anne, this accolade? "This makes me RBS, instead of ARBS, one less letter to write on every label I send to shows."

12

The Balloon Goes Up

Just a couple of months after being granted her Fellowship of the Royal British Society of Sculptors Anne Acheson would have heard the immortal lines from the Prime Minister Neville Chamberlain. Speaking from Heston Airport, just to the west of London and not far from where the M4 motorway services of that name are situated, Mr Chamberlain announced that following his meeting with Adolf Hitler: "I believe it is peace in our time."

It was in September 1938, and that autumn saw Anne working on a couple of pottery figures. A month later they were just about finished. They were for a friend, Mary Edgar, and a friend of hers, a Miss McLernon. Anne wrote: " ... I shall post Ceres and Flora to you. I am doing Flora now in *bright* blue dress, with white where the old Flora is creamy, and a shiny glaze, but it will be some time before I have another done. I have one at a show. I am marking this one at 30 shillings [£1.50] and will change it if Mary does not like it, or prefers another when I have one."

Her Royal Academy exhibit that year, the lead garden figure entitled 'Thief', was bringing in dividends as well. "I sold another lead 'Thief' last Saturday to two Australian women who had seen my Sally when they were over in 1923 and had been hoping to have one of mine ever since. They will pay £50, so I shall make about £37 on it. I had to work on the plaster a bit and it has now gone to the foundry."

One of those Australian women, Eva Waite, wrote an effusive and excited letter of thanks to Anne in confirming the sale. The letter, dated October 22nd, 1938 revealed that Eva Waite was staying in Queen Anne's Mansions, St James's Park. Miss Waite, who was from South Australia, wrote: "I feel quite excited tonight. We have wanted a garden figure for so long, but we only wanted one that gave us complete pleasure, and that, I think, we have found. Funny how, in our journeyings around the world our thoughts always floated back to your little 'Sally', and I am overjoyed that we at last took courage to find you out.... You gave us such pleasure yesterday, both in the enjoyment of your lovely work and the interest of hearing and seeing how it is done, and I can picture the continuous delight we and our friends too are going to enjoy, when our lovely possession stands in our garden ...."

She went on to explain how payment, insurance and shipping were to be organised and she hoped Anne would find everything: "... perfectly convenient, satisfactory." She also promised Anne a photo of the figure, *in situ* in her garden.

As ever Anne was frantically busy with other tasks and duties besides her studio work: "The Forum Handicrafts Show starts tomorrow, and I had all my things to label and price. Then a life class. First Epps for lunch. She is doing a post graduate course at the hospital next door, so I have had her in to lunch daily this week. After the life class there is always some confabbing about work with the cronies and pupils." As if that were not enough she then had to entertain her niece Janet 'Janey' Acheson's latest boyfriend.

At the time Janey was seeing the brother of a friend of hers, Ian Robertson, a naval officer, who turned up one day at Avenue Studios and presumably poured his heart out to her, because Anne wrote: "Ian Robertson phoned, might he come and see me, and I had a second cup of tea for him. He gave me a lift to the Forum..." Then Anne revealed: "Janet and Ian have had a row. Ian is driving her to Winchester tomorrow, but they are 'only just' on speaking terms." That romance did indeed founder, because this was the year that Janey Acheson met her eventual husband Christopher Ironside.

Anne picked up her news again: "All week it has been like this, one thing after another, with no quiet moments, so I am having headaches."

Then she looked ahead to end of the year. "About Christmas. Would you like me to come ten days before Christmas, if I could push pupils off? Then I might come back just after Christmas and ask Molly to come here after Sam goes back to Cork, as she will be so near London." Her thoughtfulness shone through as well, because she wanted to make it clear that she had no intention of dictating when she arrived for the festive season, these were merely suggestions. "Or would you rather have me later? And I might ask Molly before Christmas. That is if they still think of Brighton."

With Molly and Sam on the South Coast that December, it represented too good an opportunity to miss as far as a reunion with her sister went. "Send me a p.c. about what suits you best." In those days the postcard was considered the quickest and most efficient form of communication, and not so costly as a telegram or a telephone call.

Hazel missed out on Christmas that year and she had little hope of making it the following year as well, because she would be moving to Delhi. "Time is very short now, I hand over in another three weeks, then a fortnight with Jim in Peshawar." And a few weeks into the New Year Anne received a hastily scribbled note from Hazel explaining: "Just to let you know I have arrived safely in Delhi and am in the process of settling in. I have been staying with Epps till today, but am moving into my own bungalow this afternoon. What with hospital work and lectures and setting up the bungalow, there is little time for anything else. I have inherited a very charming garden."

Early in the New Year one of Anne's figures featured in an article in a monthly magazine called 'My Garden'. The figure was 'Puck', the portrait statue of Josephine G. Owen, which had been shown in the Royal Academy's 1931 exhibition. Eight years on, Dora Owen, Josephine's mother, whom Anne had only recently visited in Chipping Campden, had written an article entitled 'From a Boudoir Window' which opened with a fulsome description of the lead statue, a photograph of which was on the facing page.

"The lead figure of Puck on the terrace wall might be Jack Frost himself, for the shimmering of Puck's coat of hoar frost lends an elusive animation to the figure ..." and she fantasised: "... this morning might the spirit of Frost have breathed into Puck's nostrils the breath of life, for his face sparkles with mischief. Between outstretched hands some busy spider has spun a web ... the intricate threads attached to each curved elfin finger suggest that Puck may be playing a game of cat's cradle partnered by some invisible gnome...." As fanciful as it is, it is an extremely good description of what Anne Acheson had produced sixteen years before. It also demonstrated how the owners of such figures could still derive a great deal of pleasure after all that time.

Happily Anne had also had a figure accepted for the Royal Academy's 1939 summer exhibition. This one had no title, appearing in the listing simply as 'Fountain Figure', nevertheless that would have occupied her hugely for the first half of the year. After that other things would be occupying, not just Anne's mind, but that of the whole world.

The summer of 1939 was chosen for a great family gathering, which involved the majority of the Acheson siblings (Emily had died, and Hazel, who had been appointed Professor of Obstetrics and Gynaecology at the Lady Hardinge Medical College and Hospital in February, was unable to make it), most of their off-spring, a couple of Williams children (nephew and niece of Jim and Vio), and odd girl- and boy-friends as well. They rented Newport House, in the town of that name on the west coast of Ireland, in County Mayo.

Sandy Faris writes of that "Paradise in Mayo" in his autobiography *Da Capo Al Fine – A Life in Music* (Matador) "...a happy holiday for three generations of cousins through the generosity of my uncle Jim ..." For it appeared that it was James Acheson who had been the chief mover and shaker in organising this "idyll planned to last for two months ...". He was also the chief underwriter for the costs.

In his autobiography 'An Indian Chequerboard' James wrote: "I had leased the house from the widow of the last of the O'Donnells, a family of renown in Irish history; St Columba was one of them, and they used to maintain that it was an O'Donnell and not an O'Neill who smote off his own hand and threw it ashore so as to be able to claim to have been the first to touch Ulster soil; whence the 'Red Hand of Ulster.'"

Evelyn 'Muffet' Williams, the daughter of Vio Acheson's sister Betty, also penned her memories of that summer, when she was just 12. She travelled in the first instance up to London from Winchester where she had been staying with her grandmother. Anne met Evelyn at Waterloo station and put her up at Avenue Studios for the night. The following day Evelyn's brother Peter and their cousin Anthony turned up at the studio and all three made their way to Liverpool, and thence by night boat to Belfast, where they were met by another cousin, Jimmy – "so tall, good-looking and quite wonderfully dashing."

Sandy wrote: "Jimmy won all hearts; he had glamour." He certainly won Evelyn's heart. The 12-year-old was smitten, despite the presence of Roma, Jimmy's girlfriend, described by Sandy as "the decorative member" of the party. Jimmy was also driving a new car. "He had traded in his much-loved old Riley open touring car ('Rosebud') for a much larger and more impressive car." There is some confusion as what make of car it was. Evelyn was unsure, Sandy remembers it as a Lancia, but Jimmy's sister Janey recalled a Lagonda. Whatever the make and model he had definitely christened it 'Baby'.

Evelyn described the journey: "As we drove westwards the countryside became more and more beautiful and wild, with the mountains patterned with the shadows of fast-moving clouds. The hedges were of wild fuchsia and as we passed the odd isolated cottage, so the children would come running out, barefoot and ragged, to wave at us. There was virtually no traffic, maybe the odd donkey or two, and so I was allowed to sit in Jimmy's lap and do the steering."

The house sounded perfect. Sandy describes the centre of the family's activities thus: "Newport House, a large lovable Georgian Irish country house, festooned in Virginia creeper ..." adding that it slept sixteen people.

James wryly observed: "The house had its little park, including a chapel at one side and a special entrance to the principal public house of Newport on the other – the sacred and the profane."

Evelyn recalls: "Newport House was surrounded by rough grass, pitted with thousands of rabbit holes. There was a lovely old, walled kitchen garden which supplied the house with fruit and vegetables."

Sir James describes the setting more fully, including the welcoming party: "There was a long gate house at the entrance from the main street, and when we entered it for the first time, there stood the entire old O'Donnell household staff, all re-assembled in front of it with bows and wreathed smiles outside, headed by the housekeeper May Burke, delighted to see the house occupied once more, even if for only two or three months. May was a very capable person and a personage in the little town. She had no difficulty in recruiting a couple of 'girls dragged out of the bog' as she described them, to take a hand with the cooking and cleaning up and mopping necessary, when the multitude descended on Newport House."

In the front of the house there was a flagged terrace, with a flat-topped low wall at either end, and a short flight of steps leading down to the gravel drive and the area of rough grass that Evelyn mentioned.

But the place had its eccentricities. According to Evelyn there was no front door. Instead, "we came and went by way of an entrance with a huge sash window." Sandy expands on that, explaining: "Apart from one oddity Newport House still boasted its original classical entrance, with a large front doorway flanked by narrow side windows and surmounted by a Palladian pediment. All this was still there except for the door itself. This had been replaced by a couple of ramshackle contraptions ... At the base, stable-like, were double wooden half doors less than two feet high. The space above was filled by large sash windows. When the lower section of this was raised to its full extent the space for entrance and egress was no more than 5ft 6in high. We regularly bumped our heads until someone fixed two fluttering pieces of rag, warning one to duck."

Once through this strange front door the young Evelyn was struck by the gloomy interior. "It seemed then to be a rather dark, sombre house with a large staircase going up to a gallery. The staircase was lined with portraits of the O'Donnell family. There was no electricity and at bedtime one collected a candle from a table at the bottom of the stairs (an oil lamp if you were a lucky grown-up)."

Evelyn said she cannot recall any bathrooms. "I remember a dark, cavernous lavatory with a mahogany throne and a Willow Pattern bowl."

James is equally forthright in his description of the interior. "The House was indescribable, paper hanging off the walls and worn-out carpets and ragged curtains. However the ponderous plumbing, which required all hands to the old pump in the stableyard daily, never let us down. And in the evenings we settled down round the sweet-smelling turf (Anglice peat) fire, in the only elegant and undilapidated room in the house, the drawing room-cum-library."

According to Sandy, an advance party comprising James Acheson, his wife Vio their youngest child, daughter Kitty, and Harriet Faris, prepared the place for the other members of the party, which included Anne Acheson, who were to descend on Newport over the next few weeks.

The town of Newport overlooks Clew Bay, which according to Sandy is "... an archipelago of 365 islands (366 in a Leap Year, joke the locals)."

Some of them were merely small rocks, but plenty more were large enough for inquisitive teenagers to land on and explore, which is precisely what the youngsters did, laden with picnic hampers and setting sail in the fishing boat the Tope Queen to various of these islands. Beyond Clew Bay and to the South rises Croagh Patrick, the holy mountain. The landscape would certainly have caught Anne Acheson's imagination and indeed Harriet Rhys-Davies had clear recollections of her aunt taking a sketch pad out with her and drawing the youngsters at play, or her immediate surroundings.

Sandy remembers his Uncle Jim teaching the children to sail this rather ungainly sounding vessel. "The Tope Queen gave me my introduction to sailing. If there is a technical name for this type of vessel I do not know it. She had no deck, but boasted a mainsail and a jib. I suppose she must also have had a keel. She was rounded and hollow and held twelve of us. Uncle Jim supervised our first sailing trips, then left us to our own devices."

In fact James was not quite that irresponsible. He recalled: "Our boat was a redoubtable heavy open fishing boat .... She was guaranteed not to upset in any wind; we had a delightful lad called John Meany, the son of a local ex-policeman, as boatman and general handyman. The 'Queen' was easily the slowest sailer in those waters. They had a tremendous regatta in the estuary, and the Queen was out of sight of all the rest as they entered the estuary from the starting post some miles out in the Bay among the islands. But Peter Williams retrieved the honour of Newport House by stolidly winning, one after another, all the swimming races, against a large and showy field."

There was plenty for the youngsters to do, fishing, expeditions to beauty spots, surfing, as well as trips to nearby Westport for fresh supplies. In the evenings they would play card games. On the terrace, in front of the house, Kitty and Harriet invented something they called 'The Ball Game'. "...a kind of outdoor ping-pong played with a tennis ball," says Sandy. "There was no net, the bats were the palms of our hands. One player sat on each end wall of the terrace." The competitors' legs had to dangle, feet could not touch the ground ...." According to Sandy the game gave pleasure to all the family. Indoors, while the adults played bridge the younger element would play Flying Demon.

This was a special holiday for Janey, who had been accompanied to Newport House by Christopher Ironside. In her autobiography 'Janey' she noted: "It was my first experience of the West of Ireland, and in spite of the endless rain I was bewitched by it."

But this holiday had been taken in the shadow of war. The threat was growing with every day that passed. James wrote: "... the pub radio became more and more depressing. Gloom settled on Little Newport as on the rest of the British Isles. Discussions of a good September run of sea trout was forced and unreal. Cheerfulness would keep breaking in, but never for long."

Evelyn remembered how the first chilly tentacles of the impending war reached out to this happy family gathering. "Towards the very end of August Uncle Jim received a cable from the India Office recalling him to India. On the 31st, which was Kitty's fifteenth birthday, he left Newport." James Acheson, who by now had been appointed a Companion of the Indian Empire (CIE), had to report to Chester, preparatory to returning to India. He recalled: "... it was a kind of a relief."

And for all that Janey was spellbound by the rugged, romantic West Coast of Ireland, still she could not shake off an underlying sense of foreboding, one that darkened her mood. In her autobiography she notes: "Even at the time I felt that this would be our last holiday together, and there was deep melancholy mixed with the pleasure of driving around ... walking on the hills, even bathing in the icy sea. We had a period of precious sunshine at the beginning of September. It was as though fate was making the old bargain, 'Enjoy yourselves now – the bill is coming later.'"

Almost certainly for that reason, when the holiday ended she and Christopher had decided they would get married when they returned to London. Her mother, Vio, grandmother Madre and brothers James and Anthony, as well as Anne Acheson and Christopher's mother and Godmother, attended the ceremony at the Registry Office in Marloes Road, Kensington, but her father was en route for India and so was unable to attend. He also missed the nuptial tea at No 9, Avenue Studios. In her autobiography Janey wrote: "... we went to Auntie Nan's studio for the marriage tea, which she regarded as essential. She had done marvels and had produced a wedding cake with icing ...."

When Janey's father arrived in Bombay, en route to Quetta, via Karachi, there was a cable awaiting him with the news. And, in a letter at the end of September to his sister Anne, he displayed immense stoicism, with not a hint of resignation, when he wrote: "The only home news I have had was a cable awaiting me here, announcing Janet's marriage. That wasn't altogether unexpected. I have cabled my blessing and am now thinking of suitable presents. I am very disappointed I could not be there. The reasons are the same as for Colonel Field's not being at Vio's wedding. We were married in war-time and Janet was born in war-time, and now she has been married in war-time too. Well I hope it will be as happy as our marriage has been. There is no reason why it should not be for Christopher has good stuff in him and is principled and he and Janey are clearly affinities."

In that same letter he reassured Anne of his arrival on the Sub-Continent. The letter is dated September 29th and James reported to his sister: "... I have arrived safely after a most interesting, occasionally exciting (I watched the sinking of a U-boat) but very trying voyage. I don't think we are yet allowed to give details, so will keep them till later."

Back on the windswept West Coast of Ireland Janey recorded: "...on one terrible day there was a telegram for James telling him to report to the Air Force."

When Jimmy had gone up to Christ Church, Oxford he had joined the University Air Reserve Squadron in his first year. His sister Janey explained that it was because Jimmy and his friends were crazy about flying. The outcome was that he was called up by the Royal Air Force at the beginning of the war, ending up in Coastal Command, and Janey's presentiments were tragically borne out, because, like so many other young men, before and after him, the dashing Jimmy Acheson was destined not to survive the war.

Even before Anne had set off for Newport House in July 1939, she would have been well aware that war was on the way, because all she had to do was look up and in an easterly direction and there she, and pretty well the rest of London, would have seen the barrage balloons, designed to deter low flying German aircraft and dive bombers and generally help defend London against the expected air attacks. In the summer of 1939 the government had ordered that barrage balloon exercises were to take place in order to ensure a swift and orderly launch of them when the occasion demanded. The balloons hovering high over London were anchored by steel cables to the ground. By the time Anne had returned to Chelsea, in early September, Prime Minster Neville Chamberlain had made his pronouncement, on the third of the month, declaring that Britain was at war with Germany. The balloon had well and truly gone up.

13

Plus ça Change

~~~m~~~

Twenty one years after "the war to end all wars" there was a different monarch on the throne, a different resident at No 10 Downing Street, but on the fighting front it was the same old, same old. Net result, another World War. It was also a case of "plus ça change ..." for Anne Acheson. In the light of how much she gave up for the 'Great' War, it should come as no surprise that she should feel compelled, once more, to do her bit for King and Country.

But things had changed greatly. To begin with the Surgical Requisites Association was no more. In June 1919 Queen Mary's Needlework Guild had handed over the depot as it stood, with all its organisation, stock, furniture and equipment to the British Red Cross Society.

This time around it was a more mechanical war. Machines dominated, technology was developing at a gallop. The inter-war period had also seen huge medical and surgical advances being made, so there was little point in Anne seeking out an equivalent of the Surgical Requisites Association this time.

However Anne was determined to become involved in war work just as she had in the First World War, and she wanted to do something at least as important as her work had been with the SRA, so she set about finding out what was on offer. She admitted she wasn't sure quite what it was she wanted to do, but she was determined to do something. This time around 'volunteers' were paid a minimum wage by the State for giving up their regular work and careers and re-training for roles in industry. This appealed to Anne, who was a glutton for learning new crafts. There was a crying need for skilled and semi-skilled workers to enter an industry that was geared to maintaining the supply of munitions and instruments necessary to sustain Britain's ability to protect itself and, since this war was a more mechanical thing, Anne decided to go with the flow.

She thought munitions would be the trade for her, but initially there were no openings, so she applied to go on a training course run by the Women Engineers' Society. "The society runs a three month course for supervisors and I'm thinking of inquiring about that and seeing if I could start in July or after the holidays .... There is also a tool-making class at Battersea Polytechnic, but whether that ... leads to a paid job I don't know."

Of course as far as factory work went Anne was now a lot older, she had entered middle age. At the outbreak of the war in September 1939 she had just celebrated her 57th birthday. While age did not preclude her from doing anything, the factories taking on 'civilian' labour for the war work were guilty of what nowadays would be termed 'ageism'.

When she was eventually told she was in with a chance of a job she wrote to her sister Grace: "Of course it is not certain that I go there as I may be turned down on account of age." And a little later in the same letter: "There is another factory that takes lots of our trainees, but they won't have anyone over the age of 40."

It was a happy Anne who revealed, in a letter dated August 18th 1940: "I am starting tomorrow on an engineering course for war work. Three evenings a week 6.30-9.0pm for three months."

She was apparently lucky to have got on to the course so quickly, because so popular were they that there was a waiting list for the next couple of courses. According to Anne the reason she was able to jump the queue was because at her original interview for a place on a training course: "The secretary of the Society of Women Engineers said owing to my experience in kindred work they might take me." Presumably this was a reference to the fact that Anne, as a sculptress, was familiar with working with certain elements of engineering, and of course her art involved, indeed depended upon, precision. She continues: "I went yesterday to the

Institute and someone had given up owing to ill-health, so I am taking her place."

It was a busy time for her. A postscript in the aforementioned letter to her niece Harriet Faris, made it very clear just how busy she was around this time. "Your mother wrote – to my great indignation – that she does not think I can be doing much work these days. I have 'checked in' at 8am daily, except Saturday and Sunday, for three weeks, and left after 5pm ...". Her engineering course was held at the Beaufoy Institute in Black Prince Road in Lambeth, South London. It was formerly a technical institute for boys, had been since 1930, then during the Second World War it was requisitioned, first by the Society of Women Engineers, then subsequently by the Ministry of Labour to train women, so that shortages of personnel in the engineering and munitions factories could be filled.

There is an inscription on a tablet which is laid on the foundation stone of the building that reads: "Those that do teach young babes, Do it with gentle means and easy talks." The women who attended night school to learn engineering were quite possibly babes, but they took their lessons seriously.

Anne certainly must have done because just a few weeks into the course she informed the family that: "I am on the munitions training course now from 9.30 to 4.30 daily." She followed that with a letter to Grace, which had some positive news, and clearly indicated that she had mastered everything she was taught, because she wrote: "On Friday the secretary of the Women's Engineering Society – a real engineer – asked me to come to see her at the Regent Street office, and is arranging for me to go to a firm in Aldgate in East London as a learner at 30/- (£1.50) a week in perhaps six weeks' time. I shall have to get there at 8.45am but shall be doing definite war work." She was clearly thrilled at last to be able to have something positive to look forward to. However, she did temper it with a rider: "She had several other women to interview after me, so did not say quite definitely, but seemed practically certain. After being a learner the WE Society will find me a job, she thought, easily."

Despite the rheumatism and her advancing years, any doubts over her ability to meet the exacting work demanded by precision engineering were rapidly dispelled when, with not a hint of arrogance, but rather with the suggestion of a teenage pupil's pride, she reported on her progress at the classes. "At the engineering class I always finish first in my section and can sit on the bench while the others finish. The instructor very wisely puts me last when starting anything that we have to do in turn." Later in the same letter she wrote: "What we have been doing has been easy to me because it is hand tools mostly so far."

Any fears she harboured that her stiffening joints might militate against steadiness and accuracy in her work were to prove groundless: "My filing pleases my instructor." Then, deeper into the course, she wrote: "My work is generally rather a show piece. I am very accurate, eg My brazing joint exercise – jigsaw two pieces of iron, evenly filed, but leaving a tiny, even, gap for the brass – were so symmetrical they fitted when reversed. ... other pieces I get to within 1/1,000 of an inch all over, by hand."

In the later letter to her niece Harriet, Anne displayed a rare moment of vanity: "I wear a light boiler suit at work – iron filings got into my shoes, and trousers prevent that. It is lucky that I am thinner than I was. I don't look too dreadful. I really prefer a skirt for comfort. My boiler suit is a thinnish, cotton one and I am going to get some warm slacks to go in before it gets much colder. Can you imagine me in this garb? My head tied up in an Indian silk handkerchief. My studio overalls looked dirty in a day."

She also listed some of the things she had produced in the machine shop: "... have made by hand a spanner, a tri-square, an angle gauge, a plate gauge, a brazing joint etc, etc some accurate to 1/1,000th of an inch measured by micrometer screw gauge. These are all exercises, though some are useful." She certainly deserved a job after demonstrating such skill, but all the time her obvious pride in her work was accompanied by an uneasy feeling that there would be no job, nothing for her at the end of it all. Unsurprisingly she added: "If I don't get a job after all this I shall be wild."

The course was far from perfect and she was quite scathing about aspects of it. At the beginning of October, with four or five weeks of the course remaining, and no news of the promised job in Aldgate, Anne wrote: "Our lectures are a joke to me. We are a mixed lot and get a sort of elementary geometry and arithmetic – strictly what we need in work – I *did* know before, that 3/32 was half 3/16." Her frustration spilled over. "I usually learn about two things, technical points, in about half an hour. The lecturer is very bored at the Ministry of Labour scheme. We are fitters and are not allowed to have lectures on machines – which were interesting,

I was at one before the scheme changed. We have two lectures a week. He cut them down to half hours this week."

The Ministry of Labour had eventually decided to take over the running of the engineering course and the students were told that they were free to stay on or to leave as they chose. Anne opted to stay on. The course changed slightly and so four weeks into the old one Anne found she was the equivalent of ten days into the new one, which was scheduled to last for a further eight weeks, but at least the money went up again. Anne explained to Harriet: "... the Ministry of Labour voluntarily pay us maintenance 24/- (£1.20) a week and our fares and lunches ...".

She began to become fretful about a job. The one she had been 'promised' had not materialised. She wrote in early October: "If I were penniless I could get a job in a factory now, half-trained – as some of our batch have done. Two sisters were turned out of their houses in the Channel Islands and after a lot of bother about having no proofs that they are British (no identity cards or birth certificates) they have got jobs today, on half the training. I ought to be finished about November 8th."

She would be happy, she insisted in another letter, to do pretty much anything and go anywhere. She was accepting of the fact that she might not get the work she wanted, as she wrote in another letter: "... I realise that I may get some monotonous, unskilled job for the duration when I go to a factory. I said I would go anywhere, but preferred London when the Ministry took us over. Now I don't mind leaving London if they offer me a job elsewhere."

There was one unwelcome intrusion on the training course when the Ministry of Information decided to use the workshop, where Anne and her fellow students were based, as a backdrop for a film. There were still some four weeks left of the course when she wrote to Grace in mid-October 1940: "We wasted a lot of time this week over a film they made of the work for the Ministry of Information. Work was very confusing and irritating ...." And she listed the nuisances: "... about six men, some up a ladder, miles of rubber covered flexes, strong lights in all sorts of places. An actress, and her dresser touching up her face at intervals etc, etc. no room to move when wanted tools etc and the actress would be pretending to use the electric drill one wanted."

It is possible to detect the contempt in her voice when she wrote: "I expect it will be on the News Reel, though it is fiction. They brought in a 'star' to pretend to work at the machines and made a story too silly for words. Mary the heroine, when she has been at work for ten days sends home a finished piece of work *daily* to her father, who does not believe in women mechanics." Perhaps the sexism in the plot irked Anne as well.

At last on October 19 Anne had some news of work. "I am probably to work in a factory at ..." here she wrote the location, then, presumably, because of wartime censorship and the obsession with not giving away crucial information that could be intercepted by a German spy, she scratched out the name of the place, although she gave a broad hint as to where it was when she added: " ... so I expect I shall stay in this room. I finish my course on October 30th . I shall be glad not to have so far to go, lately getting home has taken an hour some days, which means the shops are shut by the time I get to them. I could if necessary walk home from ...." Again the location of the factory was scratched out, but, given the fact that she felt she did not need to move and could, at a pinch, walk home, and close inspection of the words that have been scratched out by her pen make it reasonable to assume that the factory was almost certainly in Parsons Green.

She was very up and down over the issue. Just five days later, in a despairing postcard to Grace, Anne wrote: "I am disappointed at not having any further information as to a job. Officials of the Ministry of Labour have not quite kept their promises. One did not turn up, who said she would give us details today. The man who came was entirely vague. He says they will let us know on Monday."

Anne was getting desperate, and not a little angry. She had proved she could do what was asked of her. She was almost fully trained and felt she had something to offer, yet there was little or no interest in this top student's abilities. "I might push for another job for which crowds are applying," she added, "but the hours are long and it would mean leaving anywhere I could live at 6am, and getting home about 8pm. My friend Miss McWilliam and I would like to go together and say we are willing to go to the provinces. Of course I should be glad of a rest before the job, but not knowing where it is to be, if it is to be after all this work, is most unsettling. I am depressed about it."

She continued to swing to and fro, oscillating between optimism and pessimism as regards her job prospects. "... I should wait for a while as new workers are wanted in sudden rushes when a new place opens ..." and similarly workers "are not wanted when supplies are held up." But she reiterated that ageism was the root cause of her frustration. "My age bars me from a lot of places - 'No one over 40.'"

Throughout all of this the Ministry of Labour emerged with little credit. Apart from wanting some 'action', albeit of a tamer kind than that being experienced by the military, Anne also had her life to sort out and run. "If I knew I was leaving London I would start packing up and getting rid of extra possessions in the studio. If it is in ... London I might get a cheap unfurnished flat and have my own things, or just stay here."

The note of desperation intensified the nearer she got to the end of the course. On Sunday October 27th she told Grace: "I finish the training on Wednesday. I want *war* work of course, but would be satisfied to release a skilled man from other work." As a footnote she added: "I am now semi-skilled."

Not unnaturally in the midst of such uncertainty, she began to be assailed with self doubt. "Of course the Ministry should never have said 'No age limit' at the beginning without consulting factory owners. I am now losing confidence in myself. I shall probably be too slow."

And two days after the course had finished Anne was even lower. "I am very depressed today," she told Grace on the Friday of that week.... my job is not definite yet, we are to go to the Ministry of Labour place again on Tuesday. We went today and they have not heard from the factory. It gives me a breathing space to pack up in the studio, but that is a most depressing job, mildew and damp upstairs and downstairs and not knowing whether I am really going to the provinces."

The 'where' did not really matter to Anne. "We were prepared to go to Birmingham on Tuesday, now it might be Reading (or neither). Anyhow we shall go to see this Mrs Howse of the Vacancy Department every two days till they place us. A depressing way of spending time, taking about three quarters of an hour to go and then waiting, and three quarters of an hour to come back."

That she remained as enthusiastic about working in a factory as she did is remarkable, especially given the hours some of them expected these 'volunteers' to work. "One factory works 7.30am to 7pm daily. Some are paid with bonuses for quick work. Sunday work is voluntary, paid but not insisted on. Friday and Saturday are free from 5.30pm. Alternate weeks are night shifts." Anne was certainly prepared to take anything. "If one like that is offered us Miss McWilliam won't take it so I shall have to go alone."

As low as she clearly felt, Anne added: "One good thing about being sent to the provinces is that we don't have to go for an interview. The firms at a distance take Mr Ellis's word for our suitability. When Beaufoy Institute was a boys school for engineers no boy left till he had a job. Mr Ellis [her previous instructor in the Women's Society of Engineers] had a list of 80 firms and sent them the sort he knew each wanted. Now of course the Ministry of Labour people have taken it over and they are dealing with strange new firms and women workers."

Two postcards to Grace separated by 17 days both began with the now familiar lament. Tuesday November 5: "I am still uncertain as to a job. May hear on Friday or they will wire me if they hear sooner."

Miserably for her, although Anne stayed in London after that, hanging on and hoping for news and declining an invitation to go up to Oxford to see her nephew Sandy, it was the same story two and a half weeks later: Friday November 22, another postcard to the long-suffering Grace: "No more word of a job. I am to go back on Wednesday."

At least this time, for the first time, she was given a reason for the delay. "They have explained that the change from two shifts to one daily in some neighbourhoods has meant that for the late night shift men are being taken on."

Anne expanded a little on this to Hazel over in India, in a letter dated November 27. "I am still out of work, but not so depressed about it as I was, as it has been explained to me that the changing from two shifts to one, daily in October, threw the night workers out of work and till these are absorbed the demand for women workers has gone, to a great extent. Of course the Institute people saw to it that those of the older women who were without any means got the few non-age-limit jobs there were and leave those of us who won't starve as a kind of reserve. They don't say so, but we have guessed it. I don't mind in a way as I am glad to have a 'holiday' to clear up business things in the studio. I am destroying piles of letters about old commissions and things, going through all my files. The war makes all estimates and prices out of date."

Even so she felt moved to write to Grace: "If I don't get a job then I shall come over to stay with you for the duration." It was not what she wanted of course, but she was beginning to believe that she would never be given the opportunity to put her newly-learned skills to practical use and in such a worthy cause.

True to her nature though Anne abhorred inactivity and wrote on the same postcard: "I am helping a couple of days a week at the Red Cross Hospital Library ... for a few hours, sorting books and pasting on labels. I am going again on Tuesday. This week I mended packing cases to go abroad (their carpenter man is ill), I washed book covers with soap, cleaned a few of their insides and sorted new lots. I always want to stop and read some of the books. They use 'Lightning soap' on the dirty covers with marvellous effect."

Anne needed more than grubby library books to occupy her though. She had been trained for better than this.

14

Blitz and Pieces

~~~~ɯ~~~~

I t must have been a terrifying, yet, in a perverse kind of way, impressive
sight, to see, as many Londoners did late in the afternoon of Saturday
September 7 1940, a staggering 348 German bombers, who, with their
'armed guard' of 617 fighter planes, formed a 20-mile wide block of
aircraft, that according to reports covered something in the region of 800
square miles approaching for a raid that was to leave 448 people dead –
an airborne phalanx of death, mesmerising to those watching on the
ground. This was the start of the Blitz, the airborne bombardment of
British towns, cities and seaports, which would continue until the
following May.

The number of fatalities during the Blitz is appalling. Coping with
the mounting numbers of corpses must have been a nightmare for the
authorities. At Smithfield meat market there is a hole in the road leading
to a series of underground roadways. In the latter part of the 20th Century
it was used as a car park, known as 'The Rotunda', a roadway winding
down, then suddenly disappearing into the dark, damp bowels of
Smithfield, serving medical and ancillary staff from St Bartholomew's
Hospital just across the square, as well as Smithfield Market workers and
journalists from nearby Fleet Street. But, according to one old market

porter, now long dead, some four decades earlier something more macabre was parked in the Rotunda. This was, said the old porter, where the dead were left initially after the bodies had been recovered from the rubble left by the bombers on their nightly raids. One report of the Blitz states that the worst night saw 3,000 people killed, and in the single worst incident 450 died when a bomb hit an air raid shelter. The London in which Anne Acheson lived for much of the Second World War saw more than 20,000 Londoners killed.

In one letter to Grace in the summer of 1940, Anne made her first reference to air raids. The 'blitz' had yet to start, but in the summer of 1940 Germany attempted to wipe out the Royal Air Force and carried out raids on RAF airfields, such as Biggin Hill, in Kent, and on various munitions, aircraft and engineering factories in the Home Counties and in the South generally.

Anne was relating her return by coach from visiting a client for whom she had completed "a little portrait figure ("... she is thrilled by the result, thank goodness)". Then she mentioned the raid. "All the return journey was during that raid on a suburb in that direction. I was thankful the coach did not stop ... it was cloudy so I saw nothing in the sky."

There was just a tinge of disappointment when Anne wrote in another letter to Grace: "I have not seen a plane brought down yet, I have seen a couple of battles, or dogfights."

If the aerial battles were just glimpsed from time to time – much of the fighting went on further south over Kent and Sussex – the bombing raids, more often than not, were uncomfortably close to Anne.

At the start of the Blitz Anne was living in Sydney Close. She was always cautious when the air raid warnings sounded; she was not trying to be brave in staying there, it was a matter of pragmatics; there was nowhere else to store all her work-in-progress, as well as her sculpting materials and her other art work and tools of her trade. "Owing to my big roof window and the shakiness of my other big window I leave the upstairs studio when the warnings sound," she explained in one letter at the beginning of September.

"When things sound bad we go into the Budds' 'shelter', which is now the narrow staircase, and get on with knitting. We sometimes play the world's worst bridge with them." Anne even took to sleeping, for a couple of nights, on a stretcher that spent the day propped up against one wall.

The air raids, though, appeared to have their bright side, because it is undoubtedly the artist speaking when Anne added: "The searchlights were marvellous when we came out."

As the night-time raids intensified, so sleep became an increasingly precious commodity. Time after time in her letters Anne would tell her correspondents how little she had slept while confined to an air-raid shelter. A letter dated September 2 1940 began: "I meant to write sooner but have missed a lot of sleep this week."

Her nocturnal, voluntary nursing duties had their advantages though. "I went on duty at First Aid Post last night," she wrote, when the Blitz was building up momentum in mid-September 1940, "and had the best night's sleep for a week, on the emergency operating table! I only wakened for nearby bombs, and when the table felt too hard thro' the mattress."

It was also at the beginning of September that Anne first considered the possibility of leaving the studio at No 9 Sydney Close temporarily. In yet another of her infamous postscripts she wrote: "Am thinking of going to cheap lodgings or hostel when I go on full-time [war work]. This place with raids on means too many precautions."

Anne flirted briefly with the idea of spending the nights in the reinforced shelter of an empty house which was next door to her friend Mary Morton, also an artist, but unfortunately, before she had time to discuss the idea the empty house was reduced to a wreck.

On September 16 she reiterated to Grace the idea of moving out of Sydney Close: "I am getting on all right, but thinking of taking lodgings as I have to leave the studio so often it is difficult to get housework done or to get sleep."

Two days later her mind was made up. Possibility had turned to certainty. "I slept several hours last night, but only one the night before. If there are planes directly overhead, or the [anti-aircraft] guns one has to take shelter on the way to and from work so often that there is no time to do anything, but feed quickly and gather rugs etc for the night out. One is thankful if the evening raid is late enough to let us clean our teeth, or the all-clear in the morning is early enough for one hour in bed."

She reasoned that with the frequency of the raids increasing she was spending more time going in and out of her studio at No 9, to a shelter and back, than she was actually working in it also, as prosaic as it may sound, it left her too little time to complete her housework, a fact which irked her.

It was rare for Anne to be able to spend any time in the evenings in her own home. One such occasion was when she and her neighbour and fellow artist Helen Budd benefited from later air raids by the Germans. "Once or twice we were able to stay in my studio till nearly 9.00pm, but not often."

Just before she was forced to move out of Sydney Close, Anne was invited to someone else's shelter because, as she said, there was invariably a raid on by the time she got home from work. "Miss Geddes invited me to the shelter under the flats, but the people all sat up till 12 midnight talking or playing bridge – I had to leave at 6am to get ready for work. Also they kept a *bright* light on all night and my two chairs were not really very much better than the stairs."

Her underlining of the word 'bright' has a double significance, because not only did it keep her awake, but also the black-out prohibited even the merest chink of light escaping from any building to give the German bomb aimers a clue that there were any buildings below on which they could drop their deadly cargo.

She finally made the move from Sydney Close (although she held on to the lease), becoming one of the estimated 1,400,000 made homeless by the Blitz, in early October 1940, but she didn't go too far, certainly not significantly closer to Lambeth, where she was working on the engineering course.

Her temporary abode was at No 11 Oakley Street, on the south side of the King's Road, near enough a mile from Sydney Close, which itself was off the Fulham Road.

"I have had to leave the studio and am very depressed about it," she wrote in her first letter from her new address. "No time to pick and choose where to go as there is generally a raid on ... I came here because there is a shelter in the basement." While in a subsequent letter to her niece Harriet Faris, she explained: "I have left the studio as it was not safe at night during raids ...."

Her room, she said, was on the first floor of the "biggish" house. Safety, her safety, was paramount and she continued: "... the window, a French one, has shutters and the bed is in a safe-ish position far from the window. I slept quite well last night."

She had to pay for her new-found accommodation; her rent was one guinea (£1.05), with an extra 4 shillings (20 pence) per week for what she described as a "light" breakfast. Her earlier vexation at being unable to find the time to do her housework at Sydney Close because of the hours she worked and the hours she then had to spend ducking into air-raid shelters, suggested she was a fastidious person when it came to cleanliness. This is borne out when she mentions the furniture in Oakley Street. "... the armchairs are grubby so I fetched something to cover one."

In a sentence she captured the bleakness of the war and of being forced to leave Sydney Close. "Avenue Studios are now deserted altogether at night. One ceiling in No6 came down on Friday night (October 4th 1940) either vibration from our nearest gun, or one of the time bombs, of which there were said to be five fairly near."

In a way she was relieved to have moved. "I was glad I had decided to leave when I saw the ceiling down as we had considered a roof and a floor above enough protection from shrapnel on our uncomfortable stairs in the Budds' 'shelter.'" She did however, acknowledge the inconvenience of moving. "I do hate being turned out. I shall have to spend all my weekends packing up the studio."

Cleanliness, lightness of breakfasts and cost apart, her new place in Oakley Street held a trump card over the studio as once again she returns to the theme of uncomfortable nights and lost sleep, although on the heels of that recent experience in someone else's shelter comes the contrast with her new, albeit temporary, 'home': "Last night it was lovely to be in bed all night." That was her first in Oakley Street. She put out her light on the night of Saturday October 5th and judging from what she wrote to Grace, had no need to interrupt her sleep by getting up again and seeking a shelter when an air raid started. "It seems to have been quite a bad raid, but I must have slept except when they were in this district. I heard no bombs, but the noise of the guns sometimes covers the bomb noise."

That first letter from No 11 Oakley Street closed triumphantly: "There go the sirens. Thank goodness I can stay in this openly lighted room and go on writing, instead of getting ready for an evening on the stairs when the guns begin."

Even in the midst of the horror, the misery and the inconvenience, Anne finds something positive to write home about, perhaps help to ease her family's minds as to her well-being and safety. On one occasion she talked up the guns, making it clear that these anti-aircraft batteries, which were there for her protection – and she emphasised their proximity as well, thus heightening the sense of her being safeguarded – did not displease her. Indeed she described them, or rather their noise, in a quite fanciful way. "The guns make weird noises now and seem to change. There is one like a gigantic sigh. You expect a bang at the end and there is none."

Still she missed her own home. "I hate living in a bed-sitting room. There is a disguised basin stand but no running water, no towel rail. I have a gas ring on the floor and a little gas radiator. If I could get them to put power plugs in this room it would be all right. It is clean – cleaner than I thought. I spilled water on the carpet and the cloth I mopped it up with remained perfectly clean." And in case anyone in the family wondered why the floor was so clean Anne added: "They use a vacuum cleaner." The source of hot water for a bath was "a geyser, with a penny-in-the-slot meter."

All of this traumatic upheaval in Anne's life was taking place slap bang in the middle of the most intensive part of the blitz when, according to reports London was bombed every day or night from September 7 to November 2 in 1940.

In another letter, this time to Hazel, in late 1940, Anne referred to her First Aid work: "Casualties are much fewer than were expected, specially the minor ones. Our post has had only about 50, mostly shock and broken glass cuts."

The horrors of being bombed were not confined to the immediate shock of the explosion and the instant damage. When Mary Morton was out one day a time bomb was dropped on her studio. Anne described the aftermath: "Morton ... was evacuated with what she happened to have in an attaché case. All her roof glass fell and then it poured so her place must be a ruin." It was everyone's nightmare. After the bomb's initial destruction, there was the terminal destruction by nature of the battered, shattered buildings to cope with.

In her friend Morton's case Anne relayed the latest news to Grace. "[Morton] has been three weeks out of her studio after the roof was wrecked, waiting for a time bomb across the street that has now been dealt with and not exploded."

As a postscript at the top of one letter to Harriet Faris she instructed her niece to: "Address letters to 9, Sydney Close, as I may get another room."

There is more evidence of Anne's determination to reassure all members of the family that she is relatively safe in the bomb-torn city. She adopted a somewhat cavalier approach when telling Harriet: "I am getting philosophical about raids. So many bombs fall harmlessly as far as people are concerned. Anyhow 75 per cent of London is open space so the Germans waste a large number."

But in case anyone imagines that she was being an ostrich about the perils of the Blitz she did add: "There have been horrible disasters of course, but to a very small proportion of London's millions." She also suggested that the reason everyone had to go into an air raid shelter was not because of the bombardment, but rather because of the anti-aircraft retaliation: "We have to keep under shelter when our guns are firing on account of falling shrapnel."

Then in another cramped postscript she informed Grace: "A time bomb in Sydney Street has hurled a piece of paving stone, about 14lbs, at my bathroom window, how it got over I don't know. Only a small hole. It must have just touched it. I had pasted linen net on it so there were hardly any splinters."

She also made it clear to the family back home in Northern Ireland that she was aware that they were also in the German bombers' sights when she squeezed another of her famous postscripts onto the bottom of a letter in November: "I was sorry to see that the raiders were over Ulster. Where were they?"

In Anne's eyes, but perhaps more for the benefit of any worriers in the family, this new address in Oakley Street was superior to Sydney Close, in that it was far safer. "Here I have two floors and a roof over me, so the shrapnel won't hit me and I go to bed and generally sleep through the raids."

However, she couldn't resist injecting a little bit of drama into her correspondence from time to time, because while she did not want the family to worry unduly, she obviously wanted to let them know that she was an eye witness to all the mayhem and in the frontline of hostilities, hence: "Two nights ago five bombs fell near enough to shake us – " she interrupts her explanation to say: " … Ha, ha, just as I wrote that I thought a bomb had dropped but I think it was the nearest big gun – the first one in the evening is always alarming. Gentler guns are at it now. The first thing may have been a time bomb."

It is significant that when stating that five bombs dropped nearby, all they did was to "shake us". In other words, they were not actually a direct threat on her life. The family could breathe easy once more. There was no imminent danger, it was merely a way of reminding them that she was involved, or at least in the middle of, this drama that was unfolding. There was an implication in one letter that the family was anxious not just about her physical safety, but also concerned for her emotional and mental well-being. Anne was emphatic with her reassurances. "Don't worry over me. When I am at work I am quite happy."

There was just as much inconvenience (and fear) for Londoners when there was a daylight raid, as there was at night. Anne described the procedure for her and her fellow students who were undertaking the Ministry of Labour Training Scheme for Women Engineers. "We have roof watchers, porters and mechanics, who go up when the siren goes and clang a fierce alarm when the raiders come near. Then we all go into the basement in a hurry, and by the time I have got a chair and got my knitting out and picked up the dropped stitches the bell goes and we go up again. Most of us never know whether the all-clear has sounded or not.

"I am very happy at work. I expect I should be worse off if we did not get an occasional chance to sit down when raiders are dangerous. But we don't go down till our roof watchers tell us. They go up when the sirens go. Occasionally we have almost to run from the workshops across the hall, with worried-looking men saying 'Hurry please, hurry please.'"

The area where she was doing her training certainly aroused her sympathies. "Lambeth gets rather a lot of bombs. I hate to see the poor people's houses shattered ...."

She also remarked on the sight of the Lambeth inhabitants when an air raid siren has sounded and revealed a little known fact, which is that eventually places in air raid shelters were allocated by the issuing of tickets. "The Lambeth people seeking shelter for the night are pathetic in a way, with their bundles of blankets and pillows, sometimes on prams, but they are starting [to give out] tickets for their places so they won't have to stand in queues any more. I used to pass an enormous queue which waited for a big block of offices to close at 5.50pm daily. The offices needed the shelter by day and the poorer folk from across the river used it at night."

As ever where Anne Acheson was concerned, there was an acute attention to detail, even when observing everyday life in the Blitz. Anne's sharp eyes missed nothing of significance, and opened the eyes of others as to what was going on around her at the time. Her words paint a lively picture.

The destruction of property and buildings became a commonplace sight for Anne and everyone living through the Blitz, and they seemed to get closer and closer to her. She recounted what happened to the home of her secretary, Bill Baker. "[His] house had all its windows blown in (or perhaps out) and they had a Molotoff Bread Basket [a cluster of incendiary bombs that the Germans used to drop as an alternative to the high explosive bombs] scattered around too. Most houses have stirrup pumps and sand, but these things are a worry and a fuss. Bill says Carrie was absolutely calm when the big explosion shattered the windows and a neighbour's house (luckily empty)."

It was not just houses that suffered either. "Our church, St John's Kensington, has been bombed. Kensington Chapel (Congregational) at once offered to share their building, and the services are combined."

That arrangement did not last long. Three weeks later, at the beginning of November, Anne reported: "I told you St John's Church was wrecked. They combined with the Allen Street Congregational one and it was wrecked too, so they have cleared the debris out of St John's and use it now."

Amid all this carnage it was merely a matter of time before the studio at No 9 Sydney Close took a direct hit and it happened in mid-October. Anne asked: "Did I write to you that the studio is a bit wrecked? I got half a day off on Tuesday to see to things, but could not do very much. The caretaker was to clear up the broken glass on Wednesday. The upper studio seemed three inches thick with it." She had been moving figures and other work in progress, into more secure places in the building and that policy had paid off. "Nothing precious was damaged. We had two very bad nights Sunday and Monday, I went down to the ground floor where some of the other lodgers sleep. Some are in the stuffy basement. I had a good divan bed, but close alongside on each side, filling all the floor, to the others." This particular raid had happened apparently on the night of either Sunday or Monday, October 13th or 14th (or both) in 1940.

And she even got close, albeit inadvertently, to the action, hanging around long enough to watch intently what took place. In her letter of November 2 she reported: "I saw soldiers dealing with a time bomb today. One, only, near it at first. Needless to say I kept even further away from the barrier put up with 'Unexploded bomb' on it, which has been there for some time."

The damage to her studio had understandably upset her, but as quickly as she slipped into a trough of misery, so she would haul herself out of it. "Now that I have had supper I am a bit less inclined to wish for a 'direct hit' to end my troubles. It is very aggravating never to see any of these night battles. We are told to keep away from windows, and I do."

But she still used her ears to the full, and again there is something of the poet in her when she wrote: "Our guns are coughing and barking and sighing (occasionally, but not tonight, they say tut-tut-tut) I think I hear more than one plane overhead. One German plane makes an intermittent noise, but several make a drone."

Yet amidst all this terrifying activity Anne still found time to rejoice in her surroundings. "Today London was beautiful to look at. It is marvellous how little difference all those bombs have made."

On another occasion she made a quirky observation: "There are a lot of flies for this time of year, evacuated from their winter sleeping places in houses now wrecked I suppose."

Bombs and shrapnel were not the only perils faced by civilians in those cities targeted by the Germans for the bombardment, there was also the dread of chemical attack, a legacy of the horrors and outrages of the mustard gas of the First World War. To that end everyone had to have a gas mask, but they were hardly convenient things to carry around with one all day, every day. But Anne rejoiced in a solution.

"I got the best thing for gas mask carrying that I have met yet. I was always starting out without mine. It is a handbag with mask case below. The handbag part is splendid because its base is wide and you can see into it all when you open it. It is not very much larger than my old handbag and seems no heavier!"

Anne insisted that the British citizenry would never be demoralised. Everyone rose above it and just got on with life. Anne was particularly upbeat in one postcard back home: "London is wonderful." And she played down many of the problems that had been highlighted in the press of the day. "Everything upset seems to be quickly seen-to by the authorities. If a station is closed a special bus is run. Do not believe rumours. We had no gas one morning only. I heard there was no bread, but it was only in certain shops for one day."

In her letter to Hazel she enlarged on this 'life goes on as normal' writing: "When the Blitz began pessimists said they would stop electricity and gas and water supplies. Electricity has never failed yet for more than ten minutes. (I think the authorities had more alternative supply sources than we gave them credit for). Gas is off in certain smaller districts, eg my studio, but they manage to supply the shops nearby very soon after. Paraffin and meths are not scarce.

"I knew of one district where water was off for some days, but there are big tanks in the squares for fire-fighting, and long hoses and mobile pumps suddenly appeared when the big blocks of flats had their main damaged.

"London had a year in which to prepare. We have 'Hants-Dorset' buses, Manchester buses etc, all colours and shapes. When the district railway gets a hit there is a queue of emergency buses for railway passengers only to take you to the station beyond the damage. You go into your station for your ticket and come out to the bus if there is no train on that bit of the line. All very well organised now."

She was ever ready to reassure the family as to her well-being and her safety, but she could have done with a little reassurance herself from the authorities as regards her job prospects, because amidst all the entertaining of nieces and nephews, and ducking into and out of this or that air raid shelter was the knowledge that time was slipping by, and she desperately wanted to get stuck in to some form of war-related work using her newly learned engineering skills in the machine shop.

15

A Wish is Granted

~~~~~ᢟᢟᢟᢟ~~~~~

The outbreak of war had seen Anne busy with various commissions, but other matters occupied her as well, because when she wasn't working on a sculpture she was meeting and/or putting up her various nieces and nephews. Indeed throughout Anne's time there her studio at No 9, Sydney Close saw a veritable procession of youth passing through it, all of whom used to stop over long enough to savour the delights of London, before heading off, back home, or to school, or university. The thing was that Sydney Close was a convenient (and free) *pied-à-terre* for the young of the family to come and explore the big city. And come they did, nieces, nephews, and even a second cousin, Maurice Crawford, who admitted in a letter of condolence to Grace following Anne's death that he used to descend on Anne "for cheap lodgings".

While the studio at Sydney Close was 'open house' to all members of her extended family, one of her more regular visitors throughout the war was her nephew Sandy Faris, who was to become a well known musician, and composer of, among other things, the theme tune to the immensely popular 1970s ITV television series 'Upstairs, Downstairs'. He went up to Oxford University in 1940, but, later, even after enlisting with the Irish Guards, Sandy would pop in when leave allowed, to stay with his aunt. It was on one of Sandy's earlier visits, before he went up to Varsity, when there arose something of a mystery, an event which saw Anne Acheson involved in the war in a way she most certainly could not have welcomed. Unfortunately Sandy cannot now recall the episode at all, but a letter home to his mother, Grace, reveals the bare bones.

He wrote at the time: "Aunty Nan doesn't know if she told you about the anti-Polish propaganda she is supposed to be sending out. She received a book called 'The Heroic Battle of the Poles'. It had 'Miss A Crawford Acheson, CBE, ARBS, ARCA, 9, Avenue Studios, 76, Fulham Road, SW3' printed on the top of the wrapper. Lower down was the address of Mlle Somebody in Belgium, which was stroked out, and 'return to sender' written. This had 'come back' to her marked 'Passed by Censor.'" Sandy and his aunt were clearly sceptical and indeed suspicious, about the parcel, an impression which is reinforced on reading what Sandy wrote next: "Inside the book are stories of atrocities committed by Poles on the German minority, with photographs of Germans murdered by Poles, which might equally well be Poles murdered by Germans."

Anne's reaction on opening the book and reading some of its contents, was a sensible one. As Sandy explained: "When she discovered what it was she immediately sent it to Scotland Yard, and they have since rung her up about it." Sandy concludes his recording of the sinister episode with: "The publishers must have found her name and address in a slightly out of date Debrett or Who's Who." This last remark would have been prompted because the address had been changed shortly before the start of the war.

The Ireland-based members of the family were not the only ones to take advantage of Anne Acheson's hospitality. Another of her nieces Janey Ironside and her new husband Christopher, who was also an artist, were also among the visitors. Janey was later to become the Professor of Fashion Design at the Royal College of Art in Chelsea, while Christopher designed, among other things, the reverse of the decimal coinage in 1973.

In late 1940 Anne wrote: "Janet and Christopher have been here for a week's leave. They took me out to supper and 'Gone With The Wind' on Wednesday." Anne's verdict of the film was, "... rather harrowing, but very good, too long." So gripping was the film that when an air raid warning sounded Anne wrote that no one left the cinema, perhaps because, as she put it, the building itself "... was quite a good shelter really."

In addition to the family guests at Sydney Close, Anne also took on a lodger, Kathleen French. It did not appear to be an ideal arrangement, even though it was bringing in 24/6 (£1.22½p), and to judge by Anne's description of the accommodation it was understandable. "I have a largish corner curtained off round the handbasin, and the basin and draining board made a dressing table and washstand for her. The stretcher bed stays here now, so that was semi-concealed ... pushed back by day and pulled out at night."

Kathleen French slept on the Chesterfield which had pride of place among the furniture. Anne described the conditions for her lodger: "Her bedclothes are rolled up and put on my bed by day. She dresses in the glory hole, which I have cleared out a little. She leaves at 8.30am and gets her own breakfast, which is only toast and fruit."

The intrusion got to Anne and tried her greatly from the outset though, and, despite her generous nature, she was moved to write: "Kathleen got on my nerves badly at first when she was a guest and stayed on after the weekend and interrupted my work badly. She hunted for a suitable room, but hated going off *alone* to any of the places she saw. So offered to pay me and I said I must have the studio free all daylight time and nothing of hers left in it and we have settled down. She did not realise that being subject to many visitations at any hour puts one off work." The overall impression is that Kathleen French got on Anne's nerves pretty much throughout her stay. "I found Kathleen had gone to the Budds' shelter and had forgotten her key," wrote Anne tersely, in a subsequent letter that August. When Anne finally moved out of Sydney Close there was a distinct impression that she was glad to be shot of her tenant, even reducing Kathleen French to a pair of initials, as if to dismiss her. "I insisted rather on KF taking away her things so that I could pack things in her room."

Other visitors were Janey's brothers Anthony and 'Jimmy'. In early 1940 Jimmy, who was in the RAF Coastal Command, based on the Norfolk coast, decided to spend some furlough visiting his aunt at No 9, Sydney Close. Anne, who was entertaining the boys' mother Vio at the time, wrote to Grace: "James got leave and came on Friday afternoon. We expected him at tea-time and had a nice tea ready. The phone went and someone said, 'Is that Auntie Nan? Is Mummy there?' I said yes, come along, thinking it was James, and it was Anthony, who was unexpectedly up at the Wellington Mission for the weekend, playing games with the boys clubs. He enjoyed the tea most heartily and went back to the Elephant and Castle. Then James came and said in a feeble voice, 'John has 'flu and I have laryngitis.' John was his friend who motored up with him. They were both staying in the Glendower Hotel near here and spent two days of their six days' leave in bed. Vio looked after both of them. They both had a hearty tea here on Sunday and went off on Monday to Cambridgeshire to friends of John's. Vio slept in the studio."

Anthony went on to enlist with the Royal Engineers and his Aunty Nan reported his latest news to the Irish branch of the family in a staccato note form. "Anthony going in for 'Sappers', a special Army exam in November, six months at Army's expense in Cambridge from January, then Army training and probably a commission."

In August 1940 Anne discovered she was not the only one of her circle of artist friends to be involved in the war effort. In a letter to Grace Anne reported that Amy Browning and her husband TC (Thomas) Dugdale were also hard at work for the common weal. "I had a letter from Browning. They were up on duty four nights running last week. Tommy is Parish Commander Home Guard, she is his chauffeur, and they run a telephone post and First Aid post in the house. Four of their neighbouring villages have suffered from raids."

It was a salutary reminder to Anne that the war was not centred on London, that other people around the country were also suffering under the relentless bombardment. For all that there was always the impression from within the Capital that away from London things were a little more peaceful, and Anne did make the occasional attempt to get into 'the sticks', even for a day.

She had planned a trip to Bracknell to spend a night with a Mrs Barton. "A night's rest from raids would be nice," was her explanation for the visit. But a week later found Anne admitting: "I could not go to Bracknell this week as all the coach seats were booked and I don't think the train service goes near."

A second attempt to make the trip was also thwarted. "I meant to go to Bracknell today but all the coach seats were booked before Wednesday and I had no time to find out about trains ... it is difficult to get to a phone at lunchtime. There are always a row of us trying to get to it as it is our only opportunity now that evening raids start early."

If Bracknell was out of the question there was always Oxford and her nephew Sandy, now ensconced at Christ Church. "I must write to Sandy and ask him to book me a room for next Saturday. I shall take him a picture and a cushion from the studio." Sandy duly and dutifully organised accommodation for the last weekend in October 1940. "Sandy has booked a room for me, 198 Iffley Road, for Saturday."

Anne was not alone in deciding to head to Oxford on that particular weekend, although the 'spirit of The Blitz' was certainly in evidence from the outset. "The train from Paddington was packed. We had ten in seats for eight." If that were not remarkable enough, and despite all the disruption caused by the war "... we arrived five minutes before out scheduled time as they ran two trains."

After Sandy and Anne had left her bags in his rooms, " ... we ... went to a restaurant, only to be told there was absolutely no food left. It was about 2.15pm." This was one of those situations that defies belief in the 21st Century. A restaurant running out of food. Unthinkable. Fortunately there was another eating establishment which had no such problem. "Oxford is terribly full specially weekends as Londoners go to get a night's quiet."

But if Anne had thought that by going to Oxford she would escape, temporarily, the wail of the air raid sirens she was soon disabused of the notion. After doing some shopping ("... all shops packed.") the pair of them returned to Sandy's rooms for Anne to mend his chair covers and to help Sandy hang some pictures she had brought him, including something by Browning "a little oil painting of a wet, chalky road" as well as "two large framed photos of the Grandpapa and Grandmama Glasgow portraits". And in the middle of an industrious spell of repairing and re-designing the chair covers Anne's labours were rudely interrupted. "About 7.00pm a raid warning sounded to our disgust..."

But in an act of defiance "... we stayed in his rooms..." before heading out for a meal at a Lyons Corner House restaurant in the City. Then it was on to Anne's lodgings for the night, which turned out to be not quite what a lady might have expected. "My room was full of man's things. His pyjamas were under my eiderdown, but the sheets etc were clean. This morning the landlady told me he is a Shell-Mex man, said she could let his room when he is away, to help her, as she has a daughter and children evidently to support. This morning they gave me a cup of tea in bed and breakfast downstairs, 6/6 (32½p) altogether."

Anne managed to get a lift to Christ Church, finished off Sandy's chair covers, then headed for the 1.55pm train back to London. She kept her promise to send Sandy more cushions once she had returned to London though, and added four pictures to the parcel as well.

She was not the only one to keep a promise. Although there is no correspondence after the postcard on November 22 1940, which had Anne at a low ebb waiting on news of a job, by all accounts she finally got her wish and was placed in a factory in the provinces, in Colchester to be precise.

Harriet Rhys-Davies remembered her Auntie Nan working in an engineering firm which made precision instruments for the Royal Air Force, specifically bomb aiming sights for Wellington bombers, and instruments to help the observers take aerial photographs for military intelligence.

The factory to which Anne was sent was E N Mason and Sons Ltd., a family firm that had begun by selling typewriter ribbons, eventually incorporating all office equipment, and along the way they developed a photographic method of transferring blueprints and other technical drawings onto Irish linen. The company flourished and moved more and more into specialised photographic reproduction – a forerunner of photocopying – and when, with the war looming, the Ministry of Supply and Aviation realised the importance of the work being carried out by Masons at their Arclight works on the outskirts of Colchester, they requisitioned the firm to produce specialist instrumentation for them, including the photographic equipment which was to prove so vital for reconnaissance photography prior to the RAF launching their own bombing raids on towns, ports and cities in Germany.

The site of the factory was on a new industrial development towards the northern edge of the town, on the Mile End Road. Importantly it was nowhere near any residential areas, which was to prove crucial in the light of what happened to the factory in October 1942.

A book entitled 'Essex At War' Edited by Hervey Benham and published in September 1945 by Benham's of Colchester, chronicles the events of the war over the county and includes the fate of Mason's Arclight works. The book was compiled by the Editorial staff of the Essex County Standard.

It records: "Early in April [1942], in retaliation for raids on the medieval towns of Rostock and Lubeck [the so-called Baedeker raids], the

Germans began targeting English towns which contained historical monuments, Bath, Norwich, York, Exeter and Canterbury were singled out, and Colchester began to wonder whether it might be included."

There was certainly plenty of reason for the citizens of Colchester to believe this would be the case. In July 1942 an enemy plane flew low on a west-east course firing bursts from its guns. Fortunately no one was hurt and damage was minimal, but that was the harbinger of further, more serious attacks. Any hopes that Colchester would get through the war relatively unscathed were brutally dispelled on the night of August 11 1942 when according to Mr Benham's book: "... a German plane dropped a stick [four 500lb] of bombs on Severalls Mental Hospital .... The result was that 38 patients were killed, 23 others were injured, and two members of the nursing staff." The following morning it was confirmed from Berlin that Colchester, and Hastings, had been attacked as military targets. Since around 1,500 acres of farmland were requisitioned around this time to be converted into an aerodrome and the town itself was ringed by members of the Canadian Artillery and their guns it should have come as no surprise to the Colchester inhabitants that something like this was on the cards.

Another factor was that some flight paths back to the European Continent for the returning German bombers were also perilously close to the town, and when they were on their way home the bombers frequently ditched any remaining bombs along the way in order to lighten the payload and thus add to their speed, as well as helping to make their fuel last longer.

Further raids followed in August. Then came the fateful moment when Masons was hit. It happened on October 19, when a plane, identified as a Dornier, scored a direct hit on the Arclight factory. Fortunately the majority of the workers were in the shelters, so no one was killed, and apart from one broken leg and a few cases of shock there were no casualties.

Anne Acheson thankfully had long since left their employ. She must have been sent to Colchester late in 1940 or early in 1941 to work at Mason's. However, in the one letter written by Anne from an address in Colchester in 1941 that does exist, it would appear that she was none too happy there.

This would have been despite the fact that at the factory she would have been heavily involved in the war work she so passionately desired;

and because it was precision engineering it would have challenged her newly-acquired skills as well as her own innate manual dexterity, while her ability to work to a tolerance of 1/1,000th of an inch would have been critical for this kind of work. But on May 18 1941 Anne wrote from her lodgings at No 206, Bergholt Road, Colchester: "As soon as I hear from the Ministry of Education I shall give notice here. I can leave at an hour's notice I believe, and the firm sometimes say 'Leave now' when employees give notice."

The irony is inescapable; having tried to prove to the Ministry of Labour almost daily for months that her age need not stand against her and simultaneously having railed over the reluctance of factories to employ people over the age of 40, there is the temptation to smile at Anne's next remark: "They often refuse to let employees go, but that won't happen at my age."

However long it took her to quit Mason's the parting of the ways could not have come soon enough. She had clearly been forced to work with someone who irritated her to an extreme. "My annoying benchmate has wanted to go for some time as he had got a job offered in the town his mother lives in and they won't let him go, but they have got in two new middle-aged men on our bench (not testing electrically but examining after) and I am sure one of those could be trained for my job."

It had been known for sometime in the family that Grace wanted her sister to return to Belfast for a while, as much for Anne's own safety as for the family's peace of mind that she was out of immediate danger, and it would appear that things had been set in motion for just such a move, helped of course by the fact that No 9 Sydney Close was in a state of disrepair, and that Anne was unhappy in her place of work, despite having worked so hard to get the position in the first place.

It transpired that Anne, through the offices of Grace, who was the principal of Victoria College, the leading girls school in Belfast, was to become an examiner for art for the Northern Ireland Ministry of Education. She was enthusiastic, as is apparent when she makes it obvious that she was impatient to get stuck in. In that same letter from Colchester she wrote: "I want to know a lot of things as soon as you can answer. 1) What date am I likely to get the papers? 2) Should I have them sent to Portadown? Can Nora have me and give me a room?" Nora was married to Edgar and they lived in Portadown, Co Armagh, to the south-west of Belfast, the place where Anne was born and brought up.

In fact there was a tentative arrangement for Anne to join Grace and her two daughters – Katharine and Harriet – at Rosebank, their five-bedroom, detached house in South Belfast, not far from Queen's University. But Anne had misgivings. "If I am with you I shall be just an additional person and not able to do *much* housekeeping, though washing up, making bed etc would be all right as a change and rest for the eyes."

But she obviously wanted to make sure that Grace knew what she was letting herself in for. "Think this over, whether I should be a nuisance rather than a help in Rosebank...." In case her younger sister decided that Anne would be a nuisance, she requested: "... if so ask if Nora would have me. I should like to go there if there is room. She said they were dividing the house, but perhaps they have not let the new flat in it yet."

For all her wariness and seeming reluctance to move in with her sister, it was clearly something Anne wanted to do, so she wanted to make sure that her suggestion about going to Nora instead would not be taken by Grace as being her preference. "If you want me, I'd like to be in Rosebank, but you must make no preparation for my coming." Then, in typical Anne Acheson fashion, she returned to her list of questions, and almost ignoring her worries about imposing herself on her sister, she wrote as if the Rosebank move had been decided upon. In a sudden switch of mood she asks: "3) Should I bring my bicycle?" Obviously a mode of transport she has been using to get to and from her digs and E N Mason's factory. "Is there room in Rosebank for it?" If not: "I shall try to sell it." She then squeezed in one of her trademark afterthoughts, in tiny writing, between the lines of the main letter, she said she would lend it to any member of the family (the words 'give it' are crossed out): "But, it is rather a high one, would not do for a short-legged person." On the plus side: "It is new and has complete set of gadgets."

Question Number Four is more of a list really, although she prefaced it with a question: "Would any of my household goods be useful – good double aluminium saucepan, coffee pot, sheets, blankets (old, but plentiful), rugs, towels, tea cloths?" Perhaps to break up the list she itemised all the things that she felt might be useful to Grace Faris and family. "5) Camp chair? The one I got when Katharine stayed with me. 6) Eiderdown? 7) Glass with screw tops for kitchen cupboard (none very large)? 8) Shall I bring any of these which I have left in the kitchen – golden syrup, olive oil, tea – or can you get lots in Belfast? I have Hazel's tea." Then she returned to the more important question of being an examiner and she voiced one worry: "Have I any relations going in for the drawing exams?"

With so many questions out of the way Anne started to plan her immediate future by writing it all down in the letter to her sister, that way, probably, it became a *fait accompli*. "If they want me to stay on here after I give notice I shall do so till about nine days before my [examining] work should begin. I should want about four or five days in London and about three days in Belfast (in case of delays travelling) and a day to pack here and settle things."

Then she wanted to know what a particular abbreviation means. "In your letter I don't know what O.C. T. U. means." Grace had informed Anne that John, her oldest child and the elder of her two sons, who had joined the Army, had been put in an Officer Cadet Training Unit, to check on his suitability for a commission.

Then it is back to the proposed move. "I enclose a copy of my list of questions. Stroke out things not wanted, answer others and return, unless you prefer to write," was the somewhat peremptory command from Grace's older sister.

Finally, she had one last little niggling worry *vis à vis* her move to Belfast. "Do you know anything about passports and permits now? I think there will be no trouble about that if I go to stay in N.I."

16

Home and Away

‑‑‑∽∽‑‑‑

Anne duly returned to Belfast and therefore, quite naturally, the informative correspondence between her and Grace Faris dried up for quite a spell, but it is reasonable to assume that she spent the best part of 15 or 18 months away from her beloved Sydney Close, which was just as well given the state it was in after the bombing.

The next time there was any news of Anne was in a letter to Grace dated February 13 1943. Anne had only recently returned to London. The address she gave was Duke's Avenue, and from what she says about the time taken travelling between there and Sydney Close – "It is very comfortable here and nice and peaceful, but it takes well over half an hour by train ...." – it is safe to assume that it was the Duke's Avenue in Muswell Hill, North London, as opposed to the one in Chiswick.

The Studio had been a shocking mess when it was first damaged in 1940. At the time Anne described her occasional visit home in her letters to Grace. The clearing-up operation had begun while she was still doing her engineering course in Lambeth, and it continued even after that finished.

On November 1 1940 she had returned to the studio: "Yesterday was a pouring wet day, my studio was horrible, dark, damp cold and a muddle.

When the wind rose in the afternoon the studio made noises, I think it was bits of glass out of the old torn blinds, and perhaps a ceiling crack, and I fled. I have asked the surveyors about whether the ceiling is likely to fall."

Around the same time she reported to Hazel: "The darkened studio, with the holes in the ceiling gets on my nerves very badly. When there is a wind in the black felt, they covered the gaps with, flaps in several places and I just have to depart. Anything worse than rain, wind and a siren warning sounds in that studio, you cannot imagine.... It is lonely here without the Budds and other friends."

Later in the letter she wrote, miserably: "All my tools in the studio got rusted and drawers stick with damp. I am getting rid of a lot of old clothes, but I don't know what to do about studio materials, drawings etc which I may, some day, want again."

A few days later she had obviously made her decision. "I am getting rid of lots of stuff out of the studio, going through old files etc. I have brought down all the lead figures to the ground floor."

The worries still piled up for her. Her mind seemed forever to be on the state of her abandoned home and at one point, from the relative comfort of her temporary digs in Oakley Street, she had pondered: "I wonder whether the authorities had covered my studio roof before Wednesday's downpour. If not I expect to find more ceiling down."

All this damage, and protecting what was left, had given rise to a further source of anxiety for Anne, one that was experienced by anyone whose property had been damaged in the Blitz. Who was going to pay for all this? "There is a lot of worry about the claim for damages."

There was obviously only so much she could do, and any further clearing up that needed to be done was shortly afterwards put on hold when she left for Colchester. By the time her sojourn in Belfast had ended, just over two years later, it is apparent that Anne had sorted out compensation. The wording of a letter in the late winter of 1943 makes it clear that structural repairs have been carried out on the building that the studio is in, which is why Anne was able to write: "I shall be glad to be in the studio at night."

Judging by her description of what met her when she returned, after all this time, to Sydney Close, Anne had not written previously to Grace. Her depiction of the mess awaiting her is graphic and heart-rending, and she is in no doubt about the task that confronted her. Even Hercules would have quailed at the mountains of debris. "The studio is somewhat of an Augean Stables. It took about 40 buckets of water to get the dirt off the upper studio floor and four tins of floor polish to get it to shine." It has to be remembered that rheumatism would have made this clean-up operation even more daunting for the 60-year-old Anne, yet there was not a hint of self-pity in her words. "Harrie did a little bit when she was here on Tuesday. My hands have many little cuts from the bits of glass embedded in the wood."

The work was not confined to scrubbing and rubbing either; as ever Anne had to call on her manual skills as she, and her assistant Bill Baker, set to work making everything good again. "The part [of the floor that] the rain had spoiled had to be taken up by Bill and me, and the swollen bits carved to fit and then screwed down. That was most of a day's work." At least Anne had the confidence to be able to tackle this sort of work; many men would have baulked at such a project, preferring to let a professional carry out the work.

The whole studio was suffering from the lingering damp, but getting any heat into it also had its problems. "I got the anthracite stove lit today for the first time, but cannot keep it going strongly as I still have no black-out." Even getting the anthracite stove going was not a straightforward procedure. Before firing it up Anne had to get the chimney cleared and there was more than just soot for the sweep to worry about. "The chimneys were full of rubble, about a wheelbarrowful in the upper one, more in the other. The sweep could only do the lower one as he could not do the anthracite stove, and I had only anthracite coal."

Anne had an alternative, but initially, unfortunately, it was *hors de combat*. "My oil stove was out of order," she reports. As ever though Anne was up to the task, and with her natural gift of coping with all things practical, she rapidly added: "... but I mended it."

Food was not alone in being rationed. Coal was another item which came under government control. Each household was rationed to five hundredweight (a quarter of a ton) of coal per month, although in the case of houses where coal was the only source of heat, ie there was no gas or electricity, the amount was slightly higher.

That explains Anne's gratitude to, and her appreciation of, the generosity of her neighbours the Budds, whom she revealed: "... gave me a little precious coal for last week. Just a little bucketful ." It had probably seemed enough considering that the electricity engineers had been scheduled to call round in that first week back in London. "I thought all was well when the electric people turned up first last Tuesday, but both the water heater and the wires for the radiator plugs were out of order. Some days later the water heater man did that, but I had to get the shop to deal with the wires and they have to be left for a week to dry."

The upshot was that the coal-fired stove with the small supply of anthracite remained her sole source of heat for a while and Anne wrote: "Anyhow I have no radiator yet."

The poor woman has to deal with so much. It is one snag after another. "The curtain people called yesterday, after my appealing twice to the shop, and gave me an estimate for £9. 16s. 0d (£9.80)." The curtain shop would have been responsible for supplying Anne with the vital black-out drapes, without which she was prevented from spending her evenings in her own home, as she says in somewhat irritable fashion: "I can't use the place at night till they come and do the work some time. As for the telephone, that may be five weeks before it is connected."

On top of all that there was her laundry. Not her clothes, but her existing soft furnishings, those that had survived the ravages of the weather. "The laundry does not collect or deliver, but was the one bright spot, my curtains were nicely done at the promised time, and only cost 6/6 (32½p) for as a big a bundle of linen as I could carry."

Sandy was not in his aunt's good books at this time. In 1940, when he had first gone up to Oxford, she had lent him some cushions, now she wanted them back. Sandy, though, had obviously kept her waiting. "No sign of the cushions from Oxford. Please ask Sandy to send me a P.C. at once as to whether they are coming, as if I have to buy new ones I want to have them at once."

In truth nothing seemed to be going right for Anne. "I fell off my tool chest just before black-out yesterday and cut my knee, and had a miserable journey home with a hanky stuck under my stocking." She then added: "All this cleaning is very tiring."

Not just very tiring either, but demanding, because finding the wherewithal to do the cleaning was something of a trial in these straitened times, and it called for a good deal of resourcefulness on the part of Bill Baker and Anne to acquire the necessary materials. Although the basic cleaning stuffs were readily available, polish was another matter altogether.

"I found soap and Hudson's. Floor polish was my difficulty, and as I have no carpets it is necessary. Bill got the last tin in two shops and found none in several. Barker's have furniture polish. I got the coffee pot glass there after being told they had none by a stupid looking woman, so stupid that I tried in another department. That is the only shopping I have done except food – polish. I got all my rations, but omitted to get vegetables or enough bread, so tried to get bread on Sunday morning, in vain – some odd little shops are open till 10.00am but they had none left. I got some self raising flour at 9.59am and made excellent scones later with dried milk."

Her sisters tried to look after Anne, and they did not just send her food either. In one letter to Grace written by Anne early in the war she wrote: "What parcels! And I have a bad conscience about the soap as I find a store of Golleen that had been put away in a case when I had the sprained ankle." So, typical of this generous-natured woman, she added: "I hope you can use the soap coupons I enclose." She is not quite perfect though, since in the same letter she announced: "I have lots of sweets but am not returning your nice boxful." Almost as an afterthought she asked: "Whose rations am I eating?" Another sister had done her bit too. "Molly sent me spiced beef last week so we have been extra well fed."

Interestingly there were strict rules which dictated what you could and could not send in a food parcel, as Anne pointed out: "I thought of sending a food parcel to Hilda Baliman, but it has to be rationed food only and I could not raise seven pounds of rationed food. I could rise to two tins of meat and half a pound of margarine – I always get a lot of fat with my little joints and am making no pastry. We enjoyed the apples, or rather some of the apples, you sent."

Other creature comforts invariably taken for granted in times of peace, such as the purchase of magazines or the borrowing of books from the local library, became less commonplace for Anne, because while she was engaged on her engineering course in 1940, she discovered that the hours did not tie in neatly with the opening hours of paper shops or libraries. "I never can buy a magazine or get a library book, except on Saturdays, as stationers and newsagents are closed before I get home. My part of Lambeth Walk does not run to literature."

Once, when returning from one of her extended visits to Belfast a little later in the war, she wrote: "My grocer had no rations left for emergencies the first week, but I got them in Selfridge's after much waiting. I was over there for a history of art lecture."

There were no such problems with her butcher, who, Anne said: " ... welcomed me back and gave me noble rations and kidneys."

It is remarkable the sorts of things which proved scarce in the war, matches for example. Anne certainly appeared to have a problem finding any in 1943. "I couldn't get matches at first when I was cooking on a methylated [spirits] stove, so had to keep a candle lit. But I find there are sometimes little books in the automatics on the Underground and have enough for several weeks."

That mention of the matches then put her in mind of something else. "Yesterday I got a utility cigarette lighter. Has John [Grace's elder son] one or is it any good to him for pipes? I gave him no Christmas box." The reason she could not ask John himself was quickly explained: "I stupidly have not his address, or Sandy's [by now both nephews were in the army, Sandy in the Irish Guards, John in the Royal Artillery] I thought I remembered his."

At least it looked as if she would not be without a proper source of heat for too long. "My electric radiators may be working next Thursday."

It was all rather vexing though. Anne was very much on her own as far as sorting out the studio went.

In this first week back in London Anne did have a visitor. "Dugdale turned up on Thursday. He says Browning had a breakdown after Ellen's death, but is better after a relapse since. I feel I should go and see her if I can. She wrote urging me to go. They have a vicarage ten miles away from their old house." Ellen Pannifer was Browning's maid, who had been with her since 1932 when they were still at Poplar Farm. In midsummer of 1942 like everyone else in the area, the Dugdales had to leave Poplar Farm, because the area around Iken was required for military training. They moved to the vicarage in the village of Benhall, taking Ellen with them. Shortly after settling in to their new rented accommodation Ellen fell terminally ill, dying, aged 35, in November of that year, a loss which Amy Browning felt keenly.

Browning was not the only person desirous of a visit by Anne. "Janet wants me to stay with her too." Janey Ironside was living in Leamington Spa, because her husband Christopher was serving as an officer with the Ministry of Home Security Camouflage Unit, which was based there. "In the meantime she may get up to London for a night. In which case I shall climb the ladder and pin up some sort of black-out for downstairs and shall go to bed upstairs in the dark myself."

Besides having to clear up and dispose of all the rubble and rubbish left by the bomb damage there was also the matter of Anne's work in progress. Plenty of figures in various stages of construction as well as completion remained in the studio and Anne lists them for Grace, promising to bring some back to Northern Ireland with her. "I find I have a good Sacred Bull, two Argentinas, several Mermaids and a rough Ceres and a Flora. I shall bring some to Belfast. I have not had time to go to the Royal Academy yet."

It is plain that this was only to be a brief visit by Anne. In fact it appears that she spent the best part of three months back in London, and, it is to be assumed, only the shortest possible time in Duke's Avenue, just long enough to allow her to get the studio into some sort of order so that she could once more live in it. But that apparently would not be for long either, because she needed enough time to allow her to make it presentable enough so that it could be sub-let to someone else for an unspecified amount of time, as becomes evident from the following passage: "I hope to start on the downstairs ceilings and walls tomorrow and get the stair carpet down, then the agent might start letting people see the place."

Frustratingly that was to be it as far as correspondence went from Anne in London for more than a year. There are no surviving letters to her at any address in London, or from her for that matter either. It does become apparent though that she had begun to make a regular tour of duty to Northern Ireland for the summer months, obviously to carry out her duties as an art examiner, quite possibly in 1943 and certainly the following year.

Whatever she did in the intervening months by the Spring of 1944 Anne was finally back in No 9 Sydney Close, and corresponding with the family, as well as playing hostess to yet another young member of the family, in this case another nephew, Forrest, son of Edgar and Nora. "Forrest turned up before 11.00am so I took him to the Forum Club (wrecked again) for lunch (rather austere) and we walked back through the park which seemed to interest him. He is still uncertain what he wants to do."

Browning also came to stay with Anne around this time. Despite the distraction of her visitors, though, Anne still had half a mind on her role as an examiner. "I never phoned the Ministry of Education, but they have not answered my expenses claim yet," she informed Grace, and it is possible to detect a note of anxiety creeping into her words.

In a letter dated April 6 Anne was already contemplating her summer stay in Ulster, now necessitated as much by her examiner's role as it was by a desire to catch up with the family. "... it's only about ten weeks till I leave for the summer (if the Northern Ireland Ministry get my permit)." And she set out her plans for her return to Belfast in the summer of 1944. "About the summer, I think the fruit drawing exam is June 29th, so I'd better cross about June 15th or 16th."

There was also a family holiday to consider and Anne adds: "Do book for me in Donegal, but not too early. I don't like a rush after the exam work and it's a long journey." She was becoming rather more particular, but, approaching 62, she was entitled to be. She did play the bossy older sister though, her suggestions for doing this or that occasionally coming across more like Royal Commands than sisterly requests, although perhaps the pain she is in has added an uncharacteristic edge to her mood as she pens her thoughts. Generally, from reading the available writings that have survived, altruistic would describe her overall approach to life; she invariably thought of others, consigning her own sufferings to a line here, a throwaway remark there.

Her problem was getting time off from her Red Cross duties. Initially, as one would expect of Anne, she had volunteered her services for free, just as she had in 1940. "I offered one and a half days voluntary work, but they prefer more time. I told [the boss] I should leave to go to Northern Ireland in June." She anticipated one or two problems because of the hours, even though she was only working from Wednesday to Friday each week. "Shopping and delivering my laundry (who accept parcels on Wednesday mornings only) may be a difficulty." The pity of it is there is nothing to say how she did cope with it all, but coped she must have.

17

The Monkey Club

hatever else she was, Anne Acheson was something of a glutton for voluntary work, if not indeed a 'workaholic'. Even while she was contemplating, in 1940, training to be an engineer she had already committed some of her time to doing first aid work. "I am only doing four hours once a fortnight." However she must have undertaken some sort of nursing or First Aid training course. "I am on the Civil Nursing Reserve for the London Area and have told the authorities about the plaster training [for the SRA], but there is no rush of casualties of that kind and I don't expect to be called up for years."

But it then transpired that, not content with doing first aid work, Anne also volunteered her services to the Red Cross during the day, although she was honest enough to express some frustration at trying to do justice to both roles: "I was on night duty last night and got landed into Red Cross work this morning too ...."

Anne was working in the Park Lane office of the Red Cross and explained that after a public appeal for items to sell to raise money for the organisation there was "a flood of parcels ... I worked three and a half hours opening registered parcels and registering details. We started doing the postcards of acknowledgement, but it took too much time and a new office will start on that now, from our files. The pile of parcels was growing instead of dwindling as fresh parcels came in."

Some of the items were fascinating as people unearthed artefacts and antiques suitable for the sale which was to be held at Christie's auction house. "All sorts of pathetic letters came with old watches etc." Among them she spotted, "twenty autograph letters to 'Frederick David'[possibly Frederic David Mocatta a 19th Century Jewish philanthropist, who encouraged, and supported financially, Jewish literature and arts] from Mendelssohn, Berlioz, Wagner, Joachim etc, sent by FD's grandson. A lot of the gold things were packed in dentists' denture boxes – some of the spelling was strange, things were sent for 'The REALIFE (instead of relief) of suffering. I did not open a diamond necklace, but found an old French enamelled watch with pearl setting that is a museum piece."

There was little chance of anything of truly great value slipping through the net because: "The experts go over everything after they are opened and labelled by Red Cross people."

Her 'call-up' to Colchester and subsequent move to Belfast meant that the Red Cross work had to be put on hold, but Anne was a compulsive volunteer and she still managed to return to the Red Cross before the end of the war. It was, she tells the family, only a part-time job, three days a week, 9.30am to 5.30pm, in the pay office at the Red Cross headquarters, at Grosvenor Crescent, close to Hyde Park Corner. She got it late in 1944. She started it at the beginning of December, and just before commencing work she told Grace that she got it after having heard: " ... they were desperately in need of workers." The work she was doing was nothing grand, rather menial in fact to judge by her description. "It is only what ... my boss calls donkey work (probably doing insurance stamps or something) but I don't want a responsible job. I am to be paid £4 per week, which he says politely is ridiculous. It will mean about £2 a week."

However, while it was all very well volunteering her services for this or that cause, throughout the war she still had to maintain an income. That meant producing her figures, which were ever popular. Early in 1940 she wrote: "I am working at my own work properly for the first time since August [1939]. I must finish one of the fountain figures before June and I have a little portrait figure to do in pottery too."

But the sculpting and artwork alone could not support Anne adequately so it was about this time that she took on a private pupil, who

wanted to learn modelling – not the catwalk kind, but sculpture. The
pupil was Joan Weldon. "I got a pupil this morning through a bronze
caster, who once did a job for me. He phoned me yesterday and I had a
letter this morning from Mrs Hurst, the woman who runs 'The Monkey
Club' asking me to phone her as early as possible. She brought the girl for
a lesson at eleven as she had been hunting for a suitable modelling teacher."

The Monkey Club, the nickname of a finishing school for
debutantes, and so called because it was instilled into its students that they
were to hear no evil, speak no evil and see no evil, had been founded in
the 1920s by a Mrs Marian Ellison. It was based in Pont Street, in
Knightsbridge. Fees, were around 200 guineas (£210) a year at the start
of the war. In 1939 this exclusive establishment boasted three houses in
Pont Street, which had been converted into flats for its fifty or so students.
Girls were allowed their independence, even down to cooking their own
meals, but, if they so chose, they could attend meals in the club's dining
rooms, where they would be served by a butler and maids. If they went
out in the evening it was always with an approved chaperone. The school's
aim was to produce girls in the old fashioned way, well versed in the arts,
shorthand and typing and culture, in addition to being taught the social
graces, running a household, domestic science and perhaps a foreign
language. Quite clearly modelling and sculpting were high on the list of
skills it was felt that Miss Weldon should master, in addition to perfecting
her mastery of all things domestic.

However, Anne decided (probably wisely) that before she received
her pupil she had better put into practice her own domestic skills. "I had
the whole housework to do before they came, as Mrs Hawley was ill and
did not come while I was out and I was too tired to do it last night." Anne
was rewarded for her hard work though. "The girl remarked: 'What a tidy
studio!'"

The downside to the business was that Anne was paid just 10 shillings
and sixpence per lesson. Miss Weldon was to receive two lessons a week,
in the morning, up to Easter, which at least provided her teacher with
something a little more substantial towards her living expenses. In another
letter a couple of months later, Anne, who had just been invited on holiday
with Grace, admitted there might be a problem with getting away from
London: "I have taken her on, on lower terms than usual, I may find it
difficult to get a substitute [teacher]. No one will want to come to my

studio to teach her." As a footnote to taking on a member of the Monkey Club, Anne has scratched a brief note in her address book under the name of Mrs Ellison (Monkey Club), 24 Pont Street. The note reads: "... owes fees from 1939."

As the war advanced Anne began to feel increasingly restricted by this private tutelage, which was clearly regarded by her as a necessary inconvenience: "I am dying to give up modelling and teaching." But as it turned out, Miss Weldon was not her only pupil from the Monkey Club. Anne wrote early in 1940: "My pupil Joan Weldon went off to the country and is not coming back this term, but I have another from the Monkey Club – I had still another for one day, then evacuated – I wonder how long this Diana Portman will stay in London. She only comes once a week, 10/6." She later spoke of yet another pupil, who started with her in the summer of 1940. "My new pupil is the daughter of the Peruvian Minister in London. She is fresh from convent school – very nice, very clever."

Throughout her correspondence Anne frequently drifted from this or that topic of news to something which occupied her far more intensely, it would appear. This was the topic of food.

Bearing in mind that rationing was still in force, no less so in 1944 as it was at the beginning of the war, Anne revealed an 'arrangement' that existed between herself and her sisters, or at least Grace, in Belfast, and Hazel, in India. Anne was back, ensconced in Sydney Close once more: "Dear Grace, I was just going to answer that I did not need anything from your points [Grace's ration allowance] when a parcel came from Hazel containing butter and sugar (no tea or meat). So I don't, even more so, really want anything."

She also explained that some of her more regular guests, Sandy and Harrie (Forrest's sister) were both based too far away to drop in on her and consume her precious stocks of food. "Sandy is too far away to come on a day's leave now, and Harrie cannot come often as she is a long way off too and I have a grand stock of tins now .... I still have a few dried apples etc and more raisins than I have desire to cook – and actually got prunes in Gapps [local grocers] yesterday. They never have tinned fruit, but I still have those you sent me as no emergency has yet occurred."

In another letter later on in the war Anne informed Grace: "I got three large lots of oranges. I dried a lot of the skins in the oven for flavourings, not that I want to bake much." And later: "Gapps have now tinned beans, plain in brine, but not very much salt, which are useful for stews. They are cooked and" – most important to Anne in these days of rationing – "no points."

Her reluctance to bake was tempered by the availability of ready-made items. "Cakes are getting scarcer. Anne's Pantry hardly ever has any. I made Canadian Fruit Cake, and I make biscuits." There was some good news on the rationing front, "We will have an extra half pint of milk a week now."

It was a similar story a year later, when, in 1945, Anne told Grace: "I hope John told you not to send me that Australian butter. I have two tins still for emergencies. I did open one about three weeks ago, but I can only use it for cooking, of which I do as little as possible. It lasts for ages and I get very tired of it."

There was a resourceful side to Anne's culinary skills, an echo of her inventiveness when she was working for the Surgical Requisites Association. "John turned up on Saturday, just when I had finished an early lunch. I gave him tinned pilchards and grated potatoes to cook them quickly, also soup." No doubt the recipe for the Swiss dish Rosti potatoes had already reached these shores, but it was still enterprising of Anne to turn be able to turn out a dish such as this.

As the war neared its end Anne pronounced herself very pleased with Gapps shop praising them in particular once again for their stocks of dried fruit; she did seem to be especially partial to prunes. "I can usually get prunes or dried apples. They seem to keep one kind of dried fruit in stock most of the time."

There were other inconveniences for everyone, the loss of their gas supply being one irritation that affected everyone at some time or another during the war, and early on in the Blitz in September 1940 Anne owned up to not having gas for a couple of weeks according to one of her letters. She had undertaken to feed Mr Budd, the husband of an artist friend and neighbour, on weekdays. "As we had no gas the meals were rather monotonous. The meths stove has to be refilled every ten minutes, but omelette, very varied salads with banana, raw onion, celery or apple ... and a cup of chocolate were easy enough. At the same time we filled a Thermos with *very* milky coffee and one of tea to comfort us in the sleepless nights. We found the milky coffee a help about 1.00am and the tea about 4.00pm or 3.00pm helped us to sleep in spite of noises."

The lack of gas also meant that one of life's little luxuries went by the board. When the gas supply was cut off at No11 Oakley Street bedsit, Anne wrote: "Baths are off till we get gas." And perhaps the ultimate in privation of one of life's little pleasures: "No toast of course."

The Beaufoy Institute, where Anne underwent her engineering and draughtsman training also suffered from time to time intermittent interruptions to its gas supply: "The Institute canteen had no gas for a week and the staff were not terribly clever at catering without it. They had a brazier in the yard and two primuses [primus stoves were fuelled by methylated spirit]. Now the gas is on again and they rise to sausages and potatoes."

Premature mortality was a harsh fact of life in those times. There was no expectation, as there is these days, that children would survive their parents. With diseases such as diphtheria, polio and the like, parents accepted that they could easily survive one or more of their offspring. And war, of course, exaggerated the figures, robbing communities of a whole generation of men in some cases. World War Two was no exception. It left very few families untouched. So it was to be with Anne's extended family.

Her nephew Jimmy Acheson, son of James and Vio, went missing in action in the late autumn of 1940. In a letter to Grace dated October 17 Anne told her sister: "I had a wire from Janet [Janey Ironside], which said, 'Jimmy reported missing, will wire any news.' I don't know what she wired to you. I expect she cabled to India." Jimmy Acheson was just 20 years old when he and his crew failed to return from a mission, and he was eventually officially reported missing, believed killed in action.

But the family harboured faint hopes of his survival and Anne went on to speculate what the protocols might be for informing next of kin in the event of a plane not returning from a mission. "I wonder whether the official reports go out *at once* when the plane does not come in. If so we may hear again soon." Later in the same letter she added: "I hope there will be better news soon."

A week later, though, when there had still been no news of the fate of Jimmy and the crew of the aircraft, Anne's thoughts (typically of her) turned to his parents, her brother James Acheson and his wife Vio who lived in India. "Poor Jim and Vio waiting for further news of Jimmy and feeling so far away. What a blessing Kitty [sister of Jimmy and Janet] is there."

For a few weeks she waited for more news. "I keep hoping for a telegram from Janet. I suppose by now our best hope is a prisoner's letter two months hence."

And she wrote to Hazel: "It is nearly six weeks now that Jimmy is missing. If he is a prisoner of war we should learn in a fortnight's time probably. I had a letter from Mrs Field [Jimmy's maternal grandmother] today. She has given up hope really, but I have not."

But Janey had had a premonition from the moment she received word of Jimmy's disappearance. In her autobiography she wrote: "... he was on a sortie over the North Sea when he disappeared ... I knew instinctively that I would never see him again."

Sadly Jimmy would not be the only child of James and Vio Acheson, to die in the war years. They were also to lose their other daughter, Kitty.

The five years or so of the Second World War had accounted for countless lives around the world, but also for the lives of people much closer to Anne, and those war years had also taken their toll of Anne's ageing body. At least she was able to draw comfort from being a member of such a loving and supportive family in such terrible times, privately and globally.

18

In Memoriam

~~~〰~~~

Anne Acheson did not stop modelling completely during the
Second World War, even managing to have a figure accepted for
the Royal Academy's Summer Exhibition in 1944. It was a bust
of her niece Janey, entitled 'Mrs Christopher Ironside'. She also had an
unnamed fountain figure on show at the 1944 exhibition at the Royal
Scottish Academy.

But less than a year later Anne had to undertake a far sadder
commission, one on which no price could be put. One which would have
pained her, even as she carried it out.

In the Spring of 1945 Jim and Vio Acheson's youngest child, their
daughter Violet Katharine Harriet, known affectionately by the whole
family as 'Kitty', succumbed to a brain tumour. Like her brother Jimmy,
she was 20.

Kitty's father wrote movingly to Anne: "... we are only just beginning
to realise she has gone, but sometimes I forget it and think she is still alive.
We always think of Jimmy as alive. It is harder with Kitty as she was so
much with us these last few years and we were with her at the end. It was
a tumour on the brain. She had no great pain.... She was lethargic but in
full possession of her senses and just herself slowed down and incredibly

sweet. I can't bear to think of that now...."

Her death also left Anne deeply shocked. She had, unusually, received the news not by letter, but rather by telephone. She wrote to Grace: "Janet has just phoned me that Kitty has died of a spino-cerebral tumour."

Janey had, it transpired, attempted to communicate with her Auntie Nan by telegram, as Anne explained: "She had a delayed cable first that Kitty was having an operation and the other cable half an hour later that she had died – 'happy and not in pain'. She had had bad headaches lately. She had been living with Hazel."

Later in that letter Anne returned to the death of Kitty, saying: "This letter is a bit disjointed, but I am upset and keep thinking of all the sorrow – Jim and Vio and Hazel and Harriet and you." Harriet Faris and Kitty were particularly close, having attended Victoria College together.

Janey Ironside wrote movingly of her last sight of her sister in her autobiography: "The next day I was to see Kitty off [she was sailing home to India]. We took a taxi to the shed leading to the dock. I found that I was not allowed further than the gates and I had to watch Kitty walking down the long empty shed further and further away, every now and then turning to wave. I never saw her again." That last sight of her sister had been in 1943.

Anne's onerous commission came from James, asking if she could come up with a design for a headstone for Kitty. He wrote: "Nan, would you make a design for the grave? Something simple, in a plain stone, with a cross in it (Kitty was a very devout child and would like it). The wording would be: 'Kitty, beloved younger daughter of J G and Violet Acheson. Died 17th March, 1945, aged 20.' There might be a brief text, or a few words suggesting Kitty's personality. She had developed greatly the last year and everyone who met her was struck by a sort of sweetness and graciousness." After a few more painful sentences a clearly distraught James closed with: "If you don't feel like trying a design we will understand."

Just four days later, and before Anne would have had a chance of replying, James came up with more ideas for a gravestone: "We think an Irish cross, flat on the face of the stone. Kitty was a loyal little Irishwoman and Vio is part Irish – and she died on St Patrick's Day.

"Also somewhere the words: Fair Kind Gentle Brave because they sum up what scores of letters have been saying and not just our own notions. I think the words should be without any punctuation. You may not like this, or the order, but unless you feel strongly about it we would like them to stand. Indeed these are both just suggestions for you to work on, in case you feel like undertaking this commission." And he reiterated: "We will fully understand it if you do not."

The state of mind of the bereaved parents is unimaginable. However, James Acheson did manage to explain: "Vio is very well, but her heart is very sore, and so is mine. But we have both plenty to occupy our minds here and not all our memories of Kitty give pain. Poor Vio, first Jimmy her big boy, and then Kitty her baby. But we are thankful for Janet (and Virginia) and Ant."

He concluded his letter with the news that within the next six months he and his wife were to leave India for good and return to England, to Herefordshire.

Anne duly did produce a design and in July 1945 Jim wrote to her: "I have just had a telegram from Arthur Lothian [the Resident in Hyderabad and a friend] 'Ducketts can execute design from half scale drawing. No sandstone available locally, but they can provide polished granite or polished Shahabad stone which is a greyish colour.'" James continued: "I don't know what Shahabad stone is but I imagine granite is all right.... If you agree and send out the design (keep a copy if you can) I will send it on to Lothian to get it executed by Ducketts...."

Almost two months later and there was a trace of anxiety in a letter dated August 31 1945, when James asked Anne: "Is the design for Kitty's grave likely to arrive soon? There is of course no particular hurry, but I would like to get everything arranged before we go home." He and Vio realised that the gravestone could not be ready before they left India so he let Anne know that friends would oversee everything. "... we have good friends there [in Hyderabad, where Kitty is buried] who will see to it as we would ourselves. Mr Spinks [one of Jim's assistants] is due to go to the Hyderabad residency on transfer in November. He is an expert photographer and will photograph the grave for us as soon as it is completed, and will supervise the carving of the stone."

In typical Acheson fashion James just dropped into his narrative, in passing almost, news of a very special moment in his life, a signal honour. Perhaps though he had it in perspective after the loss of a son and a daughter before they had had a chance to fulfil any of their dreams and ambitions. Nevertheless his modesty is rather touching and, given Anne's own reluctance to hide her light under the odd bushel, more likely than not is evidence that it was a family trait. Anyway he wrote, somewhat diffidently: "I flew, on an urgent call from Lord Wavell, to Delhi on 23rd." Lord Wavell was the Governor General and the penultimate Viceroy of India, "and I was dubbed privately at 4.00pm, with only his personal staff (only three or four, as others are with Her Excellency in Simla) and Anthony present – also His Excellency's son and son-in-law ... I felt like Lady Jane Grey in The Tower!"

Lord Wavell had apparently ordered that Anthony be released from his duties as an officer in the Bengal Sappers and Miners in order to attend his father's low key investiture. "His Excellency then shook hands and chatted to me and Ant for a few minutes. I had a long talk with him after dinner." James was now Sir James Glasgow Acheson CIE Bt. As for the gravestone, there are no further letters, but it is safe to assume that the commission was fulfilled. Kitty was too important, too well-loved, for it to have been neglected.

The conflict and conflagration of World War Two might have been over, but there was still deprivation in the immediate post war years, and demobilisation was no overnight operation. With rationing of many items still in force, India proved a useful source of luxury comestibles and Anne's faithful sister Hazel saw to it that the family had as much variety as the authorities would allow her to send back to Britain. One letter reads almost like a shopping list, or perhaps shipping list would be more accurate.

In October 1946 Hazel wrote: "I have sent – or rather, ordered – parcels of raisins, sultanas, currants and almonds, for you, Grace, Molly and Nora. Please report on the one you get especially the quality as I haven't seen them. I can't remember whether Janet's house is 15 or 16 Neville Street. Please let me know which. She would probably prefer marmalade to the raisins etc."

The sending of parcels was a two-way affair, as Hazel revealed in a letter just a week later, on October 27th. "Three parcels of books have arrived. Thank you very much. Is that the lot? I can't find my Eden and Holland's midwifery, but I think I didn't take it home." Hazel had returned to England for the occasional post graduate course and had obviously left behind textbooks whenever she had stayed with Anne. But as early as 1925, and not long after Hazel had arrived in India to pursue her medical career in the Indian Women's Medical Service, she had written requesting a number of books from Anne, although they were not medical textbooks, far from it, and they were, in fact, not even for her: "The books I wanted you to get me were either 'Holiday House' or a historical novel for Janet (she loves stories of Roundheads and Cavaliers etc), 'The Children of the New Forest' is good so far as I remember, or one of Evelyn E Green's and another book for Jimmy. I would write direct to Smith's for them only I am afraid the other letter may turn up and you may get them too."

When that letter was written Hazel had been in the foothills of her successful career. By the Autumn of 1946 she had become Vice Principal of The Lady Hardinge Medical College and Hospital in New Delhi. But promotion or not, there still remained an element of the absent-minded professor about her when she wrote, in the same letter: "My glasses, which I thought I had left in Portmoon, turned up in one of the bags I had packed."

By a curious coincidence Anne received a letter from Sir James Acheson, which was also dated October 27th. He was in Berlin at the time, waiting to find out where he was to be based in his new role as a Regional Governmental Officer. The human touch of the Achesons is once more revealed when James told Anne: "... here it is bitter cold and I hate to think of the winter awaiting the Berlin poor."

Sir James was unhappy. "I hope I shall not be much longer here, a week is enough of Berlin ... tomorrow I'm going to see the exhibition of modern French art in the Berliner Schloss in the Russian sector of Berlin. The Berliners are very touched by this gesture of the French, sending so many of their best pictures over."

In a subsequent letter to another of his sisters, Grace, Sir James had been to the exhibition and reported: "Yesterday I went to a first class exhibition of modern French painting (including many by Renoir, Pissarro, Manet, Picasso, Braque etc) in the Berliner Schloss. It is the old palace of the Prussian kings at the Unter Den Linden. It has been hailed by Berliners as a friendly gesture by the French and a foretaste of a return to normal civilised life in the European family ... the British government ought to follow suit. The Russians have been going all out with ballets etc – of course with a propaganda bias, but by no means all propaganda ... Art counts for a lot here, especially music."

While he was in the former Swinging City of the early to mid-20th

Century Sir James also managed to meet up with one of his nephews. "I ran over to Ploen on Friday afternoon and had tea with Sandy and his friend Peter Ward in their palace ... 18th Century, but more pretentious than the Reventlow house [Jim was temporarily billeted in a castle belonging to Count von Reventlow]... Sandy was in very good form. I'm glad I saw him in his German background before he leaves for good."

Sir James already had an idea where he was going to end up. "I'm probably bound for Kiel." He was right. He was to serve as a Regional Governmental Officer in Schleswig-Holstein and among his responsibilities was that of 'denazification', a job he described in 'An Indian Chequerboard' as "distasteful". He explained just what denazification meant. "... the permanent exclusion from all posts of even a slight degree of power in any walk of life, of all Germans who had been Nazis." The decision to exclude an individual was actually made by small, local all-German committees, but all appeals were referred to the Regional Governmental Officer and James wrote: "... my decisions in appeal were final. I naturally took those decisions seriously as one had to guard against personal or political spites."

Anne was also in receipt of a letter which featured a technological advance – the biro. "This," she wrote rather blotchily, "is one of those new pens, which only needs re-filling once in 18 months." And her conclusion? "It makes my writing worse than ever..." And she was not kidding. But as ever she looked to accentuate the positive and added: "but it is an advantage always to have something that works. It is good for addressing parcels covered with cloth."

The Royal Academy still featured in Anne's professional life once the war was over and she had works accepted in three of the four years that remained of the 1940s. Disappointingly after the passing of that decade there were to be no more showings of Anne's works in Burlington House. That owed as much to Anne's eventual decision to leave London and return to live with two of her sisters, Grace and Hazel, in Antrim, in Northern Ireland as it did to anything else.

Already by February she knew the worst about her chances of exhibiting in the Royal Academy that year: "I'll have no work for the RA," she said flatly, making no further comment.

By now Anne had become a member of the council of the Royal Society of British Sculptors. She had been elected to it in 1944, but aspects of her role irked her. "I have to go to an RBS luncheon at the Savoy. I loathe functions. It is to present a gold medal 'for services to sculpture'. I am the only woman on the council, so I have to turn up." Throughout her life there had been a sense of the pioneer about Anne as far as the women's movement went at least, and now here she was again, "the only woman on the RBS council".

As ever she was hungry for family news, and by now it must have become apparent that she was in fact a lonely person when not distracted by her work. Thus it is that in her dry way she alluded to the fact that the rest of the family seemed to have neglected her. There have obviously been no letters for a while, so Anne wrote archly, if slightly obliquely: "By dint of steady interrogation I got some news of you all out of John, but he didn't know anything about the Victoria canteen. Has it started?" This was a reference to her old school Victoria College.

At least she was back in the Royal Academy the next year. In 1946 she submitted Sabrina Fair, an entirely different figure from her statue at the King's School in Worcester. The figure was priced at £150. Frustratingly for her though there was no RA exhibit in 1947. However that did give her more time to do other things, such as entertain the younger members of her family at Avenue Studios.

Her niece Katharine arrived in April 1947, by now she was in her early thirties and a full-time teacher at Victoria College, and it had been some while since she last visited London, as she reminded her mother in a letter to her from Sydney Close – as Avenue Studios was now called. "I am enjoying myself very much here," she wrote, "I have explored old haunts in Kensington Gardens and Hyde Park ... I took a Number 11 bus as far as St Paul's Cathedral and went back to the National Gallery for a short time. It is very thrilling being in London after so many years and I can hardly believe I am here, though, apart from the bomb damage and the lack of smartness in the people one sees in the streets, it hasn't really changed much."

A couple of months later Katharine's younger brother Sandy moved in temporarily while Anne was over in Northern Ireland in her role as an examiner for the Education Board and he opened a letter to his mother with congratulations. Grace had been appointed MBE in recognition of her work in education in Ulster.

Earlier that year, when Sandy had enrolled as a student at The Royal College of Music, it was his Aunty Nan who sorted him out with digs, although they probably fell a little short of the luxurious, as he recalled: "Aunty Nan had gone to some trouble to find me digs in Oakfield Street, near St Stephen's Hospital, which was on the Fulham Road. It was typical of Aunty Nan to befriend and take trouble to help her nieces and nephews, the latter in particular (brave fighting boys). Janey Ironside was installed in nearby Neville Street ... I became a regular visitor."

Shortly before leaving for Northern Ireland to fulfil her duties as an art examiner, Anne would certainly have shown some pieces in the first major exhibition by the Royal British Society of Sculptors. The theme that year was 'Children', and according to an RBS document there were exhibits from 57 of the Society's members. Given Anne's prominence in this specific field it is highly unlikely she would have been left off the invitation list to show some of her works, and even more unlikely that she would have refused to submit anything.

The correspondence among the siblings, and indeed the whole family, rather tailed off from here on. But Anne at least found herself accepted for the next two years for the summer exhibition at The Royal Academy. She also sold a copy of The Thief for £120 to a Mrs Sydney Harvey, who lived in Wall Crouch, near Ticehurst, which is not far from Tunbridge Wells. And so impressed was she with her first garden figure that Mrs Harvey then wrote again to Anne, placing an order for "the lead figure of the little child with the fish under his arm..." This figure was 'Water Baby' and carried a price tag of £90.

In 1948 she had a head, called 'Eliza', on show, and that particular figure went on to do the rounds in the ensuing months. Anne's records show that Eliza was exhibited all over the country, from Blackpool to Lincoln to Gateshead as well as Northampton and Sheffield. That was also the year that she showed 'The Imp' and 'Harriet Emily' at an Exhibition of Contemporary Sculpture at the Russell-Cotes Art Gallery and Museum in Bournemouth.

The following year Anne modelled another head, this time that of Janey Ironside's five-year-old daughter Virginia, who was herself to go on to become a distinguished author and journalist. This figure appeared in the the Royal Academy's summer exhibition in 1949, but that was to be the last appearance of any of Anne's work at Burlington House.

The summer of 1949 also found Anne acknowledging the purchase by the Belfast Art Gallery of a glazed earthenware figure 'Sacred Bull'. She was in Co. Antrim on a holiday at the time and wrote: "As an Ulsterwoman I rejoice in knowing that one of my works is in the Belfast Art Gallery and I thank the Committee for the honour. I have received the cheque from City Hall."

'Sacred Bull', which had been exhibited the previous year at the Ulster Academy of Art, had cost the gallery £21. A couple of months later, in September of that year, Anne sent the head of Virginia Ironside to the Ulster Academy for exhibiting. There was, as ever, another Forum Handicrafts Show where Anne showed a number of porcelain figures, ranging in price from two guineas to ten guineas.

There were still commissions to be fulfilled however, and the post war prices were a lot higher, hovering around the £140-£150 mark for garden figures. To judge from the brief notes made by Anne in her 'Studio Records' which she maintained to the end of her life, she had a system for obtaining commissions. Photographs of different figures would be sent to the potential client, who, if interested, would then be asked for the preferred medium, lead or bronze in the case of the garden figures – after the war Anne added Portland Stone to the portfolio.

In the summer of 1949 Anne's niece Harriet needed somewhere to stay in London while she undertook a three-month course in Paediatrics at Great Ormond Street Hospital. "In June 1949," Harriet recounted, "I asked Aunty Nan if I could live in her studio while she was over in Northern Ireland examining art for the Ministry of Education. She generously and immediately agreed, only stipulating that I would pay the fuel and telephone bills and keep on her charwoman [that's what they were called in those days]. She asked me to keep an eye on the Budds whose studio was just across the corridor from her. She was concerned because Mr Budd had just gone into hospital. Not long after Aunty Nan's departure Mrs Budd broke her ankle, so I was kept quite busy."

By then of course Hazel, over in India, had experienced partition and the concomitant rioting. It must have been a terrifying time for her. She, by now Principal of the Lady Hardinge Hospital in New Delhi, which was specifically for women, had made the decision to open the doors to men when the violence flared up. She took in hundreds of casualties, victims of the riots on the streets of Delhi as the British left the country. Her life's work in medicine in India, coupled with her act of mercy during the troubles in 1947, saw her appointed OBE.

After leaving India, the early part of 1949 saw Hazel staying with her sister Molly in Cork, and while there she received a letter from her brother Jim, now living in Herefordshire, who gave some news of Anne. "Nan was in very good form for her, though she complained of rheumatism. I succeeded in getting her quantities of old, seasoned walnut wood here in Ross, which has cheered her up considerably. She's working against time now on her new figure for the RA." That figure of course was the head of Jim's granddaughter Virginia Ironside.

Hazel was able to catch up with her sister's doings later in 1949, when she returned to England in order to study for another post graduate qualification, the DCH (Diploma of Child Health) and while doing so she obviously joined up again with Anne, sharing her studio accommodation, just as she had done at the beginning of her medical career.

According to the archives at The Royal Free Hospital, Hazel had given Avenue Studios as her address in the United Kingdom from 1947/48 to 1950/51; this was because she was clearly on the move after leaving India, and anyway she had to be in London in 1947 in order to attend her investiture for her OBE.

One thing was sure though. Hazel would not be spending the next decade in India. Instead, and after consultation with Grace and Anne, it was decided, when Grace retired as head mistress of Victoria College, Belfast in 1951, that the three sisters would move into a house together, in Ulster.

There is precious little correspondence on this subject, but thankfully one key letter from an excited Anne to Hazel has survived. It is undated, however, given that Anne also talked later on in the same letter about a private viewing at the Royal Academy it is most likely that the letter was written sometime early in 1949; it is written on lightweight blue airmail paper, so Hazel was most probably over in Cork by then.

The point of the letter was that Grace had enjoyed some success with her househunting and had earmarked an ideal house, which the sisters would be able to rent, although no move would be made until she retired. But Grace had obviously been rather economic with the details of the house. What scant few details there were for Anne to ruminate over were that the house that Grace had found was a former rectory, Glebe House, in the village of Glenavy in County Antrim.

Thus in her letter Anne had much to ask. "I've a lot of questions to ask: a. Where is Glenavy? There seems to be no map of Ulster here. What are bus and rail and village shopping facilities?

"b. If we get the rectory shall we need my *high ladder* and my high cobweb brush (I just might manage to sell them to Mr Dickinson, who cannot afford to buy the blinds, but knows he must have a ladder and a high brush, and shall we need blinds? Should I bring some black ones over with fittings.

"c. What repairs have to be done? Roof or gutters or drains or dry rot or drainage?

"d. Is there any possibility of the place being ours by May 31st so that my household goods could go straight there? And would they be safe there if we were in Portmoon? Or is the house liveable in as it is?

"e. Is there electricity and gas and mains water?"

It is a breathtaking list of questions, most of which are perfectly reasonable. Indeed it is to be wondered just how much, or more correctly how little, information her younger sisters have imparted to her about what would be the final move of all their lives. But at least Anne could see the humorous side of things and actually managed to laugh at herself by inserting after question e. "(Candidates must answer all questions and add any other information, such as, Have you heard of the price of the rectory?)" The fact that Anne had not been told the what the rent would be was a little naughty of Grace and Hazel, although Anne made a joke out of that as well.

Then it was back to Anne's latest news. "I have had a lot of fuss and two trunk phone calls over Mrs Owen's figures, but they are going in Burchett's van on Saturday, and now I hear from her that the stone tank is not in place, and won't be for months, but I had promised to go for two nights. I hope my going can be planned for before you come here."

Anne then goes on to write of another artist: "J D Revel offers us one of his Indian pictures. I said you would be thrilled. I have two here to choose from, I hope you will be here before his pictures go to Blewbury so that you can choose. One has white oxen in white dust, and the other dark people and one spot of brightish blue. He says we can appreciate his Indian things more than people who have never been there."

Anne also shared news of Mrs Budd's health. Mrs Budd painted under the name of Helen Mackenzie, and this was confirmed by Anne, because a photograph of a still-life painting. which appeared in a magazine called 'The Gentlewoman' in June 1923, and featuring a tabby cat, had some additions to the caption in Anne's hand-writing. Under the artist's name Helen Mackenzie she wrote in brackets, Mrs Budd, and under the cat is the name Simon.

The Budds and Anne shared much in common, not least a love of reading, and they would exchange library books regularly, according to Sandy Faris, generally thrillers, romance and P G Wodehouse. However, while the Budds clearly enjoyed feline companionship, that enjoyment was not shared by Anne, who expressed a most uncharacteristic desire, when writing to say she had been looking after the studio at No10 Sydney Close and that caring included the Budds' cat "... I am afraid I wish the cat would die – the smell! I was careful to clear up when I knew Browning was coming, but Browning was horrified."

That letter eventually closed with a reminder, "ANSWER all questions". She wanted to know more about her next home that she would be sharing with her two sisters.

19

The Mould is Broken

~~~~~₥~~~~~

I n 1950s Britain austerity was still the order of the day, yet there was the faintest stirring of something fresh, a new independence, a sense of freedom. In 1951, at about the time that Anne Acheson finally bid adieu to her beloved studio in Sydney Close, the Walker Art Gallery in Liverpool, scene of a crime against Anne almost half a century earlier, reopened after a twelve year closure. Britain was on the threshold of the second Elizabethan Age.

It would still have been a fairly bleak time for Anne. Leaving the studio behind was a big enough wrench, but actually leaving London after more than forty years of living and working there, was possibly the toughest step Anne had had to take in all her life. As one of her nephews, Professor John Faris, commented: "Apart from anything else she was essentially a Londoner."

But there was little left for her in the capital. By the looks of her records the start of the decade had been a fairly thin time for Anne, with just three exhibitions, one in Bradford, another staged by the Royal British Society of Sculptors and of course old faithful, The Forum Handicrafts Show. The figures exhibited in this last comprised earthenware and pottery, whereas the RBS exhibition was exclusively large figures in bronze and lead. She gave them a choice, sending photographs of nine statuettes in all. However she was nearing 70 by now, her hearing had deteriorated; from a professional standpoint her joint problems were compromising her far more, making modelling more and more of a chore. Equally as importantly, early on in the decade there was not as much money washing around as there had been before the start of the Second World War. People were still finding their financial feet after years of tight belts and limited opportunity. Men could still be seen in their 'demob' suits. As a consequence no one was looking to spend a sizeable sum of money on as obvious a luxury as a garden ornament.

As an indication of that there exists a letter to Anne from a gentleman by the name of Dudley Saward, who lived in Welwyn, in Hertfordshire. If Mr Saward's letter is anything to go by, there is a suggestion, not only that people were less prepared to purchase garden figures, but also that Anne had found a way not to clutter up Glebe House in Glenavy with too many of her figures. Apart from the space they would take up, the cost of insuring so many figures against damage in transit would also have been an important factor in her decision, which was to send as many of them out on loan as she felt reasonable. Whether there was a modest charge for the loan is not known, nor is it possible to ascertain how many other similar arrangements she made with other clients, but it is reasonable to assume that she probably did not take as many lead figures over to Northern Ireland as might have been in her studio at Sydney Close.

Mr Saward wrote on April 6th, 1951: "This is just a line to thank you very much for indeed the loan of the statue. She arrived safe and sound, and at present we have her in the house in a position where she is particularly well placed, because in one's normal movements around the house one sees her from so many angles and elevations.

"When the summer weather is really here we may put her in the garden as we originally intended. You know, she really is quite unbelievably lovely.

"As agreed, should you require her to be delivered anywhere for a copy or for return to you or any other reason, you have only to write to me here and I will see to it that your wishes are executed, and will personally arrange the delivery. But we sincerely hope, because we love her so much already, that our child is here to stay with us for always.

"Once again very many thanks indeed for the delight and happiness you are giving us by loaning us the child ...."

There was no question, though, that in moving back to Northern Ireland, Anne Acheson was intending to stop working. However, the expectation was that there would be fewer commissions. As things turned out, there were to be no more exhibits at the Royal Academy.

When she had left Portadown in 1906 to attend the Royal College of Art, Ireland was one country. Now, in 1951, when she crossed the Irish Sea she returned to two countries.

One of the first things that happened after Anne moved to Glenavy was that she was made a member of the Institute of the Sculptors of Ireland, which, according to a notice to members dated November 1955, must have been set up in the early 1950s, because this document carried the agenda for the fourth annual meeting.

The Festival of Britain was also staged in 1951 and Anne and every other member of the Royal Society of British Sculptors, received a circular informing them of a proposed Open Air Exhibition as part of the nationwide event. The RBS had suggested that the Open Air Exhibition might be held "in the Chelsea Hospital Gardens during the Flower Show. But there was a drawback, which might well have put Anne off. "Owing to many difficulties this proposed exhibition will not be sponsored by the Royal Society of British Sculptors ...." As a consequence "... artists would have to bear their own costs and insurance." And the circular closed with: "This is only a tentative suggestion and depends entirely on the response of sculptors to this circular." It is not known whether such an exhibition went ahead. There was certainly an exhibition of sculpture at the Festival; it was organised by the Arts Council, and it was staged at Battersea Park, where works by Henry Moore and Barbara Hepworth featured prominently, but whether this was the same one as that mentioned in the RBS circular is not known. It also not known whether Anne was even interested in the idea, let alone whether she submitted a piece for it. However, she had held on to the circular, so it must have aroused her interest, at the very least.

She was certainly keen on another exhibition in London a couple of years later. This one would have been sponsored by the RBS, although shipping figures over from Northern Ireland must have entailed a certain amount of risk, and invited fairly hefty insurance premiums. A letter from the RBS, dated January 26th, 1953, referred to the forthcoming Guildhall Exhibition, to be held between March 9th and 28th, 1953.

For some reason this was a reminder to Anne. The letter began: "As you do not appear to have offered to exhibit at the forthcoming exhibition at the Guildhall, may I inform you that there is still time.

"If you have available a work of sculpture of general interest and/or photographs of works related to civic affairs, buildings, parks etc will you please forward photographs and particulars to the office not later than the 31st January."

Anne's response was immediate. To the back of the letter she attached a carbon copy of a list of photographs of five suggested figures – "Fountain Figure, bronze, Height 30 inches, £200; River Nymph, Walnut Wood, (two views sent) height 20 inches, £140; Harriet Emily, lead, height 30 inches, £150; The Thief, plaster, height 33 inches (replica in lead would be £200)." And above the list Anne has handwritten a note: "Photos for Guildhall exhibition sent Jan 29th 1953 to sec. Roy. Brit. Sculptors."

This list was the first mention of a wood carving, although that had been on her syllabus at the Royal College of Art. However among her papers are photographs of two wood carvings by Anne Acheson, one is the aforementioned River Nymph, with the two different views of the figure, as sent to the RBS. The other figure was called Moonbeam, carved from a piece of walnut, the bottom three inches or so being left, complete with bark, to act as a plinth.

Of course Anne's standing in the art world was well known and appreciated in her native Northern Ireland and some twelve months earlier, in April 1952, she had received a letter from The Council for the Encouragement of Music and the Arts (Northern Ireland), a mouthy and unwieldy title which was mercifully reduced to the acronym CEMA. The letter from the organiser, a Mr Jack Loudain, had been sent originally to Sydney Close. It began: "CEMA has under consideration the possibility of holding in Belfast late this year or early 1953 an exhibition of sculpture. We would very much like to include in it two or three examples of your work. If you have nothing new available, it may be that owners of your sculpture might be willing to lend. CEMA would, of course, be responsible for all expenses in connection with transport, insurance etc. I would be glad to have your views on this matter.

"It would be a help at this stage if you could give me some

information about the number of works you might wish to show, their respective measurements and where located ..."

There is just a suspicion of admonition in Anne's reply, a mild rebuke that CEMA did not have a current address for her and had sent the letter to London, when she had been at Glebe House for some months.

On May 14th 1952 she wrote: "Thank you for your letter of April 6th forwarded to me from London with some delay."

The rap on the knuckles delivered, she continued: "I am very much interested in the possibility of CEMA holding a sculpture exhibition in Belfast. I should be very glad to contribute some of my works, or help in any other way as I am now living near Belfast.

"I have the plaster originals of the works I should like best to show, here at Glenavy. Bronze and lead casts from these originals are in England (except three further overseas). With one exception these have been mounted on stone so that I could not ask clients to dismantle them and leave a gap in their gardens. The plaster originals I can colour exactly like metal – lead or bronze – for indoor exhibition.

"Would you like me to send photographs or would any members of your committee like to come here (Glenavy, Co. Antrim) and choose what works would suit the exhibition?

"The works I suggest are: 'Fountain Boy'. A seated figure, 31 inches high. In plaster, at Glebe House, Glenavy. In bronze at Ross-on-Wye, Herefordshire, not yet mounted on stone – available.

"'The Thief'. Standing figure, 34 inches high. A child, lifesize. In plaster at Glebe House, Glenavy.

"I have other figures in lead here and smaller works in other materials."

In 1952 she entered the month-long Royal Ulster Academy of Arts exhibition, which opened in October that year. A letter from James Ferry, the secretary, attests to that. While the sculpture she was submitting is not named, Mr Ferry advised her of a suitable date for sending the figure to The Art Gallery, Stranmillis Road, in plenty of time for it to be catalogued. He also thanked Anne for her cheque, which was presumably the payment of her annual subscription.

There was some personal sadness for Anne and the whole family in the New Year of 1953, when Hazel lost her battle with cancer. The cause of death was given as carcinoma of the liver due to primary carcinoma of the bile ducts, a particularly rare form of the disease. She died at home in Glebe House on January 21st, aged 57. Sandy Faris recalls that while the rest of the family had tried to keep the diagnosis from Hazel, she, being a doctor herself, had known all along.

Hazel's premature death broke up the happy *ménage a trois*. Although another of the Acheson sisters, Molly, eventually moved in to take Hazel's place, after the sudden death of her husband Sam in 1956. But she too pre-deceased Anne and Grace, having suffered from severe dementia in the final months of her life, and because her sisters could not cope with her, she had to be moved out of Glebe House and into a hospital at Holywell in Co Antrim, where she eventually died in 1958.

Anne exhibited again with the RUA in the autumn of 1953, this time making a note of her entries, which were: 'Fountain Boy' in plaster, with a price of £220 for a bronze replica; a lead figure of 'Tangles' (£30); and these two were accompanied by an oil painting entitled 'Ram's Island', and alongside it a valuation of £50. If any of the works of art were sold at the Exhibition the RUA collected a 12.5 per cent commission on the sale. There is a footnote at the end of the notice of Annual Exhibition, which explains that anyone wishing to join the Academy as an exhibiting Member had to submit three works to the Council of the Academy who would then decide on eligibility. It is therefore likely that Anne was applying for that with her three works for 1953, because, as in 1952, she only submitted one figure, 'Thief' in bronze or lead (£200) for the RUA's 1954 Annual Exhibition.

In the Spring of that year Anne also had a figure in the Sculpture Exhibition that was held by The Institute of the Sculptors of Ireland (Foras Dealbairi na hEireann) in the City Hall. There is a letter to her from the secretary John D Bourke. Anne must have asked about any bureaucratic problems when sending works of art across the border from Northern Ireland to the Republic. Back came the reply: "There is no trouble in exporting from Northern Ireland, but at one end there is red tape, at which we are expert cutters." He then advised her: "On the customs declaration write 'No commercial value' (this is quite true – artistic value, unfortunately, is not counted commercially) ...." The writer then mentions that the annual subscription to the Institute is one guinea, before closing the letter with an assurance that the Institute would be able to arrange for the safe return of her wood carving. There is no doubt that

Anne submitted the figure, because in the top left-hand corner of the letter she had scrawled "cheque sent, May 15th".

The figure is not mentioned by name, but Mr Bourke's letter revealed: "We would be delighted to have your walnut figure..." and, as it turned out, it was 'River Nymph' and priced at £100.

It is probably safe to assume that Anne entered the Royal Ulster Academy's 1955 Annual Exhibition, although no documentary evidence has survived; then, the following year, she resurrected her 1913 Royal Academy figure 'Echo Mocking' for the RUA's Diploma Works Exhibition, which was held in January 1956.

A month later there was a little landmark for Anne. She finally bowed to her deafness and after attending the Hearing Aid Clinic at the Royal Victoria Hospital in Belfast received her first audio device, complete with the standard issue battery book. Disappointingly there is never a reference to the hearing aid in subsequent correspondence to or from Anne.

In the winter of 1956 Anne received a letter from a member of the Portadown Civic Week committee, seeking works of art from "... citizens, or former citizens of our Borough." There is a wonderfully ingenuous flavour to the letter with the writer adding: "I understand you have an interest in Sculpture." Anne's reaction can only be imagined, but it is almost certain that the understatement, worthy of one of her favourite writers P G Wodehouse, would, at the very least, have raised a smile. So the request is made: "... should you possess any pieces of sculpture made by you, our committee would be very grateful for the loan of such articles..."

The following Spring it emerged from another member of the Civic Week committee that Anne had offered to lend the Borough four of her figures. These included a bust, in plaster, of her brother Sir James Acheson; in addition she sent them 'The Thief', 'Mischief' and 'Fountain Figure', this last being the one which had appeared at the Royal Academy's 1939 Summer Exhibition. She had put a price against three of the figures (she did not put a price on the bust of her brother James) 'Fountain Figure' and 'The Thief' being valued at £200 each and 'Mischief' £50 cheaper. It is likely that these prices had been added in order for the Borough Council to insure them against theft, loss and damage. And 1957 was also the year that the Ulster Society of Women Artists was founded, by Gladys MacCabe. Anne submitted her wood carving 'River Nymph' at the

Society's inaugural exhibition that year. The figure was photographed in an unidentifiable newspaper, and the caption contained the information that 'River Nymph' had a price tag of £100.

The Royal Ulster Academy of Arts, having decided to take part in the 1957 Ulster Festival, invited members to submit two works for what the RUA had named The Festival Exhibition, which would run from May 10th to May 18th. For this Anne decided to submit the wood carving 'River Nymph' and a bronze figure 'A small conceit', a statuette which she had first exhibited at the Royal Academy's Summer Exhibition in 1915 and 1916.

She also made another appearance at the Institute of Sculptors of Ireland Exhibition in September 1957. In addition to a lead figure of 'Mischief', which Anne helpfully informed the organisers was insured for transit and exhibitions in the British isles, there was an earthenware figure called 'Dryad' as well as the bronze portrait medallion of her mother Harriet Glasgow Acheson. But a footnote advised that "These works are sent out for exhibition purposes only." So while they had a value, again that was for insurance, they were definitely not for sale.

Anne's sister Grace and nephew John unearthed a flattering reference to her in a huge French history of art. Apparently Anne had lost her copy of the section in which she featured, but Grace then spotted something when she was attending a committee meeting of the Senate of Queen's University. She wrote to her sister-in-law Mary Faris in early December in 1958: "I remembered that one day in the Queen's library at a committee meeting I noticed on the shelves around the room a set of big volumes entitled 'Histoire d'Art' and I vaguely wondered if that was the one. So last week I remembered this and thought it was worth exploring and asked John to look it up, with the result that he arrived proudly last week with Volume 8 (dealing with art in Europe and America, 19th and early 20th Centuries). Nan was quite pleased to find her 'Sally' chosen for illustration, along with Thornycroft, Epstein and Frampton's works." The Thornycroft in this instance is Sir (William) Hamo Thornycroft, the son of the sculptor Thomas, whose works include the statue of Oliver Cromwell in London and that of King Alfred at Winchester; the third member is Sir George James Frampton, whose statue of Peter Pan stands in Kensington Gardens and that of Edith Cavell in St Martin's Place in London. Sir Jacob Epstein, who was born in New York, but became a naturalised British citizen in 1911 was knighted in 1954. His early work tended to provoke outrage, his 18 large nude sculptures in 1908 on the front of the building that is now Zimbabwe House in Trafalgar Square, caused shock at the time and subsequent works of his were often labelled obscene, but he exhibited throughout his career and also painted and gradually his challenging of traditional taboos affected people less and less. He achieved recognition in his later life, and among his later works is an aluminium figure 'Christ in Majesty' at Llandaff Cathedral in Cardiff.

That same volume of the 'Histoire d'Art', which mentions Anne Acheson in the same breath as this trio of 'greats' also sees the author André Michel describing her as: " ... parmi les meilleurs sculpteurs d'Angleterre..." ("...among the best sculptors in England.")

There was a further submission of an unspecified number of figures which Anne entered in the 1959 Royal Ulster Academy autumn exhibition. But 1959 was more important to Anne for an entirely different reason. As a famous former pupil she had been invited, in October 1959, to unveil the plaque to commemorate the centenary of the founding of her old school Victoria College, Belfast, where Grace had been head mistress from 1930 to her retirement in 1951, a distinguished reign for which she was appointed MBE. The Centenary celebrations included a number of events, including a pageant staged by the pupils to mark various moments in the College's illustrious one hundred-year history, a Centenary Thanksgiving Service and a Centenary Dinner that began with grapefruit and subsequently featured among its six courses, a supreme of sole mornay and roast chicken and ham, followed by fresh fruit salad and cream. There is a photograph in a newspaper showing a behatted Anne pulling on the drawstring that opened the curtains and revealed the plaque dedicated to the memory of the College's founding by Margaret Byers some 22 years into the reign of Queen Victoria, whose name the College took in 1887, the Monarch's Golden Jubilee, by Royal Command.

So Anne Acheson was still a celebrity even as late as this in her life, when her work had been cut to a minimum. A month before unveiling the plaque at the Victoria College Centenary she found herself the subject of a feature in the Belfast Telegraph. The reporter, who went up to Glebe House in Glenavy to conduct the interview, must have had a hard time wringing enough material out of Anne though, since she wrote: "Modesty makes Anne Acheson reluctant to talk about herself and her career. As we strolled through the garden she was much more anxious to draw my attention to beauties of the view."

This feature appeared on September 10th when, despite the heatwave that had dried up the British Isles that summer, there was still plenty to see in the old rectory.

The reporter describes how the house was hidden from the road by trees and she continues: "The old world garden makes an ideal setting for ... the work of Miss Anne Acheson, who lives here in retirement with her sister Mrs Grace Faris."

It was in this article that Anne also revealed how she had changed her policy on the number of replicas she was prepared to produce for sale. "At one time," she told the reporter, "I did only six copies because I thought I couldn't possibly sell more, then I increased it. But I never had more than 14 copies of any one piece."

At the time of the article Anne was working on a head of one of her great nephews, Paul Faris, son of John and Mary. "He is very proud of it, and loves to show it to all the family," Anne was quoted as saying. A photograph of her at work on the figure complements the article, but she revealed to the reporter that rheumatism made tackling new work difficult.

She was also still an active member of the Royal British Society of Sculptors and in the midsummer of 1959 she received copies of a leaflet for the Sir Otto Beit Award for sculpture "in the British Isles and Commonwealth *outside* London, and would be glad if you would kindly send them to any individual or body, who might be interested, in Northern Ireland...." says the secretary's letter. Sir Otto Beit was a German-born financier and philanthropist, who moved to England in 1888 and became a naturalised British citizen eight years later. Among many generous donations to public institutions Sir Otto helped the Victoria and Albert Museum purchase numerous works of art and gave his name to an award for excellence in sculpture through the RBS.

As Anne entered the 'Swinging Sixties' she also entered Who's Who. In April 1960 she was sent the proof of her biography for checking and correcting; strangely she omits to mention her school, Victoria College, unless the editors of Who's Who felt schools were not to be named.

Sadly, though, there is precious little evidence of what she was doing by this time. Thankfully there is a letter from her brother Jim late in 1960,

and from what he wrote it is apparent that Anne has kept her hand in with
her own Christmas cards, something which she had been doing for a good
number of years. The last was a view of Lough Neagh, and there was
another, earlier, card of a squirrel, as well as views of a bridge at Glenavy.
"We keep them all," wrote James, "and have an idea of framing and hanging
them when we can decide on where." In that letter Jim enclosed a cheque
for £30, being interest on a loan of £500 from Anne, a financial
arrangement he confirms in a subsequent letter, just over a year later

In general though, clues as to Anne's movements in 1960 and 1961
are scarce. However, in late Autumn 1961 she was able to visit Jim on his
fruit farm in Herefordshire. Although the letter is undated Anne wrote:
"I got £160 repayment from the Income Tax people for 1959, 1960 and
1961." So it had to be late in that last year that she went to see her brother
at Holly Bush House, because of the mention of the income tax refund
and also because she talked of Janet (her niece Janey Ironside) visiting
Ulster "... about December 1, and wants to come to Glebe House, so keep
that date free ." There being an implication that it is not too far in the
future. According to Vio (Lady Acheson), Anne's visit was "... an
unqualified success, and she seemed so happy and interested in everybody
and everything in Much Birch."

Anne's hand-writing is remarkably neat, belying her 79 years, and she
admitted: "I rest a lot. It is very cold today." She returned in time for
Christmas 1961 at Glebe House, before, shortly afterwards being taken
ill, although she might have perked up at a letter from Jim and what it
contained.

It was dated January 24th and in it he referred to the £500 loan. At
the top of the letter he has added a postscript in which he acknowledged
his gratitude: "I haven't thanked you for the loan! It was a great help during
the lean years. Thank you again." But in the body of the letter James also
mentioned the loan. "... I have been meditating returning your £500. We
have had another good year, the market prices having more than made up
for the very light crop of apples, ie unlike most other growers we had
enough apples to sell to take advantage of the high prices. So we really do
not need the £500 any longer and can finance our development plans (the
biggest item this year is building a cold store) with possibly some
temporary help from the bank. Possibly without if crops and prices are
reasonably good. So I am enclosing our (ie JG and CA Acheson) cheque

for that amount. I think it may come in useful to you for increased expenses on household help etc."

There was also news of her great niece and nephews. "We had Fenella with us for supper and bed last night. She is growing up rapidly, but hasn't quite lost her attractive baby ways. Malcolm and Nigel have gone back to St Edward's and The Elms respectively. Both looking enormous (better for the holiday and good home food). Malcolm is a huge boy now and his voice has broken – it sounds just like his father's on the telephone."

As for Jim and his wife: "Vio and I are flourishing. We are going to stand ourselves lunch in Monmouth today to celebrate my 73rd birthday."

But before any of that family news and talk of the money Jim had opened the letter to Anne by alluding to her health. "I was delighted to hear from Grace of your improvement. I do hope it will continue...."

Sadly his hopes were in vain. His sister's illness could no longer be managed by Grace alone at home and Anne Acheson had to be admitted eventually to the Lagan Valley Hospital in Lisburn, Co. Antrim, where she spent the last few weeks of her life, before slipping quietly away.

20

Innocence and Health

~~~~✧~~~~

Anne Acheson was no hypochondriac. In fact she was generally
stoical about her various ailments. Whenever she mentions them
in her correspondence it is more by way of observation, than of
complaint. Nevertheless many of her surviving letters contain at least one
reference to her state of health or an inquiry into her correspondent's
fitness; in fact the impression is that the physical well-being of her family
and her friends was of greater import and interest to her than her own
health.

For instance when visiting Hazel in Jubbulpore in 1932 Anne had
some worrying news for the family, because it transpired that Hazel had
not been too well. "She has much less of those sick turns she was having
regularly when I arrived." But according to a subsequent one, in March,
shortly before she was due to return home things had changed. "Hazel
had a slight recurrence of her tummy trouble with a very slight
temperature, so I fussed a bit and Captain Irvine examined her, and the
pathologist at the military hospital is making some tests. She is ... very thin
and a bit nervy."

Much later, in 1941 Anne revealed remarkable ignorance or
innocence when she stated: "Hazel has been in hospital for a D.C. I don't

know what that is." She presumably meant a D and C, a medical abbreviation for Dilatation and Curettage of the uterus. "She went to Agra for it and was a week in bed."

On another occasion Anne wrote to Grace: "I am sorry to hear from Harrie that you have had 'flu .... I was ill for a week or more with that throat and cold. I nursed myself as well as I could, but could not do any work (by work I mean studio work)."

But she was equally solicitous of her friends. "I have been extra busy ... as Edie Leppard had a big operation last week," she explained to Grace in a letter in 1937, "and wanted me to go to see her often. She got a bad cough so had a very painful time. She could not bear her noisier friends – I am not an intimate friend – but Browning was in quarantine as she had been with someone who had scarlatina, and I suppose I took Browning's place."

She even began the letter in which she, eventually, told Grace about her being made a Fellow of the Royal British Society of Sculptors with: "I hope you are not all ill."

At the end of the war she heard alarming news about two more of her friends. "Hytch phoned me on Saturday morning about Toolie, it is terrible, I am anxious for more news. She seemed to have hope from the new treatment." Hytch, a medical student friend of Hazel's, was also a cause for Anne's concern. "I wonder how long Hytch's own operation (don't mention it as Jane does not know about it) can be postponed." And then: "I have just heard that Dorothy Hilder's husband has died in India."

Anne was forever taking care of her neighbours and fellow artists the Budds. Not long before she was due to leave Sydney Close Anne told Hazel: "Mrs Budd is definitely better today. She greeted me with that news, which was a great change. She is to stop the penicillin ointment now. She has been getting liver injections (District Nurse said that is what they were). She cannot do without veganin every four hours yet. I wish she could get out."

During the Blitz she had also become fearful about the potential of epidemics, becaused so many people were crammed into air raid shelters, and the conditions in the shelters were also a cause for concern. "I am afraid the hospitals will fill up from the shelters soon. I heard of two pleurisies yesterday. The little original shelters, which were really meant for people in the street in daylight are cold and dampish – they were when we 'slept' in one months ago. I had to lean against a damp wall. The bigger one we tried was warm, but very crowded." And here she revealed a twist of fate. "It got a direct hit a fortnight after ... I had given it up."

Anne found her body did not enjoy the often cold and damp places that the air raids forced her to seek. "I go to a shelter under some flats at night. I sleep (or don't) on the floor or on steps, much too close to the crowd.... I slept several hours last night, but only one the night before." And: "I got an awful cold sleeping in public shelter and on stairs." And again: "Last night was 8pm to 6am in the shelter. I got about three hours' sleep and one in bed." Her temporary move to Oakley Street after Avenue Studios were damaged during a raid, was a step into luxury for Anne, because she no longer had to go to a shelter during a raid, her bedsit in the house being deemed safe enough to allow her to remain their while the Luftwaffe dropped their bombs, and Anne told Grace: "... now that I sleep in a bed my rheumatism has disappeared almost...". Throughout her adult life Anne was plagued with chronic joint problems, which impinged a great deal on her work, and there are several references to her frustration when trying to model this or that figure.

The earliest manifestation of her arthritis – she referred to it variously as neuritis, fibrositis and rheumatism in her letters – was when she was in her mid-thirties and visiting Browning at her friend's parents' home in Bedfordshire. Anne broke off in the middle of a report on her activities in the latest edition of The Budget to inform the family of a problem with her back: "Excuse my writing, I think I have lumbago, can't stand straight or turn around. I have Em's plaster on and Hazel has got anti-phlogistine in case it gets worse." Just a day later she added: "The crick in my back is better this morning though I am still very stiff. I am able to go about. I expect it was the bitterly cold drive to the station yesterday morning. I never warmed up after it all day."

During the Second World War, when she was preparing a figure for exhibiting at the Royal Academy in the summer of 1944, she wrote a rather poignant letter to Grace, informing her sister: "I ... tried to finish the big figure in plaster of Josephine Owen. Today was sending-in day, and I finished it, more or less, last night with a coat of distemper, and saw it break as they loaded it on the lorry this morning. It was a war substitute for the proper van and I expect the figure was worse broken before it got to the Royal Academy. So all the pain in my hands from working was for nothing." And later that same year, when she is without her home help, there was another reference to her condition. " ... I have given up hope of getting my hands well enough for anything skilled while I have to do my own housework."

Rheumatic pain is bad for anyone, but for someone whose job is based on manual dexterity and accuracy, it has to be hell incarnate. Frustration and misery do not begin to cover the feelings that beset the victims of this crippling disease. Anne underlined just how bad it was: "I have had less pain in my hands than ever today, but still cannot finish this letter at one sitting."

By this point, at the bottom of the second side of the paper, her writing had deteriorated into an uncharacteristically untidy scrawl. She started the third side the following day, a Sunday. She expanded a little on her hands and their condition. "If I don't use my hands for a day (eg when I spent a morning shopping without carrying things, as when I went to eight shops to look for a hat) my hands are almost well the next day."

There was only one moment of what might be termed self-indulgence, when Anne explained to Grace why she had to take a break from writing letters. "I am too rheumatic to sit long. I have a lot of trouble with my right wrist, which has a swelling on it. As every occupation, housework and work, is a strain on it I am slightly sorry for myself ...."

She tried to do what she could to ease the suffering. One terse sentence informed the family: "I wash vegetables in warm water, doctor's advice to save pains in hands."

During the war years Anne underwent a course, but this one was not re-training her for another career in voluntary war work; rather it was an attempt to ease, if not cure, her painful joints. She called it 'light ray' treatment, which would almost certainly have been infra red therapy. "I have two more of the twelve treatments to get. The right hand is much better, though writing still hurts, but I am much better otherwise and can stand it better. The three medicines I have had to take may have had that result."

However her upbeat mood was somewhat dampened by the pronouncement of the mother of her pupil Daphne Wingate Morris. "Daphne's mother, who was head of an electric treatment department and has been working at a hospital in Kensington, depressed me thoroughly last week by saying I should do absolutely nothing with my hands for three months. Dr Eva Morton does not agree with that, thank goodness."

A fortnight later it was all over, but it had not quite done the trick, as Anne told Grace. "I have finished my course of light ray treatment. The Doctor is disappointed that I am not quite cured, but says people often go on getting less and less pains after they have stopped having treatment. I am still to take a complicated system of drugs. One this week, none next week, a different one the next week and none the week after, and repeat. And halibut oil tabloids all the time."

In February 1945 came another reference to her increasing incapacitation and her consequent inability to do much work. "I never really get back to modelling; my neuritis stops me, though I don't have it badly. I couldn't work in the cold weather." And later: "I had a cold before I went to Leamington and felt the effects of it for weeks. That may have brought the hands' neuritis back."

Precious few letters have survived from the years when she was involved with the Surgical Requisites Association, and perhaps because she was dealing directly with patients whose medical problems were far more grave, far more acute than her own, there was not a single reference to her state of health, Not until the early 1920s did she broach the subject, but when she did so it sounded fairly serious, because in 1923 she found herself in hospital.

On January 12th Anne wrote to Molly: "Of course Hazel and I would love to have you, but it is not a necessity. I should like you in one way to be with Hazel while I'm away, but she is often out from 8.20am to 9 or 10pm, so you would be rather wasted so to speak."

It transpired that Anne was scheduled for an unspecified operation at the King Edward VII Hospital in Marylebone towards the end of the month and she had been organising hers and others' lives around it. "Browning will sleep in the flat probably two or three nights a week and she may get Epps [Dr Phyllis Epps, a medical friend of Hazel's] for a weekend."

Meanwhile Anne had arranged for her convalescence to be at the "Duchess Home, 2, Beaumont Street." This establishment was just around the corner from the hospital. Anne wrote that she expected to begin her convalescence "... about the end of the month, so I should leave there about February 21st."

She obviously felt fine in herself, because she was able to state confidently to Molly: "... I expect to recover quickly .... If you do plan to keep yourself free, if it is convenient, from February 15th in case I get in a day or two early and get out a day or two early."

Anne perhaps felt a little guilty about dragging her sister away from her husband Sam Faris, because she added: "I must confess, for Sam's sake, that you would be a luxury, not a necessity, but wouldn't a change be good for you too? And Hazel would be easier in her mind the first week or so if you were there while she is away all day."

She then revealed plans for herself and Hazel to go and stay with the aforementioned Epps and Hytch, for a long weekend down in East Grinstead. "I was afraid my op would have to be sooner on account of the room in the nursing home and that would have upset this plan of Hazel's, but we got it settled for later."

There are numerous mentions of colds and 'flu throughout her letters, but more so as the 20th Century picked up its skirts and pulled away from the memories of the First World War. The victims of 'flu were invariably knocked off their feet by the affliction. Anne was no exception. And of course it had a bearing on her work.

"My temperature goes up to 100 daily," she disclosed in 1935, "and now I have an awful cold in the head as well as the pains ... I have still got the headache ... I am horribly weak after six days' temperature...", before adding: "My big work should have been cast yesterday in plaster – but it has to be done in the studio. It is not ready really anyhow... I am wild at wasting a whole week."

A couple of years later she was just recovering from another bout of something 'flu-like: "I am now fairly well alternate days – chest still tickly and knees shaky when I work too long.... Nurse's bill was £5 for the week." Her health certainly affected her professional life, and in quite significant ways. "I moulded (cast) a figure (which had been spoilt for the third time by drying up while I was ill) on Friday, and cut my hand when finishing the second of eight mixtures of plaster. I had to go on all day with the job as soon as I had first aided the cut, but it hurt all the time as it was at the base of the first finger. It was rather a heavy job anyhow, but would have cost about £3 so I thought it worth doing myself, also I wanted to work in the mould. I can leave it in the mould stage next week."

The following year it was pretty much the same story: "I got up and dressed yesterday morning, much against my inclination, but things had to be sorted and priced and listed for a show. The doctor came in the

middle, took my blood pressure and says it is terribly low, she says that is
as bad as having it high. I said does that mean the tonsils are not the
trouble (I meant the temperature business) but she settled down again
and said she was tactfully not mentioning that just now as I must get
stronger before anything can be done to the tonsils. I am to go away now,
to feed up, when back at work I am to have a large midday meal and rest
after and she hopes to get the tonsils out before next winter."

Influenza was invariably complicated by secondary chest infections
in those days, because London still experienced smogs because of all the
atmospheric pollutants (coal fires being one of many contributors to the
thick, choking, yellow fumes of the toxic combination of smoke and fog)
which swirled around the streets of cities throughout the country during
the autumn and winter months. Smogs were the underlying cause of most
respiratory ailments, in 1952 in the London area alone 4,000 deaths were
attributed to smog, and it was not until four years later that the 'Clean Air
Act' was passed which saw councils banning the use of bituminous coals
and instead using so-called smokeless fuels.

In addition to her arthritis and her regular battles with colds, 'flu and
numerous headaches Anne was afflicted with a far more distressing
condition – deafness. This affected her deeply, bringing her very low at
times, most acutely when she was doing her training in 1940.

She was working in the machine shop at the Beaufoy Institute when
she first refers to her hearing loss. "I am afraid I must get a hearing
apparatus. I do not hear 'all clears' when there is traffic and am not sure
of warnings ... learning a new job among machinery may be difficult."
And not long after this admission, and well before the course had finished
she confessed to Grace: "... my age and deafness make me feel a bit
depressed."

Even before the war Anne was aware of some loss of hearing and after
making a telephone call to Grace in Belfast she wrote: "I could not hear
you very well on the phone part of the time ...." Harriet Rhys-Davies
remembered: "As the years went on her deafness caused her great distress,
especially when unable to participate in a hilarious family conversation.
She would often say, plaintively: 'I'm very deaf today.'"

Anne's emotional state was generally fairly stable. However she did
let herself go on a couple of occasions, and quite out of the blue as well.
In the summer of 1929 Anne took time out to write a sombre note. It was

on August 11 that Anne contemplated her mortality. She wrote on two small sheets of headed notepaper bearing the King's House Studios address.

The envelope is addressed "To my heir or heirs. <u>Instructions as to works</u>."

The note begins: "<u>Instructions to my heir</u> as to the disposal of my works after my death.

"All plasters [this is a reference to the plaster models of her figures] should be broken up, especially 'Mischief' and 'Sally', whose limited edition is disposed of. These should be broken up <u>at once</u>.

"'March' 'June' 'October' and 'December' are limited to ten in the British Isles and to fifteen in the United States of America." Anne then went on to list the ones that have been sold and the name of the purchaser. Then, touchingly, she referred to the busts of her sister Hazel and brother James. "The plaster busts of H E Acheson and J G Acheson are the only plaster works I wish kept."

At some later date Anne returned to this note in order to cross out various instructions that have been overtaken by events and time, but she then wrote: "Break up 'Rags', 'The Slide', 'Thirteen O'clock', '1914' and 'Puppy' as I do not like them." There then follows a suggestion for disposal of two more figures: "Gazes or John White (Bond Street) might pay for plaster of 'Watersprite' and 'Hosepipe', with copyright." She did not forget her great friend adding: "Give Browning something after brothers and sisters." But the apparent finality of these instructions was then relaxed when Anne wrote: "Except as regards the limited editions these instructions are only advice – need not be followed, but do not let the plaster of limited editions out of your possession (though they may be kept by a reputable foundry till the editions are cast, then destroyed.) If you cannot sell metal replicas destroy at once. As ever with Anne, she always managed to find a postscript to add and she squeezed in the following: "Harriet Emily and Rags are limited to ten in the British Isles and fifteen elsewhere." The note carried her signature and the date, but what prompted her to write out these instructions when things were still looking up for her, from a professional standpoint at least, remains a mystery.

There was a further allusion to her mortality towards the end of the second World War. Again there is nothing to explain why she should suddenly introduce the subject into an otherwise cheerful and chatty letter. But there it is, squeezed into one of her trademark, *non sequitur* postscripts at the bottom of one letter that said: "When I die Harrie Acheson is to have my 'Christening' ring, French-marked ACA, if Hazel, my heir, does not mind."

It was early in 1949 that Anne made a final mention of her physical well-being. It was a short comment, but perhaps it helped her to make up her mind about leaving London and returning to her native Ireland. "Dr Frances gave me more medicine for fibrositis, says I need a long rest – everyone does need a long rest nowadays, but I'm all right when not fussed with business.

21

Post Mortem

~~~~ॐ~~~~

I n the Spring of 1962 a brief note arrived at Glebe House for Anne
Acheson. It was from Grace Carter, the secretary of the Royal Society
of British Sculptors, as it was still known in the middle of the
Twentieth Century. It was dated March 15 1962. The note reads: "I have
heard that you are ill, so this is just ... to send you very good wishes from
the Society for a speedy recovery, and we hope that we may be hearing
better news soon ..." The fact that the note was written at all at least
suggests some presentiment, albeit tardy, on the part of the writer;
unfortunately by the time it arrived at Glenavy, a day, or even two days,
after that, it was certainly far too late for the concern it expressed to have
been of any comfort to Anne, or Grace for that matter, because Anne had
passed away on March 13th.

The certified cause of death was given as myocardial degeneration,
or heart failure, with a secondary diagnosis of "senility certified", but
medical jargon changes over the years and this could be interpreted simply
as old age, which wording often appears on modern day death certificates
as an underlying cause of death.

The RBS did make up for their unfortunate timing. According to Dr
Emmanuel Minne, Archivist and Historian of the Royal British Society

of Sculptors, the selfsame secretary Grace Carter, wrote in the council's minutes that when Anne's death was "announced at the AGM on 27th March ... all present stood and observed a minute's silence in honour of your sister ... . A number of tributes were paid and amongst these the President [Edward Bainbridge Copnall] said that Miss Acheson's memory would be kept green by the many delightful works of sculpture she had left, and Lady Muriel Wheeler also spoke of her with affection."

And an obituary in the RBS's Annual Report and Statement for the year 1962-63, stated: "Miss Acheson's broad modelling of her favourite material, lead, gave sculptural dignity to works in which she considered playfulness and fancy necessary requirements, and indeed gave charm to her work. ... her services to Art and the Society will be recognised in the affectionate memory of Members for many years."

Anne had been ill for some weeks before her death. At first she was nursed by Grace, but as Sandy Faris noted in a letter to his mother at the beginning of February 1962, when he wondered whether she could break away from caring for her sister to see a performance of Gilbert and Sullivan's 'Iolanthe' which had just come out of copyright, "I wish you could come and see 'Iolanthe', but it is obviously difficult with Auntie Nan ill. Is there anyone who could look after her for 24 hours, which is all you need be away for? It would surely do you good to get a little break. The strain must be tiring for you."

Anne Acheson had always given a lot to her family. Her main beneficiary was her sister Grace Faris, but she did not forget her nieces and nephews, of whom there were originally twelve, be it her time, somewhere for them to stay, encouragement and an interest in their education and their subsequent careers. In death so it was in life. All ten of them were named as the beneficiaries of her will, which she had made in September 1952, and practical to the end, she divided her estate equally among all of them.

Newspaper obituaries were full of praise. According to The Times: "... she was an accomplished craftswoman with a special talent for decorative garden figures in lead ..." and later "... she never descended to the mere quaintness, which has produced so many monstrosities in terra cotta for the adornment of suburban gardens, and when her figures – of which 'The Imp' and 'Sally' were the most popular – were shown in a garden setting, as they were at the British Empire Exhibitions at Wembley in 1924 and 1925, they had a very pleasing effect."

The obituary writer in The Times went on to acknowledge that Anne "... was not limited to lead, and her Academy contributions included several heads, statuettes and medallions in bronze."

More touching, and nearer to the real woman, were the letters of condolence, with which Grace was inundated at Glebe House throughout March. Perhaps the most poignant, and most important, was that from her oldest and dearest friend and colleague Browning. "I am grieved at the death of dear Ach, yet I have hesitated to write to you, for I know only too well that nothing one can say will be of any comfort to you for the loss of such a dear one ... I have had Ach so much in my mind for weeks. I wrote to her at Christmas time, and had no reply, which made me wonder if all was well with her. How I wish I had written to find out.

"I don't like to bother you, but it would be so kind of you to send me a note. I do hope she had not much to suffer, it would be a great relief to my mind to know, for I loved her ..."

And Helen Budd, for so many years a neighbour and a friend, was also moved to write to Grace. Her letter was short and to the point: "I need not say how very, very sorry I was to see that our very dear 'Ach' had died. I do hope that she didn't have to suffer much. We were always hoping to see her again, and Brownie and I often talked about it. You have all my sympathy as I have recently had a bereavement, which does not grow less, with love and sympathy ...."

Even one of her pupils, Daphne Wingate Morris, was moved to write to Grace to express her sadness at the news. Her respect for Anne is evident in that some 20 years down the line she still referred to Anne as Miss Acheson. She wrote: "I was shocked to read of Miss Acheson's death ... and do hope she did not suffer too much. I have been wondering about her ever since Christmas, as it was the first year I had not heard [from her] and was just about to write and ask how she was.

"You may remember that I was a student of hers for some years. I remember her with great affection. She gave pleasure to so many people through her work, and with her wonderful personality. She was always so kind to me and I hate to think I shall never see or hear from her again."

Anne Acheson's willingness, indeed insistence, on doing her bit for King and Country during two World Wars, reveals a great deal about the woman and her character. She was independent-minded, yet she certainly possessed a team ethic. When confronted with a problem she proved to be persistent and extremely resourceful; she was also blessed with imagination and consequently an inventive mind, on top of all that, even in her advanced years, she was not so much a willing learner as an avaricious apprentice, eager to add this or that skill to her already formidable range. It would seem from her work with the Surgical Requisites Association, that she was also a natural leader. The responsibilities of taking charge of a project or a situation clearly did not bother her in the slightest; indeed management seems to have been something she took in her stride and even welcomed. She was of a stoical bent, as her attitude to her ailments bears witness; she might have written of them, but she did not wallow in too much self pity.

However, those whose lives she did touch have been able to flesh out the bare bones of Anne Acheson's personality a little more with some of their memories of meeting, and of being, with her.

One or two things are consistently touched upon by her young relatives (as they were then) and those were her kindness to everyone, her generosity of spirit and her patience even when at a critical stage of her work.

John Faris also recalled how Anne helped him with a project for School. He described how she assisted him: " ... in connection with a handicraft competition at Royal School Dungannon: in effect she did it, and I got the prize."

Another of her nieces, Janey Ironside, perhaps found Anne taking a little too much responsibility for her, remembering a time when she was 17 and had just had her portrait painted by Thomas Dugdale. In her autobiography Janey wrote: "As a thank you gesture, Dugdale invited me to dinner at the Cafe Royal. And my aunt announced that she was coming too in case my head was turned by his silly compliments – 'which of course he doesn't mean,' she added, joining herself yet again to that careful league of Nanny Barnes and Madre [Janey's maternal grandmother], who were so anxious to eradicate any trace of vanity in me. I have not mentioned my aunt before the episode of the portrait, but she was a fully paid up member of this league."

But Anne was also remembered fondly by Janey, who was always aware of the tolerance and indulgence shown to the younger generation by the childless Anne Acheson.

"To give her her due we were fond of Aunt Nan," wrote Janey in her autobiography, "and I realise now how maddening it must have been to have nephews and nieces asking for a bed in her studio, and when very young, expecting visits to the zoo and to Peter Pan's statue and to Piccadilly at night to see the lights, and causing interruptions to her work."

John Faris certainly found in his aunt an amiable companion, despite the age difference, and he added: "Throughout my childhood she was a frequent and, to me at least, a welcome visitor."

And when it came to his turn to visit Anne he had nothing but pleasant memories. "I spent a weekend there for example between two scholarship exams. We went to a theatre."

John also recalled an episode that Anne wrote about and has been recorded in an earlier chapter. He went into a little more detail, although perhaps the passage of time has left him a little confused as to the identity of the fish in question. He wrote: "I remember one occasion when we were sitting down to a delicious dinner that she had prepared, chops, roast potatoes and so on, everything splendid. Suddenly she shrieked 'John there are some sardines [Anne had written of the fish being pilchards]!' It had come to her that she might not have provided enough to satisfy my supposedly voracious appetite."

That she was always mindful of others and concerned to make sure that everything was just so for her guests merely reinforced the impression that she was a giver, not a taker in life.

Even when Harriet Rhys-Davies was a grown woman she saw the softer, gentler side of her aunt in one rare moment in 1951, just after Anne had moved to Glebe House. "Though not normally demonstrative of affection she would sometimes put her arm around me when making an important statement. I remember one occasion in 1951, just after the three sisters had moved into Glenavy. Aunty Nan and I were standing in the drive surveying the rather dreary laurels alongside it. I said that I planned to plant loads of daffodils to cheer it up. 'Well,' she said, putting her arm around me, 'be sure you throw them carelessly, so that they land in clumps, not rows, so that they'll look like a poem, not a dictionary.'" There was a great deal of her poet mother in her.

Most summers between the two wars found Anne sharing a holiday with Grace and her family. Portballintrae was one of their favoured haunts and one of her nephews, Sandy Faris says his earliest memories of her: "... are of her sketching on the beach ... Auntie Nan (and Auntie Hazel if she was on furlough from India) would both sit at their easels doing watercolours of Faris and Acheson children playing around the coble, the flat-bottomed salmon fishermen's boat. Their pictures were, I thought, equally charming, but Nan got more credit; she was an *artist*, Hazel a mere amateur."

Yet, for all that can be gleaned about Anne Acheson's character, somehow the personality underlying that character has an elusive quality. Relationships outside the working environment are rarely referred to in any of her correspondence. However, it is safe to say that she was a private person. Nowhere in the letters which have survived, is there ever any mention, not even a hint, of what her love life was like. Or indeed whether she even had one. And despite all her contributions to 'The Budget', there was never the slightest allusion to any 'special' person in her life, no suggestion from Anne of any deeper, more meaningful or more personal relationship with anyone. Any reports she might make of visiting the theatre or going to restaurants or concerts are when she is entertaining one or other members of her family, or going out with her friends and colleagues; yet from what she wrote of those outings, they were obviously something she enjoyed immensely, so it was not as if she were an agoraphobic, or even shy.

However, her death did turn up one name, one person whom she had never spoken about, and yet, on reading his letter of condolence to Grace Faris, it would appear that Anne had certainly enjoyed the company of someone who signed himself J C Arnold.

John Corry Arnold was the only son of the Rev Robert James Arnold and came from Dunnurry Co Antrim. He was a member of the Irish Bar, and completed his BA at St Johns College, Cambridge.

He was a barrister and a member of The Honourable Society of the Inner Temple. He was also the author of a number of books on law including 'Vendors and Purchasers of Legal and Leasehold Property' (1929), 'The Landlord and Tenant Act of 1927' and 'The Settled Land Act' (1937). He must have been about the same age as Anne, and although he obviously misremembered an early London address of hers, confusing Kensington Crescent with Kensington Terrace, he had never forgotten Anne Acheson.

In his letter to Grace, dated March 18th he wrote: "Will you allow me to say how sorry I was to read of the death of your sister Anne.... fifty years ago I met her in Newcastle with your sister Molly and again in 1910 when she was living with two other girls ... in Kensington Terrace and I had left Ireland for London." John Arnold had been admitted to the Inner Temple on April 10th that year, being called to the Bar in May 1911. And he must have been glad to have stumbled upon someone else from Ulster. He certainly admits to feeling a bit down upon first arriving in London.

His letter continues: "She was kind enough to ask me to call to see her there. For some years we met fairly often, sometimes going to plays together and taking long walks over Richmond Park on Sunday afternoons. She was full of gaiety and kindness, and looking back now I valued her friendship very much at a time when I was lonely and rather homesick. After the war, when I went back to Ireland ... I am afraid we lost touch, but I always looked for her beautiful statuettes at The Academy, and was delighted to hear of her success in the world of art, of which I was myself so ignorant.

"I hope you will not feel I am obtruding myself into your private grief in writing to you, but I would like you to think that I look back upon her memory with gratitude and also on that of your sister Molly ... how I hope that you and your family, of whom I sometimes hear, are well. I think I once met you at a debate at Queen's when you supported some motion of mine and, thanks to your help, it was carried. We were both probably wrong but what is the use of being young if you can't make mistakes?"

There is nothing in what he related to Grace to indicate that the relationship with Anne was anything other than Platonic, and certainly if there had been a greater depth of feeling then neither would have allowed the other to "lose touch". The fact that the mysterious Mr Arnold never once featured in any of Anne's letters is more likely because, however kind she was to him, and however much she enjoyed his company on long Sunday afternoon walks, he did not represent anything more than a casual acquaintance; someone who had felt a little homesick for Ireland on first arriving in London, and had latched on to Anne for a short while. It is still intriguing though, and simply by sending a letter to Grace, would seem to indicate that Anne had still made a huge impression on Mr Arnold for him to have harboured such memories for half a century. So quite possibly Mr Arnold could have been a victim of unrequited love, but without any evidence from Anne the depth of their relationship does not merit idle speculation. In fact in the end what this letter to Grace does, is merely to underline another facet of Anne Acheson's character, that she was essentially a private person. There were things that she was happy to talk and write about, and obviously things that did not warrant the time, the effort, the ink or the paper and postage.

Anne Acheson was a remarkable woman, who had lived through remarkable times. She beheld the end of the Victorian Age; endured the horrors of not one, but two World Wars; she witnessed the birth of the Jet Age and international air travel; she had been a subject of six Monarchs and she saw the beginning of the end of the British Empire.

Her spirit endures in the eternal children she created; the pictures she painted; the pottery figures she crafted; the car mascots she sculpted. There is also the fact that almost a century later the Plaster of Paris splint is still used throughout the world.

Quite some legacy.

Appendix
Anne Acheson's Academy Exhibits

ACHESON, Miss Annie C.   Sculptor
8 Kensington Crescent, W.

1911	1864	The Pixie	Statuette
1912	1837	Will o' the wisp	Statuette, bronze
1913	1979	Echo mocking	Statuette, bronze
1914	2120	Thirteen o'clock	Statuette

12, Redcliffe Road, SW10

1915	1816	A small conceit	Statuette
1916	1928	A small conceit	Statuette, bronze

6, Wentworth Studios, Manresa Road, SW3

1920	1474	Mrs Wingate	Bust, bronze
1922	1454	The Imp	Lead garden figure
1923	1502	Sally	Lead garden figure
1924	1560	Boy with hose pipe	Fountain figure, lead
1926	1285	Rags	Garden figure
	1309	Mrs Spafford	Portrait medallion, bronze
	1392	April	Statuette
1927	1615	Tangles	Statuette, lead

	1644	Mrs Dugdale	Head
1929	1547	December	Garden figure, lead
	1548	June	Garden figure, lead
1930	1538	March	Garden group, lead
	1540	Leveret	Garden group, lead
1931	1546	Annabel Cundall	Head
	1650	Josephine G Owen As Puck	Garden figure, lead
1935	1551	Harriet Glasgow Acheson	Medallion, bronze
	1576	Water Baby	Garden figure, lead

9, Avenue Studios, 76, Fulham Road, SW3
| 1938 | 1428 | Thief | Garden figure, lead |

9, Sydney Close, 76, Fulham Road, SW3
1939	1198	Fountain figure	
1944	1147	Mrs Christopher Ironside	Bust
1946	1200	Sabrina Fair	Garden figure
1948	1361	Eliza	Head
1949	1351	Virginia Ironside	Head

Index

~~~ꟼꟼ~~~

Acheson, Anne Crawford (also known as 'Annie' 'Nan' 'Ach'): *appointed CBE 1; birth 2; early academic and artistic prowess 7-8; attends Victoria College, gains honours from Royal University of Ireland, assistantship at Victoria College, attends Belfast Municipal Technical Institute, wins free studentship to Royal College of Art, Kensington 9; student years at RCA 9-16; meets Amy K Browning 11; job searching 15-16; appointed as art teacher at The County Secondary School, Putney 18; Grand Tour with sister Grace 18-23; life as an art teacher 23-27; learns the 'Tango' 27; models for Browning's The Red Shawl 29-30; confirmation of first Royal Academy exhibit 30; second RA exhibit 31; becomes Aunt for first time 33; becomes member of Union Internationale des Beaux-Arts et Des Lettres 33; joins Surgical Requisites Association 42-43; devises papier maché splint 47; takes first plaster casts of fractured limbs 48; invents waterproofing for papier maché limb baths 53-57; turns down chance to profit from waterproof limb baths 57; gets letter from Dugdale 57-58; with sister Hazel visits Browning at her family home 58-59; appointed Head of Plastics at SRA 60; finally realises that Plaster of Paris can be used for splints 62-63; receives CBE at Buckingham Palace from King George V, and describes ceremony 67-68.*
Starts making car mascots 71-73; completes portrait sketch in bronze of Dugdale 75; elected Associate of Royal Society of British Sculptors 80; reveals how she captures her child models in action for her garden figures 82; more on her methods 84-85; sees Hazel off to India 86; off to Darlington to see Mrs Fanny Spafford who has commissioned a bronze portrait medallion of herself 86; to Amalfi with Browning 87; commissioned to model a bust of Gertrude Bell 89; bust of Gertrude Bell is completed 94; praise for the bust of Gertrude

Bell *95*; bust unveiled in Iraq by King Faisal I *95-96*; visits Browning in
Suffolk *97*; admits to financial worries *98*; made an Academician of the
Ulster Academy of Arts *99*; given commission by The King's School,
Worcester and produces 'Sabrina' *99*; visits Dora Owen *100* and *121*; takes
up teaching post at Norland Place School *102*; doll making and Royal
Worcester work *102*; plays hostess to young relatives *102*; first visit to sister
Hazel and brother James in India *104-107*; second visit to sub-Continent,
this time touring which includes Swat Valley *107-111*; a haunting
experience *105-107*; makes a medallion of her mother for exhibiting at RA
112-113; problems with doll factory payments *113*; problems with Royal
Worcester contract *112-113*.
    Starts sketching for calendars *114*; moves to Avenue Studios (later Sydney Place)
114-116; lets King's House Studios *116*; visits Cotswolds again *121*; first
attempt to become an examiner for Northern Ireland Ministry of Education,
good reference from Dugdale *122*; elected first woman Fellow of Royal
British Society of Sculptors *122-123*; goes to Co Mayo for family holiday in
1939 *127-133*; lays on tea after marriage of niece Janey to Christopher
Ironside *131*; trains as precision engineer with view to volunteering for
munitions work in Second World War *134-138*; battles to find war work
135-141; volunteers to work for Red Cross *143*; forced out of Sydney Close,
temporary lodgings in Oakley Street *145*; Sydney Close takes a direct hit in
Blitz *150*; sees 'Gone With The Wind' with the Ironsides *154*; receives anti-
Polish propaganda *154*; takes on lodger Kathleen French *155*; takes a break
from London and the Blitz to visit Sandy Faris in Oxford *157*; finally gets a
job in engineering company in Colchester *158*; unhappy in job and
eventually quits *159-160*; becomes art examiner for NI Ministry of
Education *160*; returns to Belfast for a short while *161*; back to London in
1943 *163*; operation to clear up studio *163-167*; returns to Belfast again
169; back in London *169*; more Red Cross work *171-172*; takes on pupils
from 'The Monkey Club' *173-174*; commissioned to design headstone for her
niece Kitty *179-180*; member of council of RBS *184*; decides to move back to
Northern Ireland and live with Hazel and Grace *188*; offered paintings by
John 'JD' Revel *188*; becomes member of Institute of Sculptors of Ireland
192; submits works for Guildhall Exhibition *193*; submits works for Council
for the Encouragement of Music and the Arts in Northern Ireland (CEMA)
193-194; exhibits with Royal Ulster Academy of Arts *194-195*; exhibits
with Institute of the Sculptors of Ireland *195*; receives her first hearing aid
196; allows figures to be exhibited during Portadown Civic Week *196*;

unveils plaque to commemorate Centenary of Victoria College **198**; visits brother James in Herefordshire **200**; dies **201**; general health of throughout her life **202-210**; in hospital for unnamed operation **206**; obituaries and tributes to **211-218**.

Acheson, Edgar: *birth of* **6**; *persuades RUC his father's car has not been used for clandestine political activity* **32**; *writes letter to Anne from the 'front'* **50-51**; *marries Nora Brodie* **51**; *missing in action* **64**; *confirmed as prisoner of war* **64**.

Acheson, Emily: *birth of* **6**; *news of forthcoming marriage of* **11**; *dies* **112**.

Acheson, Grace: *birth of* **6**; *Grand Tour with sister Anne* **18-23**; *marries Rev George Faris* **31**; *appointed MBE* **184**.

Acheson Fenella: ***201***.

Acheson, Harrie: *recalls a stern Anne Acheson* **84**.

Acheson, Harriet: *early years* **2-3**; *literary gifts of* **3**; *marries* **4**; *supporter of Temperance movement* **4**; *visits Suffrage Movement meeting and House of Commons* **32**; *illness and convalescence in Blackpool* **35**; *death of* **37**.

Acheson, Harriet Emily 'Hazel': *birth of* **6**; *at Chelsea Polytechnic School of Art* **59**; *Red Cross volunteer* **59**; *visits Browning's family home with Anne* **58-59**; *medical student at Royal Free Hospital* **71**; *leaves for India* **86**; *appointed professor of Obstetrics and Gynaecology at Lady Hardinge Medical College and Hospital, New Delhi* **127**; *appointed Vice Principal of Lady Hardinge Medical College and Hospital* **182**; *appointed OBE* **187**; *leaves India and returns to UK, dividing time between London and Ulster* **187**; *dies* **194**.

Acheson, Sir James Glasgow: *birth and early childhood of* **6**; *'An Indian Chequerboard' the memoirs of* **6**; *frustration at being so far from the action while working for the Indian Government* **59**; *asks Anne to design and produce a car mascot for his new vehicle* **73**; *adventure while on holiday in Co Antrim* **75**; *recollections of final family holiday in Co Mayo* **127-131**; *distress of at death of Kitty* **178-180**; *knighted and leaves India* **180-181**; *appointed Regional Government Officer in Berlin* **182**; *involved with, and* responsible for, 'denazification' in Schleswig-Holstein **183**; thanks Anne for loan of £500 **200**.

Acheson, James 'Jimmy': *holiday in Mayo* **129**; *called up by RAF* **132**; *in RAF Coastal Command and visits Anne* **155**; *reported missing in action* **176-177**.

Acheson, Janet 'Janey' (*see also Ironside, Janey*): 3*-month dress-making course in London* **122**; *meets Christopher Ironside* **125**; *sense of foreboding on holiday in Co Mayo* **131**; *marries Christopher Ironside at outbreak of war* **131**.

Acheson, John: *early years* **4-6**; *businesses of* **4**; *politics of* **4**; *marries Harriet Glasgow* **4**; *Justice of the Peace* **5**; *and Ulster Liberal Party* **5**; *opposition to Boer War* **5**; *criticised for employing members of Garvaghy Road Roman Catholic community* **5**; *acquires first car* **32**; *suspicions of Royal Ulster Constabulary of car being used for clandestine political activity* **32**; *death of* **36**; *obituaries of* **36**.

Acheson, Joseph: *goes into business with brother John* **4**.

Acheson, Rev Malcolm: **201**.

Acheson, Mary 'Molly': *birth of* **6**; *brush with Black and Tans* **74-75**; *joins Grace and Anne at Glebe House* **195**; *dies* **195**.

Acheson, Vio (*wife of Sir James Acheson*): *brush with terrorists* **75**; *invited to Wali of Swat's duck shoot* **107**; *adventure on the road* **109**; *on holiday in Mayo* **129**; *attends Janey's wedding without her husband* **131**; *suffers loss of son Jimmy* **177**; *loses younger daughter Kitty to a brain tumour* **178**.

Acheson, Violet Katherine 'Kitty': *dies* **178**; *Anne commissioned to design a headstone for the grave* **179**; *Janey Ironside's moving description of her last sight of her sister* **179**.

Addresses of Anne Acheson: *Sedlescombe Road, West Brompton* **12**; *Kensington Crescent* **12**; *Beaufort Mansions, Chelsea* **71**; *Wentworth Studios* **78**; *King's House Studios* **79, 116**; *Avenue Studios (later Sydney Close) description of* **114-116**; *damaged by bomb* **150**; *clearing up operation* **163-167**; *Oakley*

Street **145**; *Bergholt Road, Colchester* **160**; *Rosebank, Belfast* **161**; *Duke's Avenue* **163**, **169**; *Glebe House, Glenavy, Co Antrim* **189**.

Alexandra School, Portadown: *7*.

An Indian Chequerboard (*memoirs of Sir James Glasgow Acheson*) **6**.

'Annabel Cundall' **100**.

'April' **87**.

'Arabella' **100**, **119**.

Arnold, John Corry (J C): *letter to Grace referring to Anne* **216-219**.

'A Small Conceit' **37**

Baker, Bill (Anne's amanuensis): **98**, **103**, **118**, **150**, **165**, **166**, **167**.

Barrie J M: *'What Every Woman Knows'* **10**.

Beaufoy Institute (Lambeth) **135**, **140**, **176**.

Belfast Municipal Technical Institute: *9*, *2*.

Bell, Gertrude: *Anne Acheson commissioned to model a bust of* **89**; *brief biography of* **89-91**; *bust is completed* **94**; *praise for the bust of Gertrude Bell* **95**; *bust unveiled in Iraq by King Faisal I* **95-96**; *replica bust at Royal Geographical Society in Kensington Gore* **96**.

Black and Tans, The: *74-75*.

Blitz, The: *142-152*.

Browning, Amy K (later Amy Dugdale): *Suffragettes sympathiser* **12**; *exhibits for first time at Royal Academy* **29**; *visited at her family home by Anne and Hazel* **58-59**; *Anne visits in Suffolk* **97**; *featured in article in Glasgow Herald* **101**; *upset at death of maid* **168**; *forced out of home by the war* **168**.

Budds, The: *112, 114, 119,143, 145, 146, 155, 164, 166, 175, 186, 189*.

Budget, The: *explanation of* **10**; *references from* **10, 12, 13, 24, 27, 30, 33**.

Byers, Margaret Morrow: *founds Victoria College* **3**.

Car mascots: *72-73*.

Carrickblacker Road: *debate of pillar box on* **5**.

'Ceres': *124*

Coggers: *Marion Cran wants a replica of Sally at* **77**; *Anne visits in order to place 'Sally' in garden of* **78**.

Council for the Encouragement of Music and the Arts in Northern Ireland (CEMA): *193-194*.

Cran, Mrs Marion: *praises lead garden figure 'Sally' by Anne* **75**; *purchases a figure of 'Sally'* **77**; *invites Anne to her house in Kent to site the figure* **77**; *applauds the concept of portrait statues* **81-82**; *praises Anne's fountain for a garden in the Cotswolds* **82**; *describes the process of Anne's creation of a lead garden figure* **83**.

Crawford, Lady Anne: *Commissions a bust of herself from Anne* **73**; *letter to Anne thanking her for the bust* **73**.

'December': *97*.

'Diana': *119*

Dugdale, Sir Thomas 'TC' or 'Tommy': *writes to Anne with details of his 'war'* **56-57**; *Anne Acheson completes 'portrait sketch' in bronze of* **75**; *featured in article in Glasgow Herald* **101**; *key role in Scottish Schools of Art* **101**; *made Associate of Royal Academy* **114**; *writes reference for Anne* **122**.

Dugdale, Amy (see *Browning, Amy K*).

Dunavon (Acheson family home): *building of 6.*

Dunham, Joanna: *biography of Amy K Browning 29.*

Durnford, Evelyn 'Muffett': *recollections of family holiday in Mayo 127-129.*

'Echo Mocking': *RA exhibit in 1913 34; Theft of from Walker Art Gallery, Liverpool 34-35.*

'Eliza': *185.*
E N Mason and Sons, Colchester: *158-160.*

Fanner, Kate: *headmistress of Putney County Secondary School 25; glowing testimonial for Anne 26.*

Faris, Alexander 'Sandy': *'Paradise in Mayo' recollections of final family holiday on West Coast of Ireland 127-130; regular visitor to Sydney Close 153-154.*

Faris, Rev George: *marries Grace Acheson 31; dies 87.*

Faris, Harriet Emily: *recalls King's House Studios 79; modelling for her Auntie Nan 83; remembers Anne Acheson scolding her nieces and distancing herself from them with her working overalls 84; stays in Anne's studio for 3 months 186.*

Faris, Professor John: *birth of 33; impression that Anne Acheson favoured boys over girls 85; visits Anne Acheson 103.*

Faris Katharine: *stays with Anne Acheson 103-104.*

Faris, Neil: *5.*

Faris, Samuel: *dies 1956 195*

'Flora': *124.*

'Fountain Figure': *127.*

Gilroy, John: *115.*

Glasgow, Adam: *joins brother, Rev Professor James, on mission in India* **2.**

Glasgow, Harriet: (see Acheson, Harriet)

Glasgow, Rev Professor James: *first missionary of Presbyterian Church in Ireland to visit India* **2.**
Gleichen, Lady Feodora: *80, 117-118.*

Gleichen Memorial Prize: inaugural award won by Anne Acheson **118.**

Gregory, Christine: *Elected Associate of RBS* **80.**

Hallé, Elinor: *joins Surgical Requisites Association* **43**; *uses papier maché for arm cradles* **43**; *recipe for papier maché* **44**; *success of papier maché arm cradles* **44**; *appointed CBE* **67.**

'Harriet Emily': *185.*

Hawtrey, Sir Charles: *Anne sees in 'Never Say Die'* **34.**

Hawtrey, Charles (comic actor): **34.**

Hirons, Margot: *praises Anne's garden statuary* **81**; *endorses the use of lead as a medium for garden figures* **85**; *admiring of Anne's bronzes* **86**; *writes about Anne Acheson's Royal Worcester figures* **93.**

House of Commons: *Harriet Acheson visits* **32.**

'Imp, The': *73.*

Industrial Art Exhibition: *75.*

Ironside, Christopher: *meets Janey Acheson* **125**; *marries Janey Acheson at outbreak of war* **131.**

Ironside, Janet 'Janey' (see also *Acheson, Janet*): *'Janey' autobiography of* **7.**

Ironside, Virginia: *model of her head is Anne Acheson's final RA exhibit* **185.**

Irwin, Rev John: *proposes marriage to Emily Acheson* **11.**

Irwin, Mrs Molly: (see *Acheson, Mary*).

'Josephine G Owen as Puck': **100, 126-127.**

'June': **97, 117.**

Kendrick, Flora: *Elected Associate of RBS* **80.**

Kerr, Rev Alexander: *accompanies Rev Professor James Glasgow on first Presbyterian mission to India* **2**

King's School, Worcester, The: **99-100.**

Knight, Dame Laura: *former tenant of Sydney Close (Avenue Studios)* **115.**

Ladies Collegiate School: (see *Victoria College*).

Lanteri, Edouard: *teaches Anne Acheson* **9**; *glowing reference for Anne* **18.**

'Larrikin': **88.**

Lawson, Jess (later *Lawson-Peacey*): **10, 12, 80.**

'Leveret': **100.**

Mackenzie, Helen: (see *Budds, The*).

'March': **100, 117.**

Matier, Anna: *headmistress of Victoria College* **9**; *glowing reference for Anne* **18.**

Morton, Mary: *elected Associate of RBS* **80**; *studio bombed* **147.**

'Mrs Dugdale': **88.**

'Mrs Wingate': **75**.

Mulberry Walk, Number 17: *acquired by Surgical Requisites Association* **40-41**; *expands* **51**.

Norland Place School, Holland Park: *Anne gets job at* **102**.

Order of the British Empire, The: *explanation of founding of* **67**.

Owen, Dora: *visited by Anne Acheson* **100**, **121**.

'Paradise in Mayo': *recollections of family holiday in 1939* **127-132**.

'Pixie, The': **30**.

Plaster of Paris: *used as a splinting material* **62-63**; *brief history of* **63**.

Queen's University (original institution): *brief history of* **3**.

Queen's University, Belfast: *John Faris Professor of Logic and metaphysics at* **33**.

'Rags': **87**.

Rationing: *general references to* **167-168**, **175-176**, **181**.

'Red Shawl, The': *portrait by Amy K Browning of Anne Acheson which was exhibited at The Royal Academy* **29**.

Reynolds-Stevens, Sir William: *proposes Anne Acheson for associateship with RBS* **80**.

Rhys-Davies, Harriet Emily: (see *Faris, Harriet Emily*).

Royal Academy, The: *brief history of* **28-29**; *Browning exhibits at* **29**; *Anne Acheson's first exhibit* **30-31**.

Royal British Society of Sculptors: *Anne Acheson elected Associate of* **80**; *Anne Acheson elected first woman Fellow of* **122**; *on council of* **184**.

Royal College of Art: *9, 10, 11, 12, 28.*

Royal Society of British Sculptors: (see *Royal British Society of Sculptors*).

Royal University of Ireland (formerly Queen's University): *brief history of 3.*

Royal Worcester: *93, 113-114, 116.*

'Sacred Bull, The': *119.*

'Sally' (lead garden figure): described and purchased by Mrs Marion Cran *76-79*; *entered by Anne in British Empire Exhibition of 1924 at Wembley 81; sold to Australian lady, letter 125.*

Singer Sargent, John: sometime resident of Sydney Close *115.*

Society of Women Artists, The: *88, 100.*

Spafford, Mrs Fanny: *Anne visits preparatory to making a bronze portrait medallion of the educationalist 86.*

Spencer Augustus (principal of RCA): *glowing reference for Anne 18.*

Stabler, Phyllis: *seconds Anne Acheson for associateship with RBS 80.*

Surgical Requisites Association: *history of 40-42; Anne Acheson joins 42; Elinor Hallé joins 43; source of inventions 46-40; Anne and team invent waterproof papier maché limb baths 53-57; expands across Britain and Europe 60; exhibition of inventions 63-64; sets up training course 66; tributes to the efforts and inventions of 66.*

Swat Valley: *visited by Anne and Hazel 107-108.*

Sydney Close: (see *Addresses, Avenue Studios*).

'Tangles': *88.*

'Thief, The': *122, 123, 124.*

'Thirteen o' clock': ***37***.

Union Internationale des Beaux-Arts et Des Lettres: *Anne Acheson becomes member of, exhibiting frequently thereafter* ***33***.

Victoria and Albert Museum: *Anne exhibits at* ***75***.

Victoria College, Belfast: *founded, changes name* ***3***; *family teaching tradition with and education at* ***4***.

Walker Art Gallery, Liverpool: *theft of a figure of Anne's from* ***34-35***

Walthamstow Hall: *school at which Harriet Glasgow was educated* ***2,3***.

'Water Baby': ***117***.

Wentworth Studios: *temporary workplace of Anne* ***78-79***.

'Will o' The Wisp': ***31***.

Women's Suffrage Movement: ***32***, ***38-40***; *first victory of* ***70***.